IMAGES
of America

RANCHO PALOS VERDES

On the Cover: Palos Verdes College opened in 1947 in a swale above Portuguese Bend. It was a seemingly casual two-year campus with an intense curriculum and a close bond between students and faculty. One of the joys of a campus away from houses—besides the snakes and skunks—is that, if you live nearby, you can ride your horse to school. This is a Peter Gowland photograph. (Courtesy Local History Collection, Palos Verdes Library.)

IMAGES
of America

RANCHO PALOS VERDES

Ginger Garnett Clark

ARCADIA
PUBLISHING

ISBN 978-0-7385-6920-8

Published by Arcadia Publishing
Charleston, South Carolina

Printed in the United States of America

Library of Congress Control Number: 2009920012

For all general information contact Arcadia Publishing at:
Telephone 843-853-2070
Fax 843-853-0044
E-mail sales@arcadiapublishing.com
For customer service and orders:
Toll-Free 1-888-313-2665

Visit us on the Internet at www.arcadiapublishing.com

To museum curators and reference librarians,
for your quest for facts and your willingness to share;
and to John Hartley and John Carroll

Contents

ACKNOWLEDGMENTS

The two historical repositories on the Palos Verdes Peninsula are the Point Vicente Interpretive Center and the Local History Collection of the Palos Verdes Peninsula Library District, so a very special thank-you to Diana McIntyre, curator and docent coordinator at the Point Vicente Interpretive Center, and to Marjeanne Blinn, in charge of the Local History Collection of the Palos Verdes Library District with its irreplaceable oral history collection. Both have been extremely generous with their collections, their knowledge, and their time. And thank you to the docents of each group who have been unflaggingly enthusiastic and helpful.

Steve Iverson, historical curator at the Rancho Los Cerritos Historic Site in Long Beach, was very generous with his time and information. And thank you to librarians Mary McMillan, Melanie Sellar, and Darren Hall at Marymount College for opening their files.

Marcella Low at the Southern California Gas Company took time to send out a photograph to her retired supervisors, and they took the time to identify it. Shannon Dean of the California Water Service Company put out the word, and Don Jensen, district manager, Westlake District, answered it, cheerfully opening his company's historical files.

The former city mayors were very helpful: Mel Hughes, both as a mayor and an amateur radio operator; Doris Hughes; John McTaggart, who held office longest; Flo McTaggart; and Ann Shaw, who was with the city from the very beginning, as was Ken Dyda, who made not only his own papers available but also boxes of Dorothy LeConte's papers and photographs.

To those who opened their photo albums, identified people in photographs, and shared their memories: Dan Colburn, W6DC; Kay Conrad; Barbara Gleghorn; Rose Jensen; Homer Meek, K6HKT; Carolyn Petru; Lynn Scollo; Brian Tilley, KA6UHM; Barbara Wallace; Jo Woods; Dennis Yonker, NE6I; Linda Cherney and her mother, Mary Robertson; Don Christy; Joe Cocke; Mike Fabian; Ray Frew; Yvonne Ishibashi; Dennis Jaconi; Rosalee McCarrell Orr; Maxine Patalano; Dr. Charles Rennie; Ed Sharpe; Sunshine; Jean Curtis Wells; Michelle Wible; Yvetta Williams; and Ken Zuckerman, and the many helpful neighbors in Rancho Palos Verdes who I missed naming but who were generous with their memories, a heartfelt thank you. And thank you to Robert Frank, city editor at the *Everett Herald.*

INTRODUCTION

Until 1913, the Palos Verdes Peninsula was just a place to graze cattle or plant crops. Jotham Bixby reaped a profit in the late 1800s in both of these pursuits with the help of his ranch manager, Harry Phillips. But in 1913, a conglomerate of businessmen led by Frank A. Vanderlip, a New York banker, bought the peninsula, sight unseen, from Bixby. As soon as Vanderlip saw the peninsula, he knew he had found the perfect setting for an enclave of 100-acre estates, with a yacht club, golf course, and more. Frank Vanderlip made plans to develop the hills. He planned to do it grandly and with care, so as to get the best from this beautiful land.

World War I and the economic depression derailed his plans. He settled for a few less-elaborate communities, which he also planned with care. Frank Vanderlip died in 1937, leaving his land to the corporation, which belonged, for the most part, to his children. In 1945, Vanderlip's second-eldest son, Kelvin, took over the family business, and the peninsula had five golden years of gentle land development, including a community in Portuguese Bend where the Vanderlips lived. In 1950, Frank Vanderlip Jr. took over the family business, and in 1953, for tax reasons, he sold the part of the peninsula that still belonged to the family. Great Lakes Carbon bought it, and the decisions that company made about land development ultimately created the backlash that created Rancho Palos Verdes.

Rancho Palos Verdes is shaped like a gerrymandered horseshoe. It includes all of the property Great Lakes Carbon bought and a little more—all of it Los Angeles County land. Great Lakes Carbon had found that the diatomite they planned to dig on the top of Crest Road, their stated reason for buying the property, was too wet to be a viable mine. They changed their focus, formed a development company, and in conjunction with the Capital Corporation, a subsidiary of Transamerica, started building houses and selling land to other developers. This turned into a building spree that many people felt the County of Los Angeles should have stemmed by restricting permits.

In 1967, The League of Women Voters published a review of peninsula land use, zoning, and land development on the peninsula called *The Time is Now*. This book, researched and written by league member Dena Friedson, became the foundation on which the Save Our Coastline (SOC) movement was built. SOC had two goals: to stop coastal development and to create a fourth city from the county land on the peninsula.

Since the neighboring cities refused to absorb the neighborhoods around them, many people were drawn to creating a fourth city. Three ideas drove them: Fear of the county's seemingly unlimited approval of all building, a desire to maintain the open space, and the belief that overbuilding would burden the peninsula's infrastructure, such as roads and water.

Save Our Coastline (SOC) drove the city to incorporation. It was co-chaired by Helene Drown, a Republican, and Dorothy LeConte, a Democrat. LeConte guided the campaign with a deft and hard-driving hand. The Steering Committee met every Saturday morning at 10:00 for three years, and the Policy Committee met almost every week. When there was word of dissent, SOC made certain it was countered immediately with a letter, phone call, or mass mailing. Fliers used the words "developer's lies," "Zuckerman agents," and "Marineland and the major developers want you to believe . . ." The campaign created an adversarial division between the large property owners, such as developers, and many of the people who lived in the very homes the developers had built for them.

Opponents of incorporation countered that a fourth city was unnecessary, expensive, and economically unsound—that it would not actually solve any of the problems. They said it meant higher taxes so the city could support itself, that it would be economically accountable should additional landslides occur, that there would be less police protection, and that it would be another—and an unnecessary—layer of government. The youngest Vanderlip son, John, opposed it, and Howard Jarvis of the United Organizations of Taxpayers, Inc. said that SOC's projected expenditures were unrealistic.

The road to the fourth city was paved in the courts. Written into the California State constitution was a provision that said a city could not be incorporated without the approval of 50 percent of its landowners. Bill Monahan of Marineland brought a petition to the Los Angeles County Board of Supervisors with the signatures of 55 percent of the landowners, opposing the fourth city. This effectively blocked SOC's drive to incorporate. Immediately after the County Board of Supervisor's meeting, rejecting SOC's petition to incorporate, a few hundred SOC members marched from the supervisor's chambers down the street to the Federal District Court to file a lawsuit against the state's incorporation law, which they charged violated the 14th Amendment of the U.S. Constitution. The Federal Court, after looking at other cases, told them to take their case back to the state. SOC took it to the California Court of Appeals and lost. In 1971, they went to the California Supreme Court and won. The supreme court decision meant that from then on, in California, those who own the majority of property can no longer control the city formed around them. Henceforth, city incorporation in California would be "one man, one vote."

Bill Monahan left Marineland in 1971 when it was sold. Those who took his place embraced the fourth city campaign, and as the campaign strengthened, more large-property owners ceased their opposition. Meanwhile, representatives of SOC successfully blocked various development proposals as they arose.

The election on August 28, 1973, was to create the fourth city and elect a city council. The fourth city campaign promised the city would be run with little overhead. They promised to contract out the work, to not build a city hall, and to generally keep expenses low by keeping employees to a minimum. The city was voted in by a landslide and the new city council put a moratorium on all building, with the exception of those structures for which concrete had already been poured.

Fifteen years later, Rolling Hills Estates residents Bill and Barbara Ailor formed the Palos Verdes Peninsula Land Conservancy, which successfully negotiated land purchases from various developers. Many, like the 155-acre Forrestal Preserve, were bought outright by the city of Rancho Palos Verdes. In the case of the 399-acre landslide area of Portuguese Bend, peninsula residents raised and donated a portion of the purchase price and the balance came from various government funds and grants. The city now owns 1,000 acres in nine reserves, and the Land Conservancy manages and holds a "conservation easement over all of the acreage."

Oddly enough, in some ways Rancho Palos Verdes has come full circle. It has land management and open spaces as Frank A. Vanderlip envisioned but without private ownership or the ability to build.

This book is an abbreviated history of Rancho Palos Verdes and the land on which it stands. Of necessity, it omits the earliest history—the Tongva Indians and the Rancheros—and has no room for many of the other fascinating stories that remain to be told.

One

Written on with Loving Care

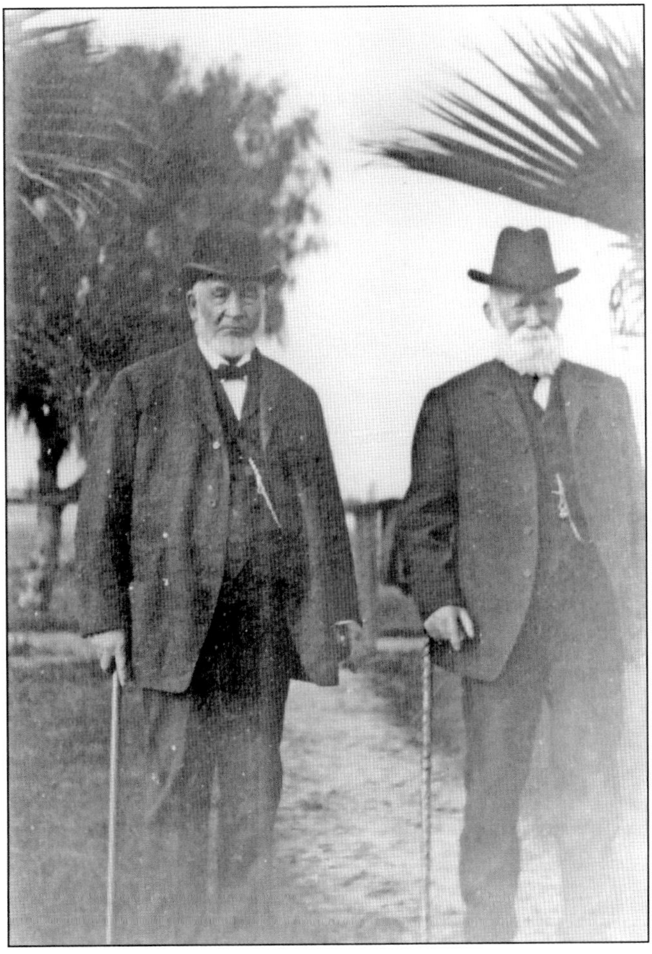

In 1852, fifty-five years before this picture was taken, Jotham (left) and Marcellus Bixby arrived in Volcano, California, aboard the sailing ship *Samuel Appleton*. They and their brother Llewellyn earned enough gold by Christmas to return to Maine. In 1853, they returned to California, having bought along the way 2,400 sheep. They lost a musket and a man to hostile American Indians. (Courtesy Rancho Los Cerritos Historic Site.)

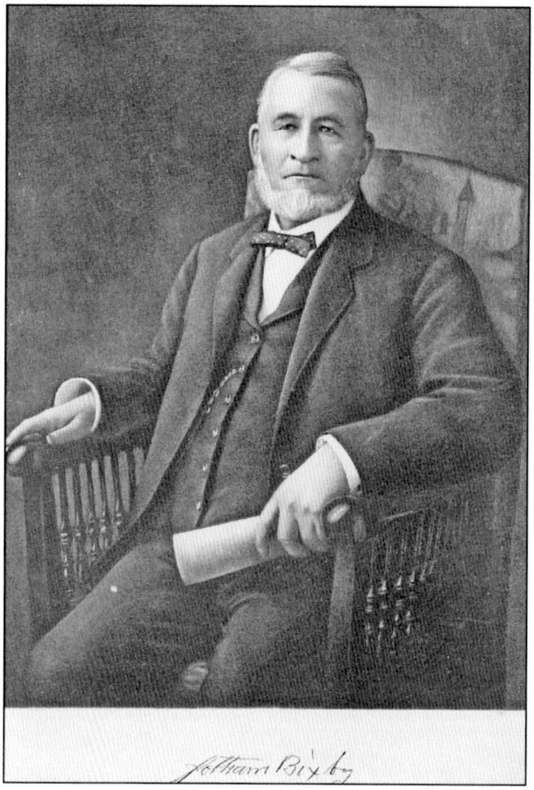

The Bixbys set up their sheep partnership in Monterey as Flint, Bixby, and Company. By 1865, they had expanded to Southern California. Jotham moved to Los Cerritos and began buying interest in surrounding lands, including Rancho de los Palos Verdes, and lending money to the cash-strapped Sepulvedas. By 1882, Jotham Bixby owned all of the Palos Verdes Peninsula except San Pedro. (Courtesy Rancho Los Cerritos Historic Site.)

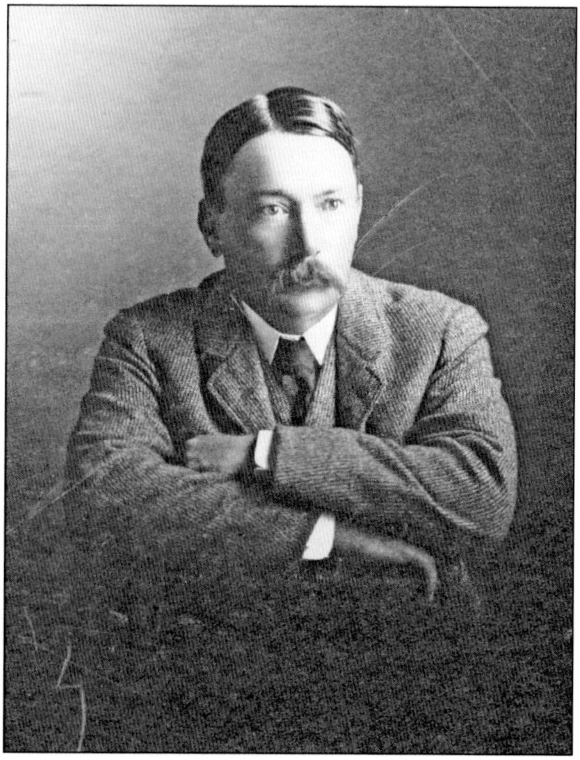

Jotham, who died in 1917, gave management of the Rancho de los Palos Verdes land to his eldest son, George H., around the mid-1880s after George H. had returned from Yale. This undated photograph of George H. was probably taken in the mid-1890s when he was around 30 years old. (Courtesy Rancho Los Cerritos Historic Site.)

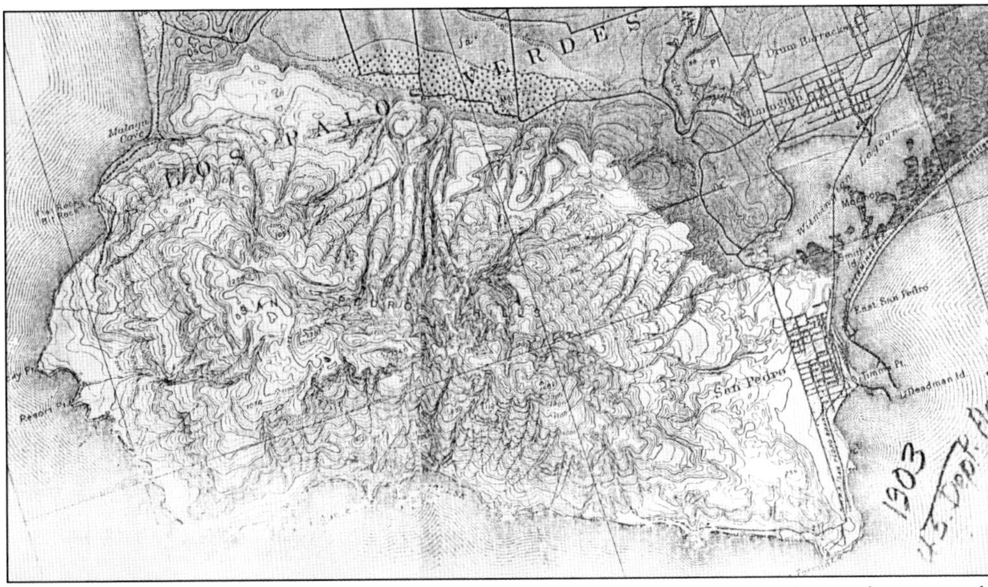

This Department of Agriculture topographical map shows the wilds of Los Palos Verdes peninsula in 1903. Point Vicente, where the lighthouse will be built, is on the lower left. On the upper right is the Bixby Slough, formerly Laguna Machado, from which the peninsula drew its water for many years. (Courtesy Local History Collection, Palos Verdes Library.)

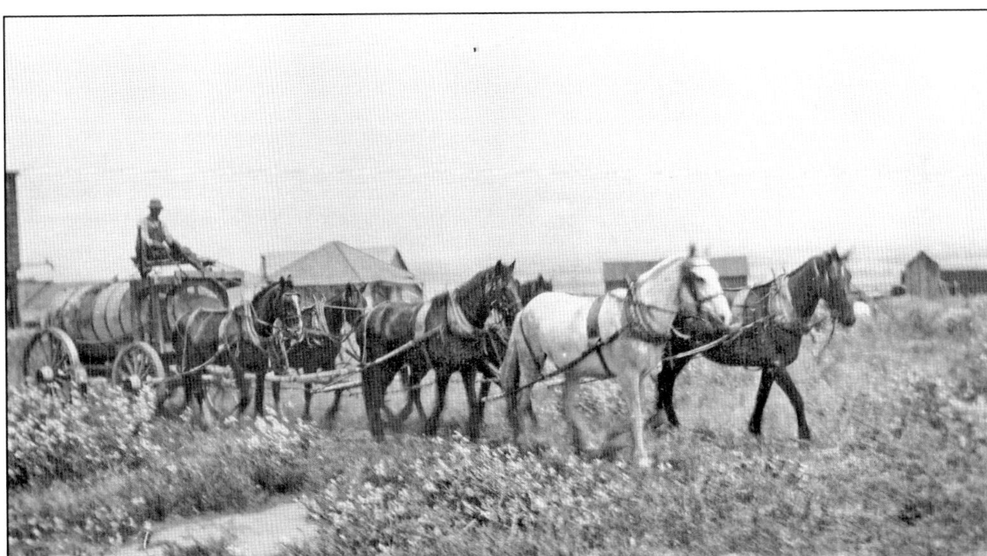

In 1894, George Bixby hired Harry Phillips, a mining engineer, as his ranch foreman. Phillips had an unusual ability to find water on the arid peninsula. Here in 1915 is a team and wagon carrying good water to their new ranch home for household use. It was drawn from a well that Harry Phillips Sr. had dug near the old ranch. (Courtesy Local History Collection, Palos Verdes Library.)

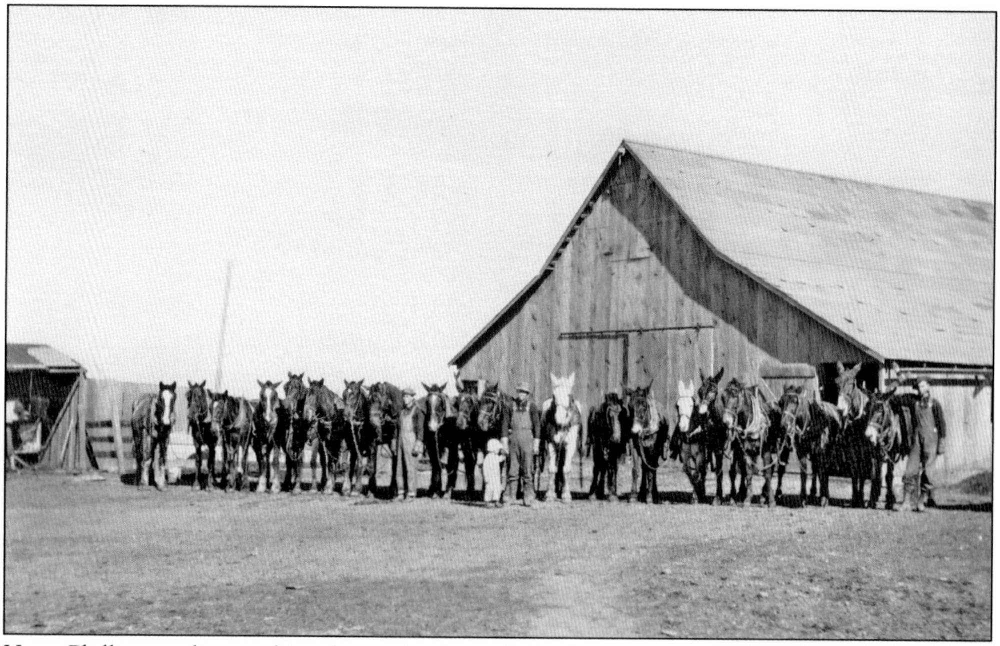

Harry Phillips set about making the peninsula profitable in many ways. He bought 10 thoroughbred Herefords as breeding stock and neutered the lesser bulls to upgrade the herd. Phillips, his two sons, and three hands worked regularly. During roundups, Mexican vaqueros from Wilmington were brought in. Harry Phillips' stock of horses and mules were used for farming and ranching. (Courtesy Local History Collection, Palos Verdes Library.)

Palos Verdes, though rocky, is fertile land. Phillips brought in Wallace McCarrell to farm the upper hills as a sharecropper. Phillips also brought in many Japanese families, who established vegetable and flower farms along the coast. Meanwhile, Harry Phillips also farmed—mostly barley. Here is Harry Phillips Jr. on a mower. The photograph is dated 1914. (Courtesy Local History Collection, Palos Verdes Library.)

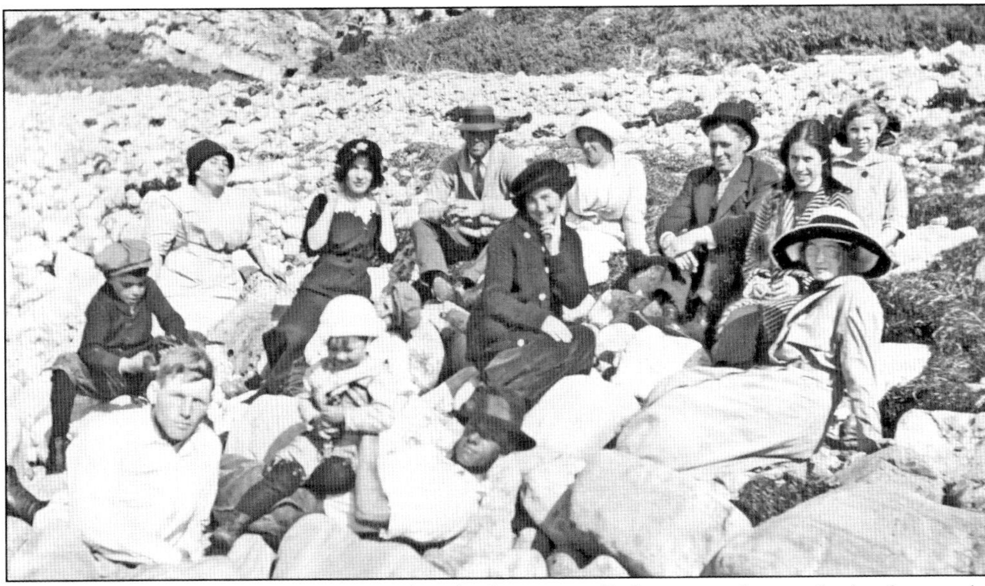

The five Phillips children were expected to do chores—milk the cow, cultivate the land, mow the hay, and in the case of the girls, help out with the housework, cleaning, and cooking. Their rare free time sometimes meant an excursion to the beach. Here the Phillips family and their friends pose for a picture during an outing near Malaga Cove around 1914. (Courtesy Local History Collection, Palos Verdes Library.)

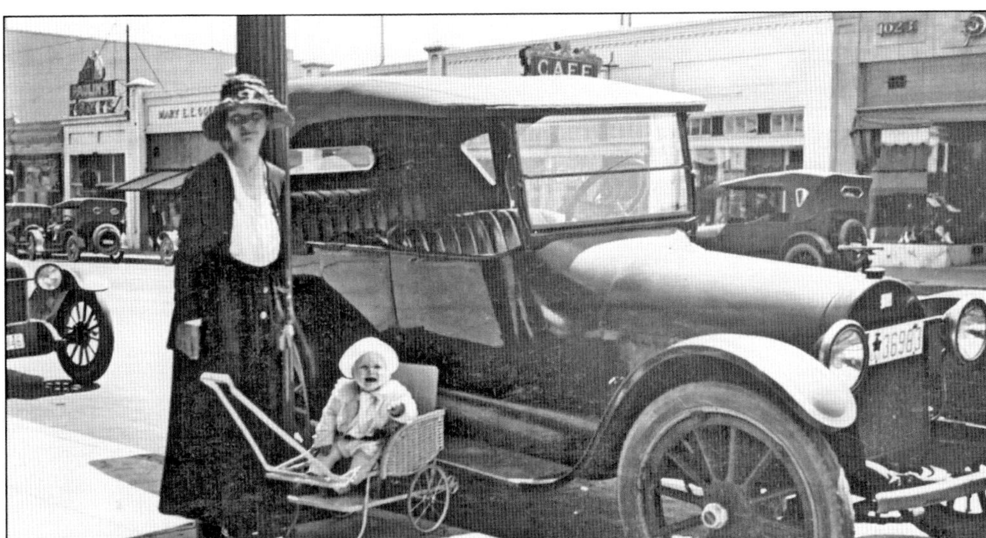

This is Hulda Phillips, wife of Harry Phillips Jr., probably visiting Ojai, according to the note on the back of the photograph. With her is the next generation of Phillipses, Harry Phillips III. The photograph is dated 1917. (Courtesy Local History Collection, Palos Verdes Library.)

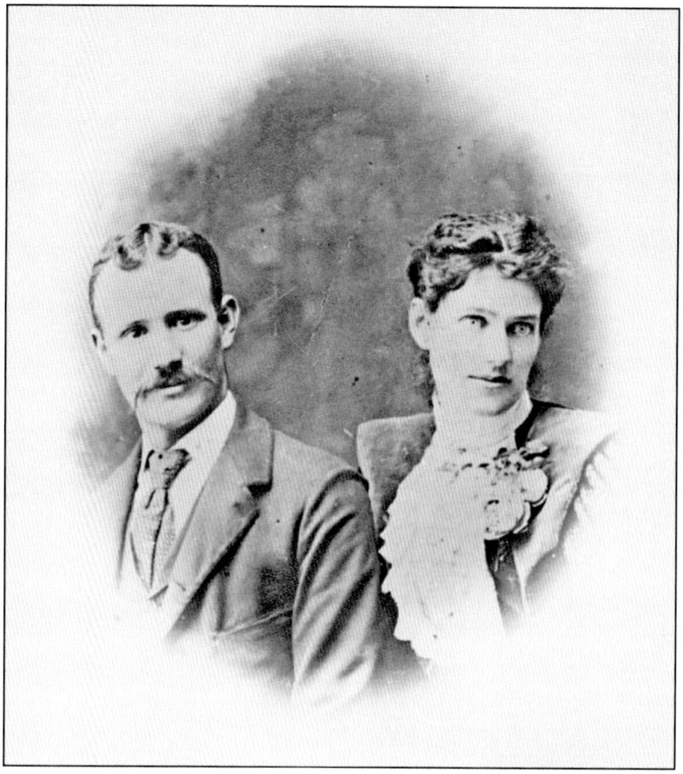

In 1896, a 27-year-old Wallace Worth McCarrell married Maggie Travolia, and 13 years later, in 1909, they began to sharecrop a few hundred acres on upper Palos Verdes for Harry Phillips. McCarrell paid one fourth of his crop, usually barley, to the Bixbys and delivered it all to a warehouse in Redondo Beach. "He was a good farmer, very successful," said Harry Phillips Jr. (Courtesy Rosalee McCarrell Orr.)

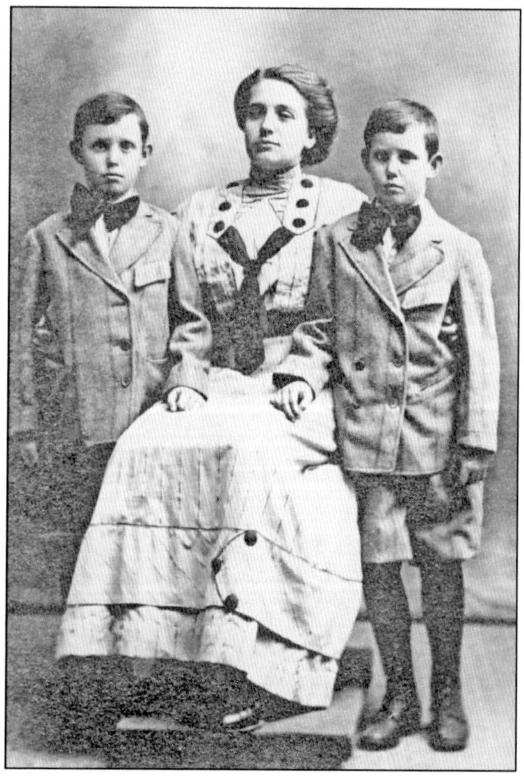

The McCarrells moved to Palos Verdes with five of their six children: Herbert, Minerva, Grace, and Roy and Raymond (twins). Maeblossom arrived shortly thereafter. This is Maggie McCarrell with Roy, on left, and Raymond. The family's farm was at what is now Highridge and Crestridge Roads. Later Maggie moved from the isolated farm to a house that Wallace built for her on Elena Avenue in Redondo Beach. (Courtesy Rosalee McCarrell Orr.)

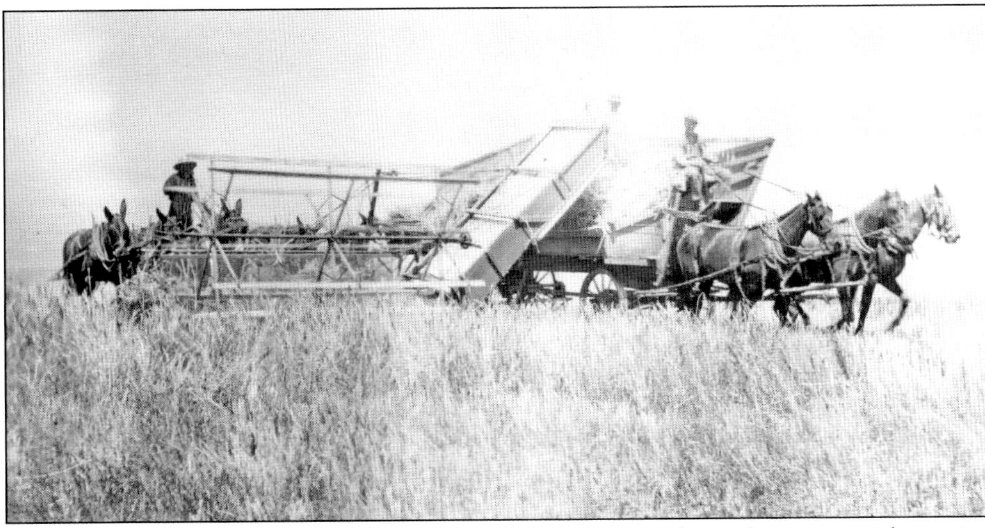

Barley was the primary crop until Roy McCarrell brought in garbanzo beans as an alternative, but that was long after this photograph was taken. Dated 1915, this image is labeled "header for barley." The method combines reaping the harvest and dumping it into a waiting horse-drawn cart. Although this is on the Phillips farm, the McCarrells used a similar method. (Courtesy Local History Collection, Palos Verdes Library.)

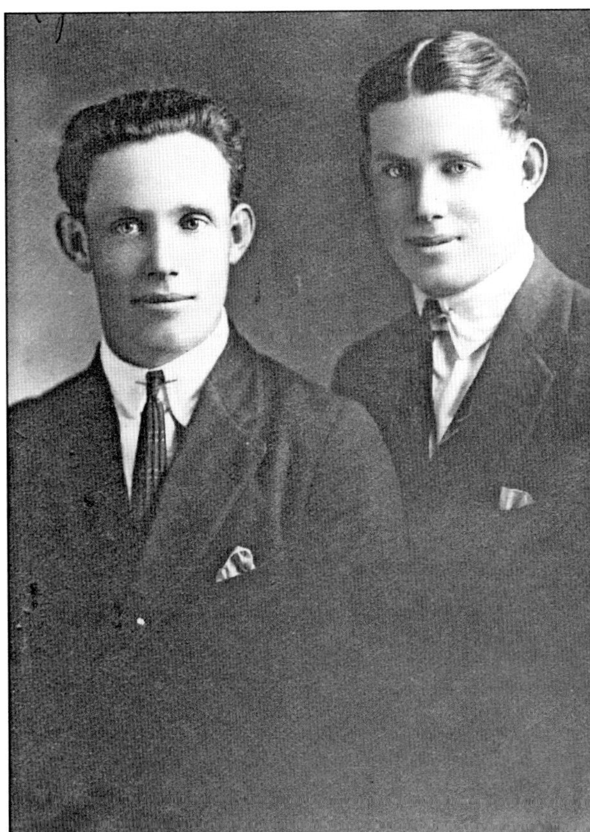

Phillips maintained yearly contracts with all the farmers. Roy and Raymond grew up as the second generation of McCarrells to farm Palos Verdes, and like their contemporaries, Lewellyn and Harry Phillips Jr., they worked alongside their father. Raymond (left) and Roy lived on what would become Crest Road and Crenshaw Boulevard. (Courtesy Rosalee McCarrell Orr.)

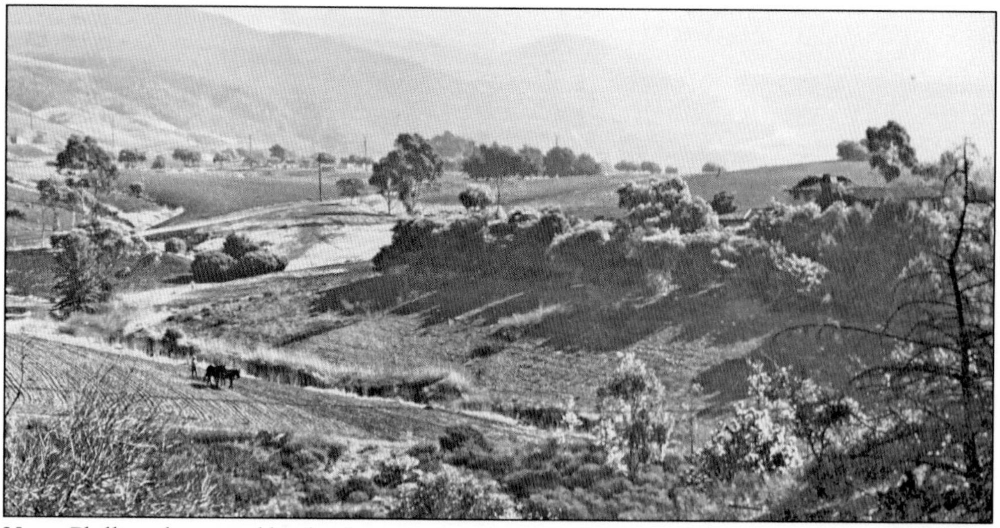

Harry Phillips also rented land to Japanese immigrants who entered the country through Canada and Mexico around 1900. The Ishibashis were among the first to arrive, and four generations have farmed here since. The Japanese were not allowed to own land but leased it for $10 per acre per year. For all the farmers, leases were yearly since the land was destined for residential development. (Courtesy Point Vicente Interpretive Center.)

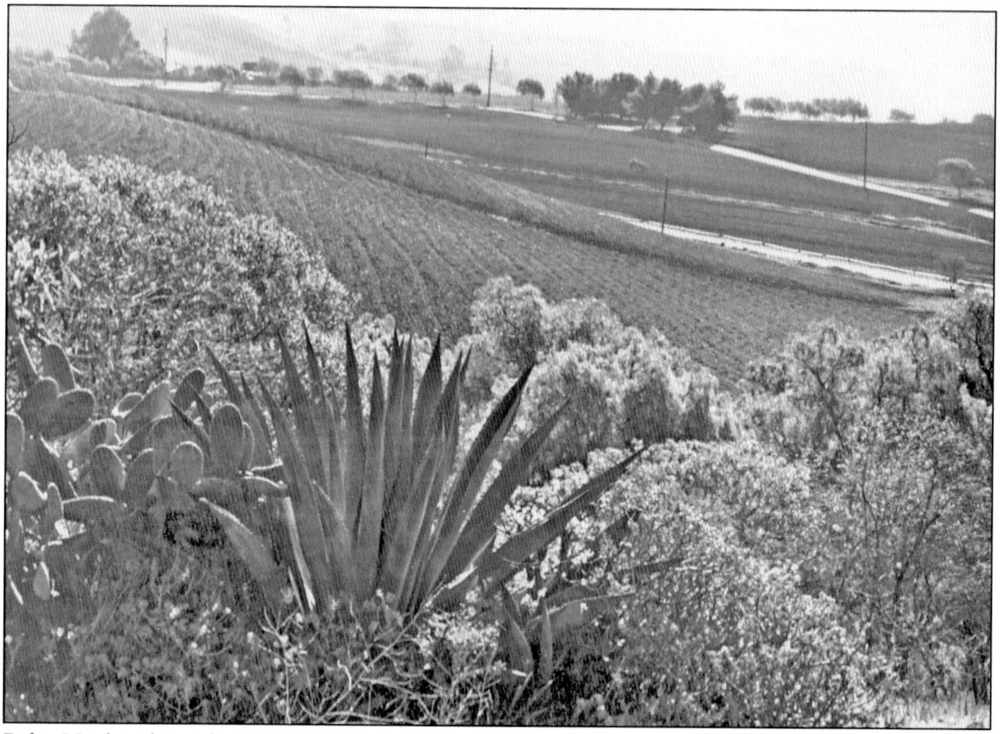

Palos Verdes along the south coast is, in the words of farmer Yukio Motoike, "the most beautiful place on earth." It is also a wonderful place to farm. Despite the lack of water, they harvested the earliest produce, and "early" meant more sales. The fog and humidity on the southern and western coastal areas provided enough moisture to grow good crops. (Courtesy Point Vicente Interpretive Center.)

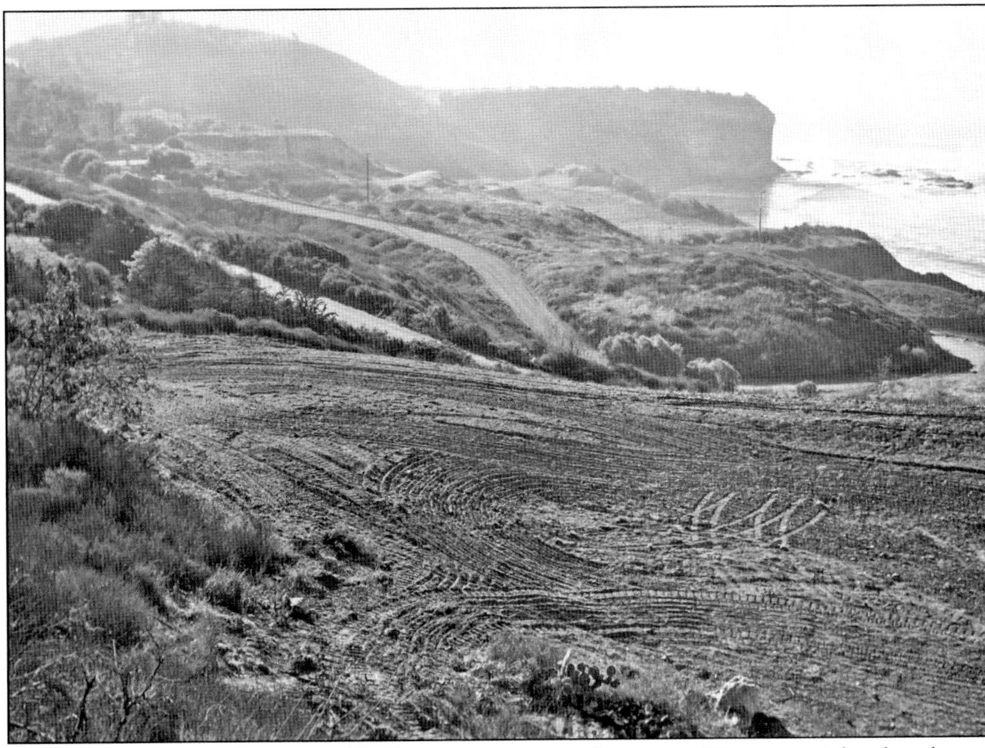

"We start with some things suitable for winter crops, such as peas. Then we might plant beans, squash, tomatoes," said Yvonne Ishibashi. "Around July, no more crops would be planted until the fall. In the summer we kept up our farm equipment, prepared the ground for winter planting, and maybe took a small vacation." (Courtesy Point Vicente Interpretive Center.)

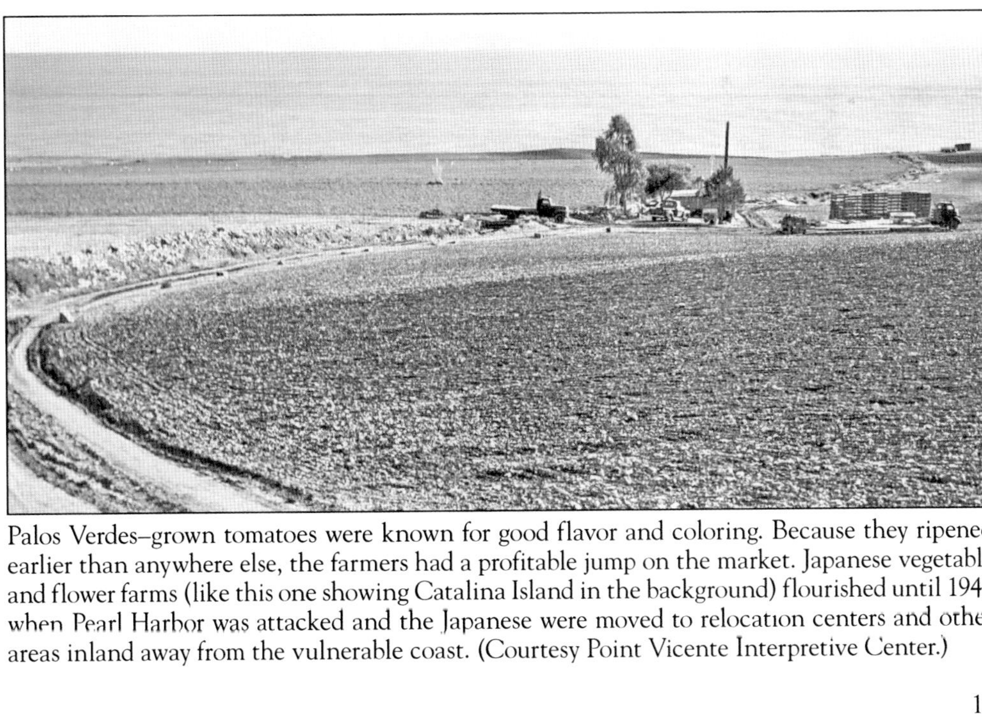

Palos Verdes–grown tomatoes were known for good flavor and coloring. Because they ripened earlier than anywhere else, the farmers had a profitable jump on the market. Japanese vegetable and flower farms (like this one showing Catalina Island in the background) flourished until 1941 when Pearl Harbor was attacked and the Japanese were moved to relocation centers and other areas inland away from the vulnerable coast. (Courtesy Point Vicente Interpretive Center.)

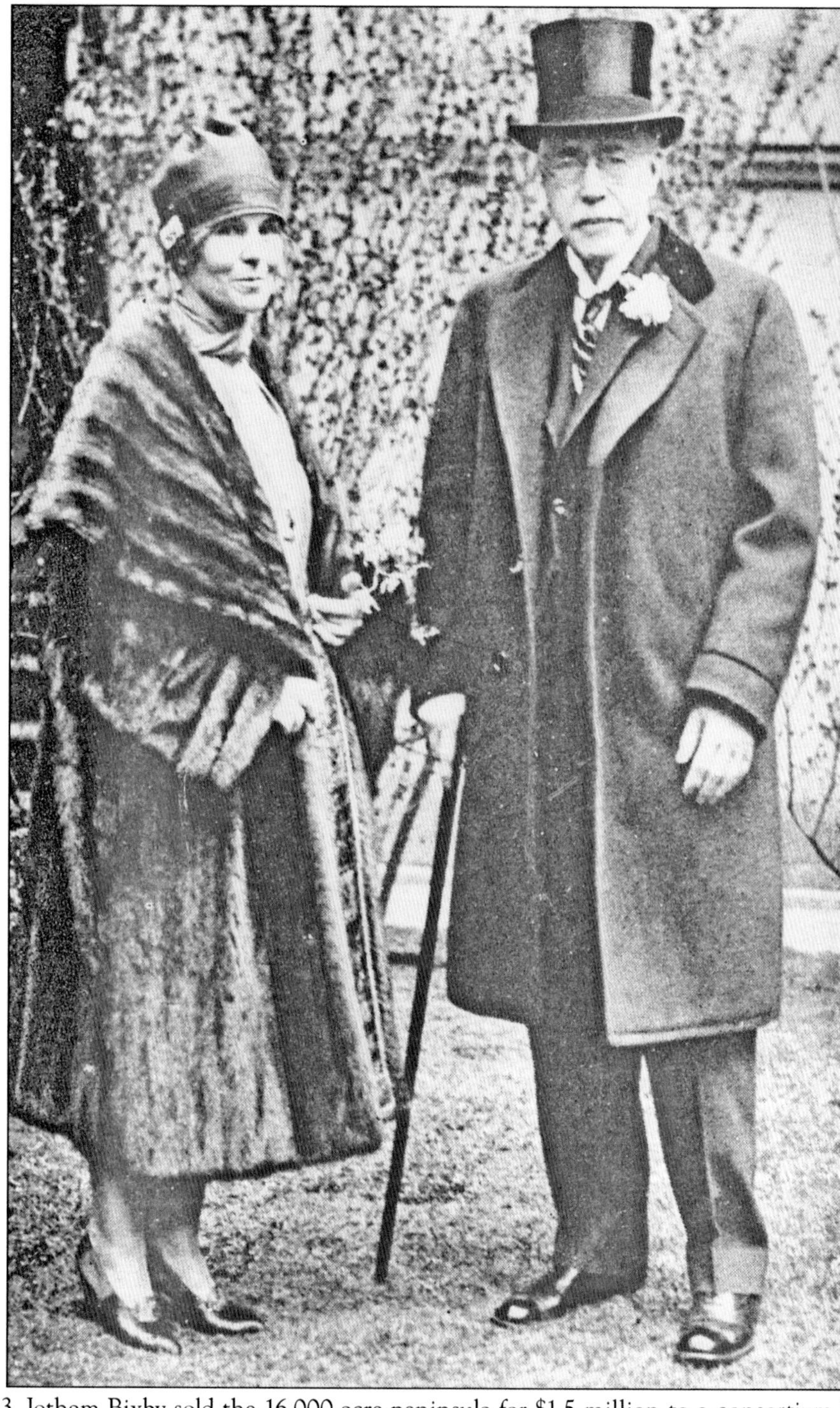

In 1913, Jotham Bixby sold the 16,000-acre peninsula for $1.5 million to a consortium headed by New York banker Frank A. Vanderlip. The 1907 stock panic had convinced Vanderlip of the wisdom of real estate. Palos Verdes was his fifth large land purchase, all chosen for their proximity to two railroads. Frank A. and Narcissa Vanderlip are shown in an undated photograph. (Courtesy Local History Collection, Palos Verdes Library.)

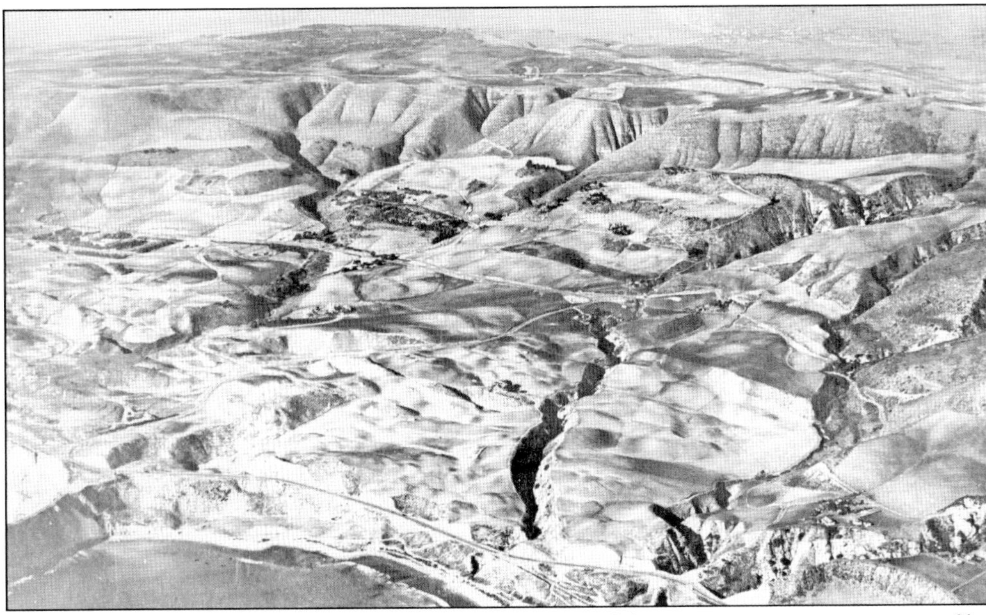

Vanderlip described his first view of Palos Verdes as one of the most exciting experiences of his life: " . . . a range of folded hills, miles of tawny slopes thrusting themselves abruptly from the Pacific; broad natural terraces with, here and there, a little farm. I was reminded of the Sorrentine Peninsula. It was an unspoiled sheet of paper to be written on with loving care." (Courtesy Local History Collection, Palos Verdes Library.)

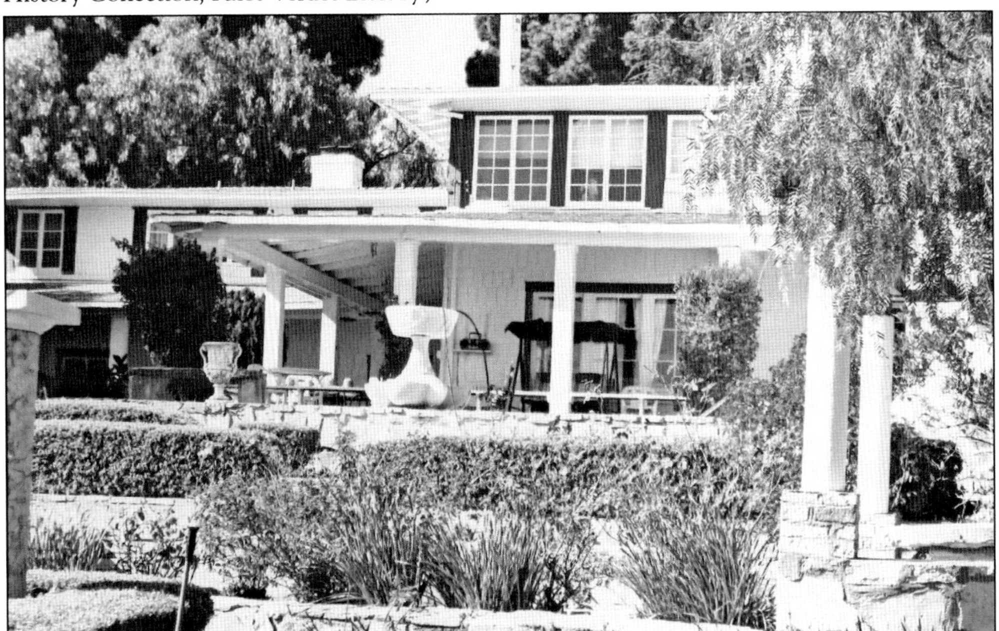

Portuguese Bend was chosen for the Vanderlip's summer home. The Cottage, as it came to be known, built in 1916, had been copied from their rustic vacation house in Scrub Oak, New York. Narcissa Vanderlip drove four stakes into the ground for the builder who, thinking she'd made a mistake, rotated the house and ruined her view. A later addition (left) corrected the problem. (Courtesy Vintage Palos Verdes.)

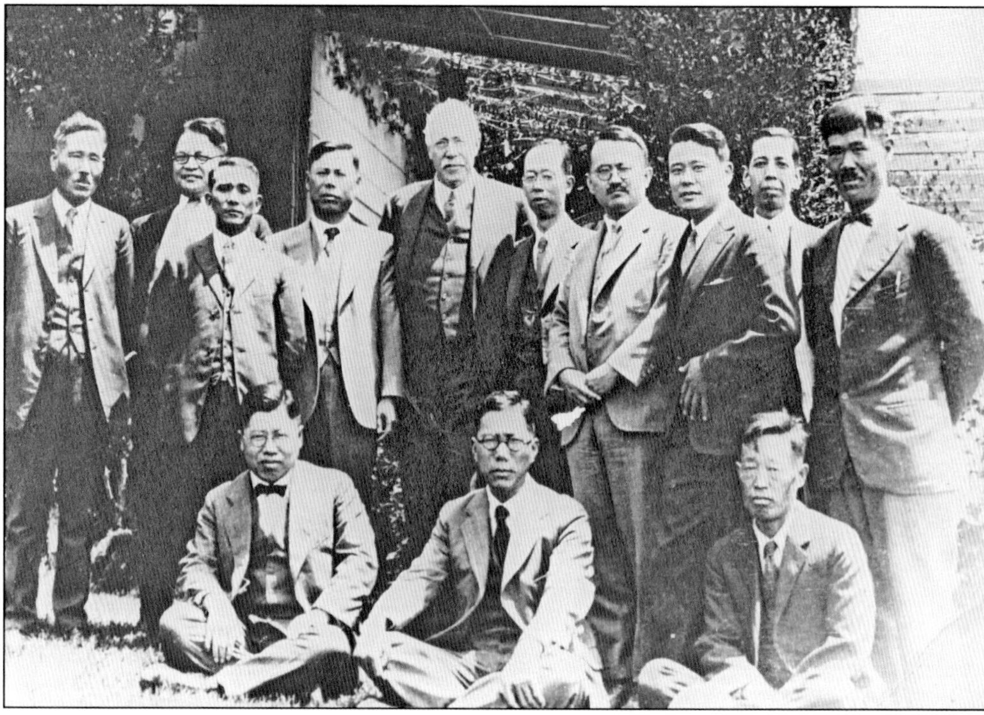

The Vanderlips had marvelous luncheon parties at their summer home. Since guests drove many miles and the roads were primitive, parties ran late. Guests included superstars Pola Negri and Josephine Baker. In this 1928 photograph, Frank A. Vanderlip hosts dignitaries from Japan and Palos Verdes. Nobusuke Kishi, who was to become Japan's prime minister in the 1950s, stands second from the right in the back. (Courtesy Local History Collection, Palos Verdes Library.)

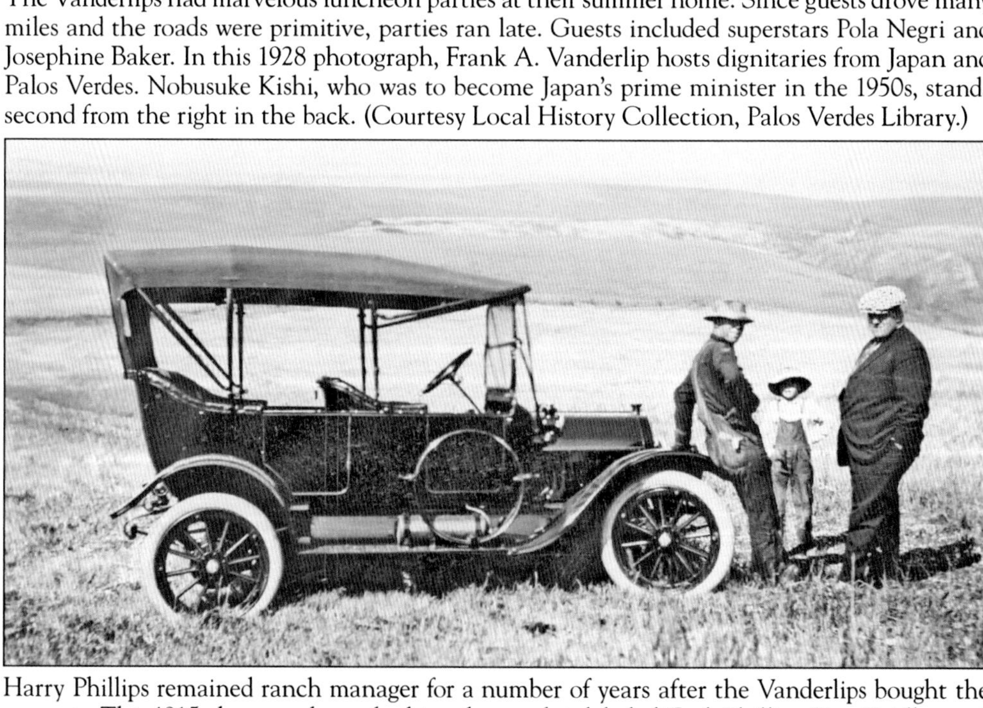

Harry Phillips remained ranch manager for a number of years after the Vanderlips bought the property. This 1915 photograph overlooking the ranch is labeled "Jack Phillips, Dan Gridley, and famous tenor." The man in the cap looks remarkably like Enrico Caruso. The Vanderlips may have requested a tour of the ranch for their famous guest. (Courtesy Local History Collection, Palos Verdes Library.)

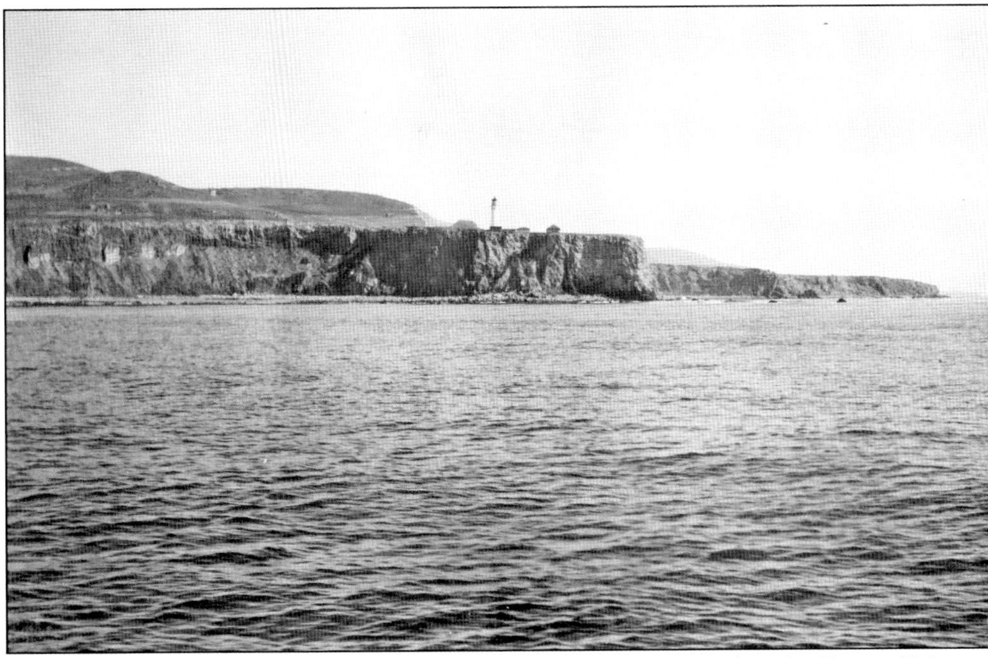

Capt. George Vancouver originally named this Point Vincente after the Friar of Mission Buenaventura. The name was changed to Point Vicente by the Pacific Geographical Society in 1933. The peninsula began as a small island several hundred thousand years ago. It rose from the sea in fits and starts. Between each rise, the sea created a beach, and with each rise, the beach became a terrace. Palos Verdes has 13 terraces so far. (Courtesy Point Vicente Interpretive Center.)

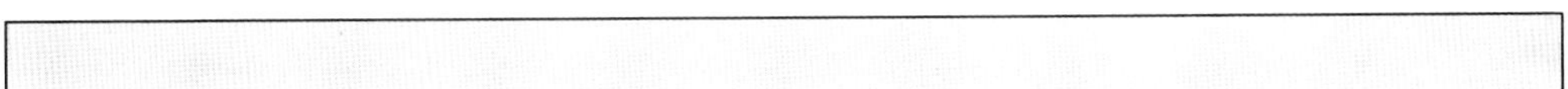

In 1916, Congress approved funding to build the lighthouse at Point Vicente. Since this was land that Frank A. Vanderlip had planned for a village, a five-year battle ensued to wrest the property from him. Finally, after threats of eminent domain, the government acquired the 8-acre property. In 1926, the lighthouse went into service with seven buildings, including an electrical generating plant to power the light. (Courtesy Linda Cherney.)

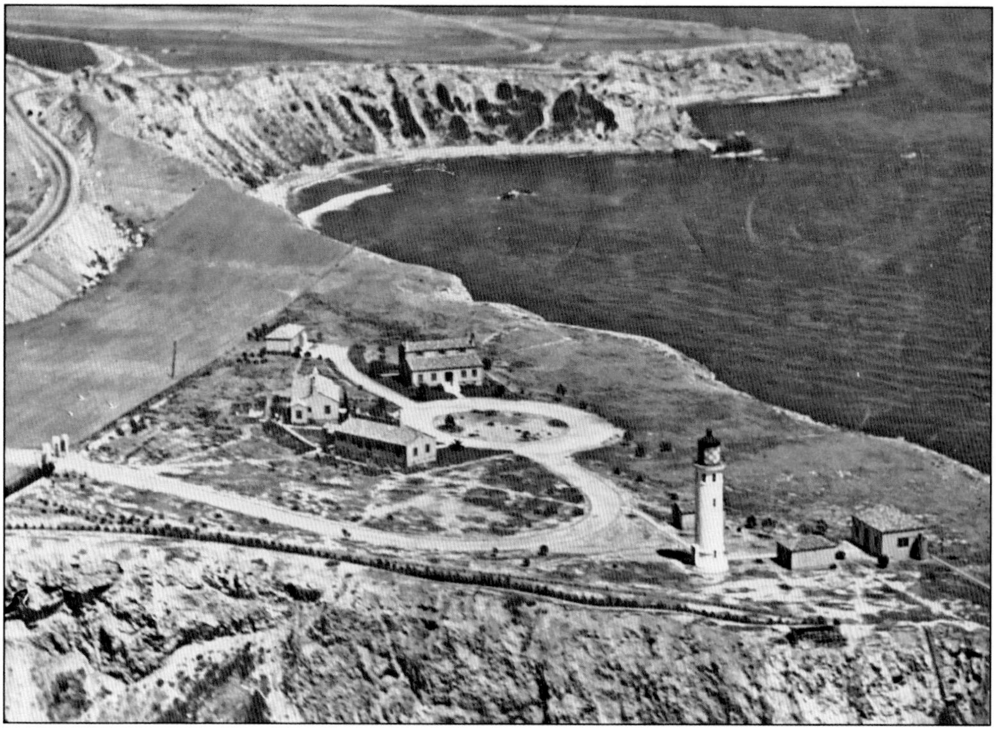

In 1789, George Washington signed an act that required lighthouses to be turned over to the central government. In 1910, the Bureau of Lighthouses was created. One of the three civilians who ran the newly created lighthouse at Point Vicente in 1926 was Raymond Deurloo, who married a Lomita woman named Heertha in 1928 and brought his bride to live on this lonely point. (Courtesy Linda Cherney.)

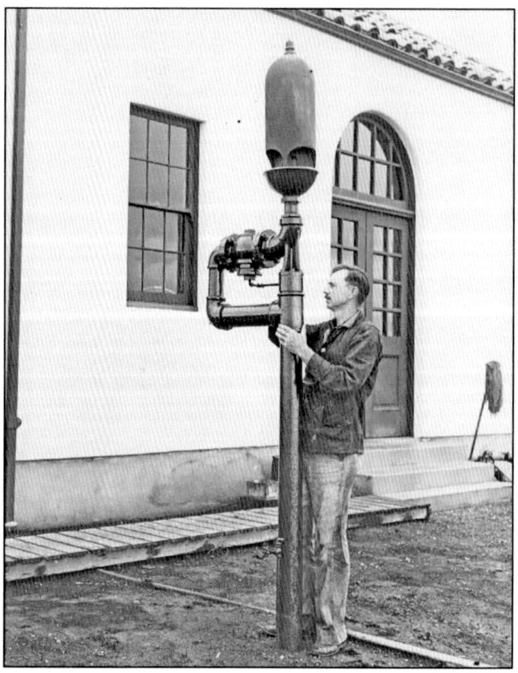

In 1930, forty-two-year-old Anton Trittinger (pictured here) took over as lighthouse keeper. He and his wife, Frieda, and their two daughters moved from the Farallon lighthouse in northern California. They were greeted by kerosene lamps, a coal-fired stove, and a fireplace for heat. The steam-driven foghorn, shown here, gave ear-piercing blasts, sometimes for days on end. (Courtesy Linda Cherney.)

Fresnel invented his lens in 1822, but it was not tested until a new lighthouse board was created in 1852. Ten years later, all lighthouses in the United States had them. This lens was hand-ground in 1886 in France and spent 40 years of service in Alaska before being installed at Point Vicente. Anton Trittinger polishes this 1,000-watt bulb. The light can be seen for 20 miles. (Courtesy Linda Cherney.)

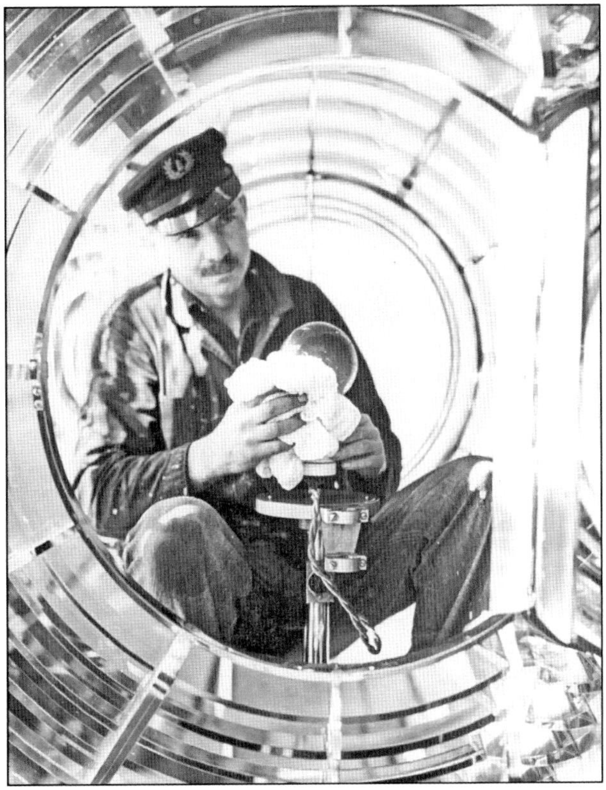

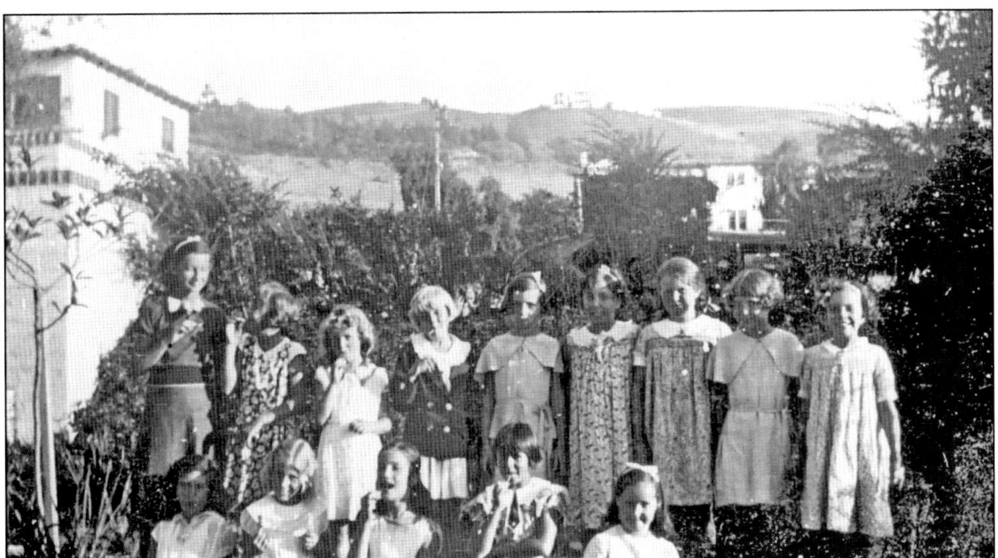

The Trittinger daughters attended Malaga Cove School. They and other grade school children from the south side of the peninsula arrived at school on a bus or in the back of one of the Japanese farm trucks over unpaved roads. Sophie was 18 months older than Mary. This photograph is of the girls at a party being held at the school in the mid-1930s. (Courtesy Linda Cherney.)

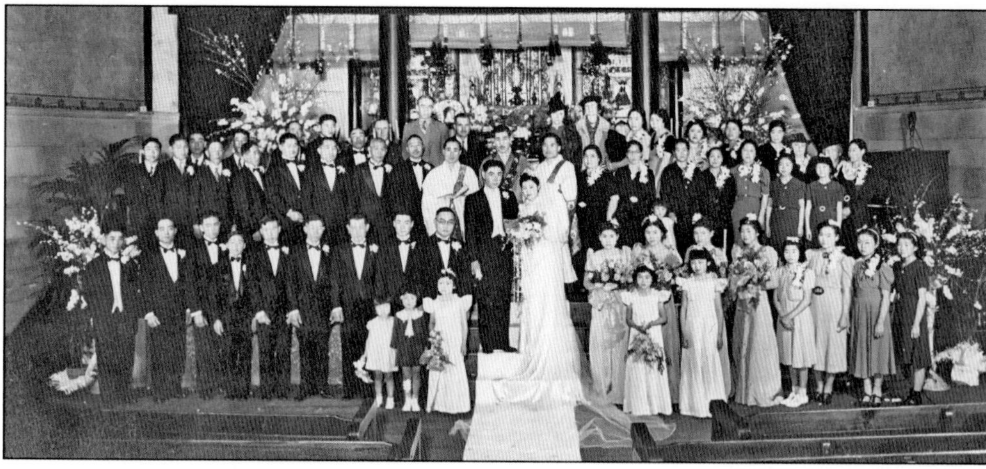

Japanese vegetable farms surrounded the lighthouse. These farmers were the Trittinger's nearest neighbors, and some became friends. These two Japanese weddings, many years apart, were held at the same Buddhist temple in Gardena. In both photographs, Anton, the lighthouse keeper, is in the back center behind the bride and groom. Frieda wears a plain hat and is in the back on the bride's side. In the photograph of the later wedding, Anton wears a flower in his lapel and the girls, who are now teenagers, stand in the very back with their mother in front of them. (Both, courtesy Linda Cherney.)

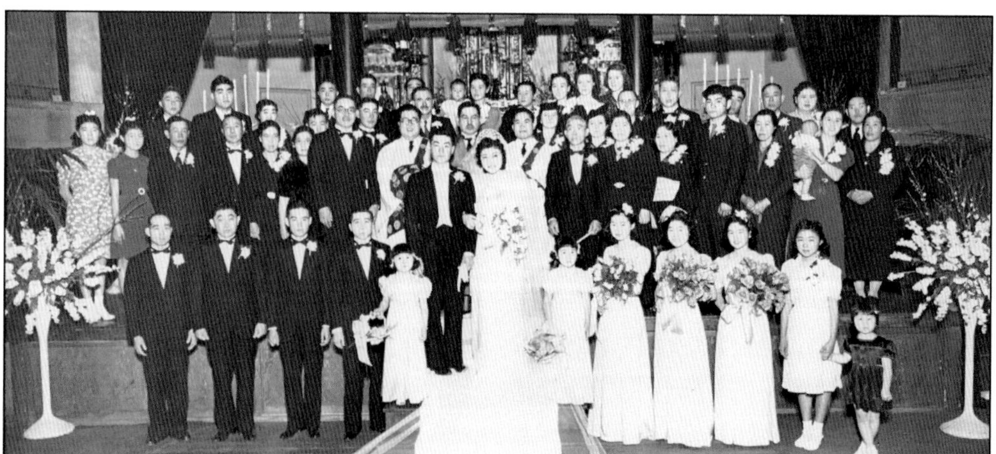

This photograph, which shows the Trittingers gardening, may be posed, but in fact, over the years they took barren ground and planted trees and drought-tolerant geraniums, creating a colorful garden on the arid lighthouse grounds. The trees and many of the plants are still there. "It was so barren. My parents wanted to make it beautiful," said daughter Mary, now in her 80s. (Courtesy Linda Cherney.)

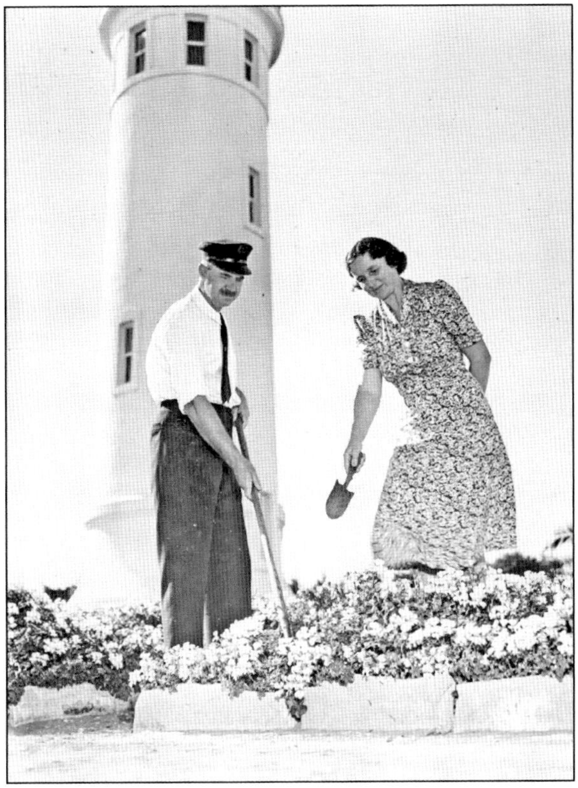

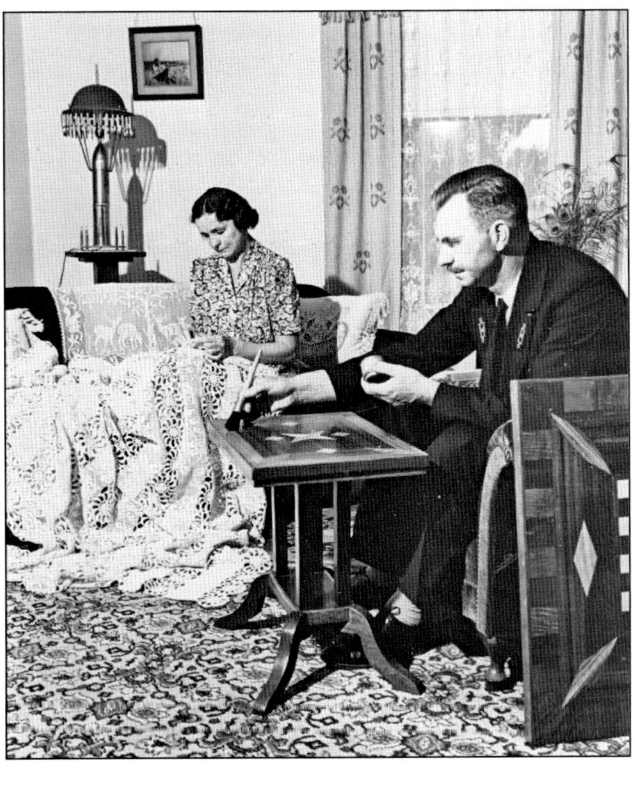

Anton Trittinger was born in Austria. When he went back to visit family, he met Freida, and a year after his return, he sent for her. They married in 1921. Anton was a lighthouse keeper almost all of his working life. Here they share their evenings with their respective hobbies—Freida crocheting and Anton completing his wood-inlayed furniture. (Courtesy Linda Cherney.)

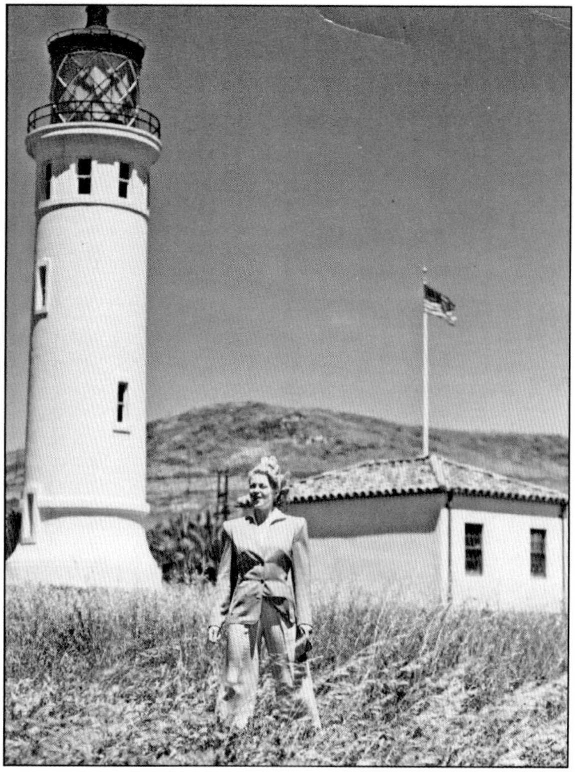

The lighthouse, like the rest of the beautiful peninsula, attracted movie stars who found it the perfect background for studio photograph opportunities. Lana Turner made a memorable visit on April 18, 1941, to the delight of the Trittinger family. (Photograph by Carpenter; courtesy MGM Studios Location Department and Linda Cherney.)

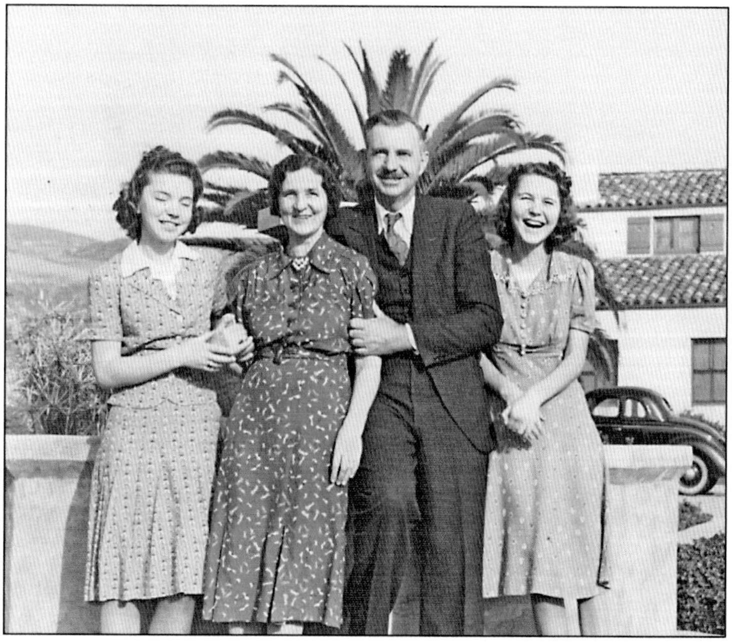

In 1939, the Bureau of Lighthouses was integrated into the U.S. Coast Guard. Lighthouse service personnel were given the option to be brought into the coast guard or to remain civilian employees. Anton joined the coast guard and stayed on as lighthouse keeper until 1945. Here he stands on the grounds with his family: (from left to right) Mary, Freida, and Sophie. (Courtesy Linda Cherney.)

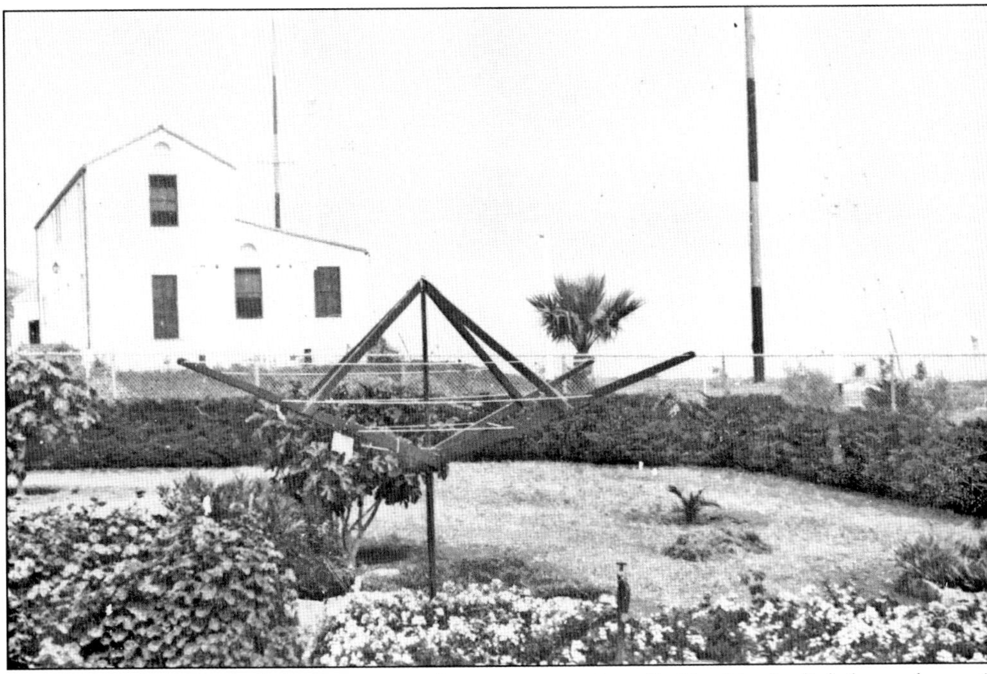

In 1934, a radio room with high towers and antennas was installed beside the lighthouse keeper's house—beyond the clothes-drying line—and was run by the U.S. Lighthouse Service. In 1939, when the U.S. Coast Guard took over, Lt. Leo G. Bellarts became the radio station's first commanding officer. It was staffed with seven radio officers, a cook, and a seaman who worked around the clock in shifts. (Courtesy Linda Cherney.)

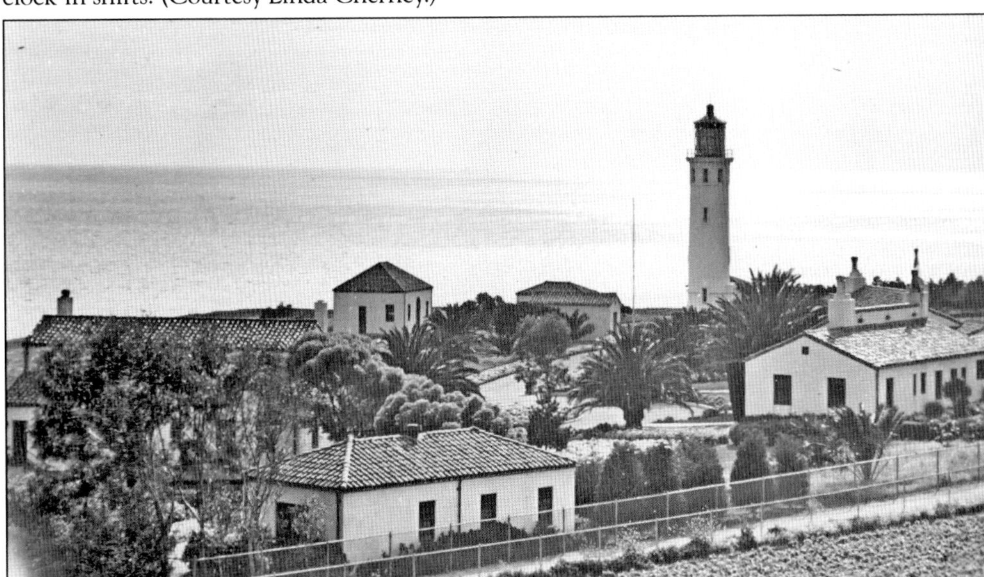

In 1945, Anton Trittinger retired from his 15 years of lighthouse duty at Point Vicente. He then joined the army, moved to San Pedro, and was stationed at Fort MacArthur for the rest of his career. He and Freida left the lighthouse grounds lovely, lush, and green with growth—quite a change from the arid, barren ground that had met them on their arrival in 1930. (Courtesy Linda Cherney.)

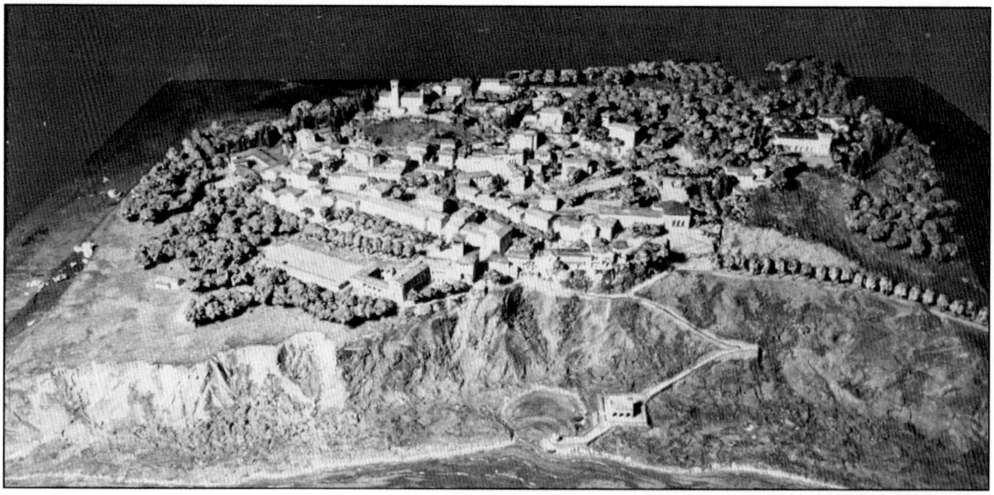

Vanderlip felt he had a mandate to protect these lovely, terraced hills that so reminded him of Italy. He set about to develop them with care, hiring landscape architect Frederick Law Olmsted Jr. to create a master plan. Vanderlip also commissioned French landscape designer Jacques Greber to build plaster models of his vision. For Point Vicente, he wanted an artisans' village cascading down the hill in steps. (Courtesy Ken Dyda.)

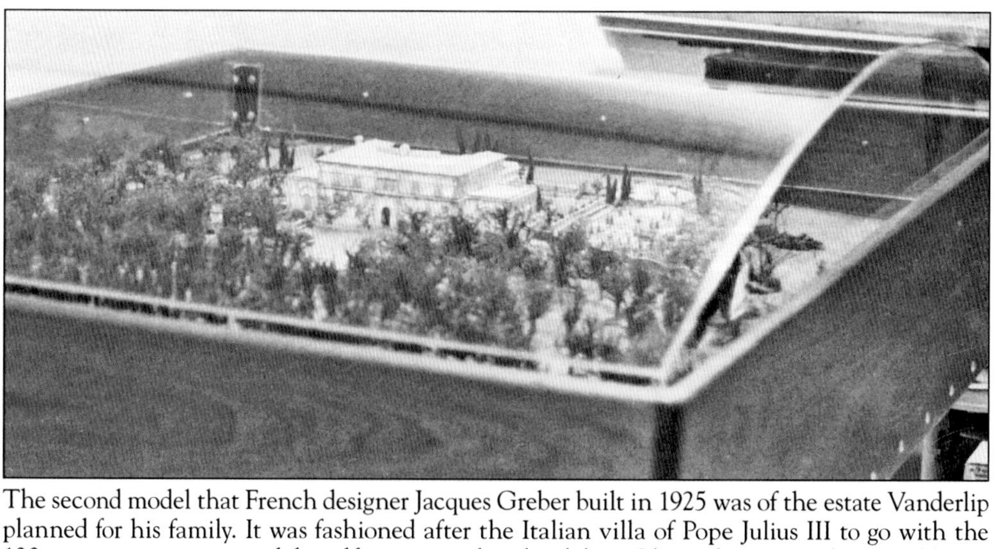

The second model that French designer Jacques Greber built in 1925 was of the estate Vanderlip planned for his family. It was fashioned after the Italian villa of Pope Julius III to go with the 100-acre estates, country club, golf course, and yacht club in Olmsted's master plan. World War I disrupted the plans, and both models languished for years at Beechwood, the Vanderlip estate in New York. (Courtesy John McTaggart.)

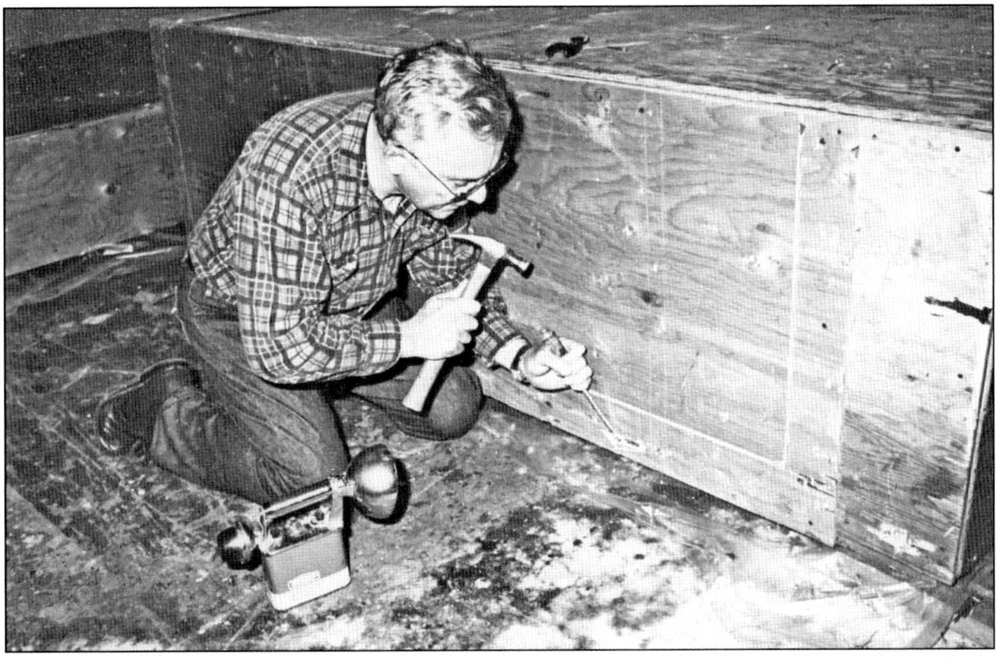

In the 1990s, the models were donated to the Palos Verdes Historical Society by Frank Vanderlip Jr. through the work of Ralph Jester and Ken Dyda. Dyda arranged for the models' trip back to California, and when they arrived, he had them stored in the bunkers near the Rancho Palos Verdes city hall. Here is Ken Dyda, wielding hammer and screwdriver to open the first crate. (Courtesy Ken Dyda.)

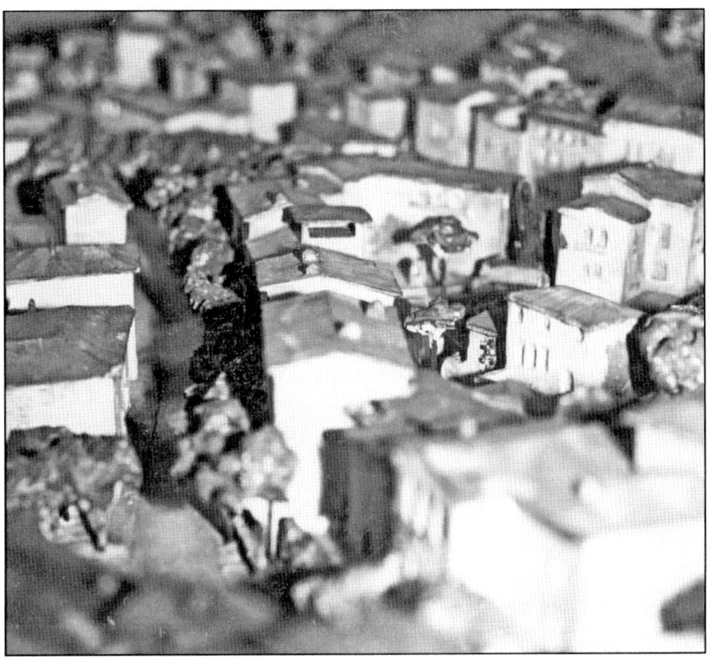

This artisans' village, a copy of the Italian village Neri, was one of the two restored by local model maker Joe Cocke (pronounced Coke) who worked at the Los Angeles County Museum of Natural History. Cocke painstakingly reglued pieces, touched up paint, and gently removed dust with a damp brush to make it look "not new, but like a 25-year-old model." The legendary Cocke was impressed with Greber's workmanship. (Courtesy John McTaggart.)

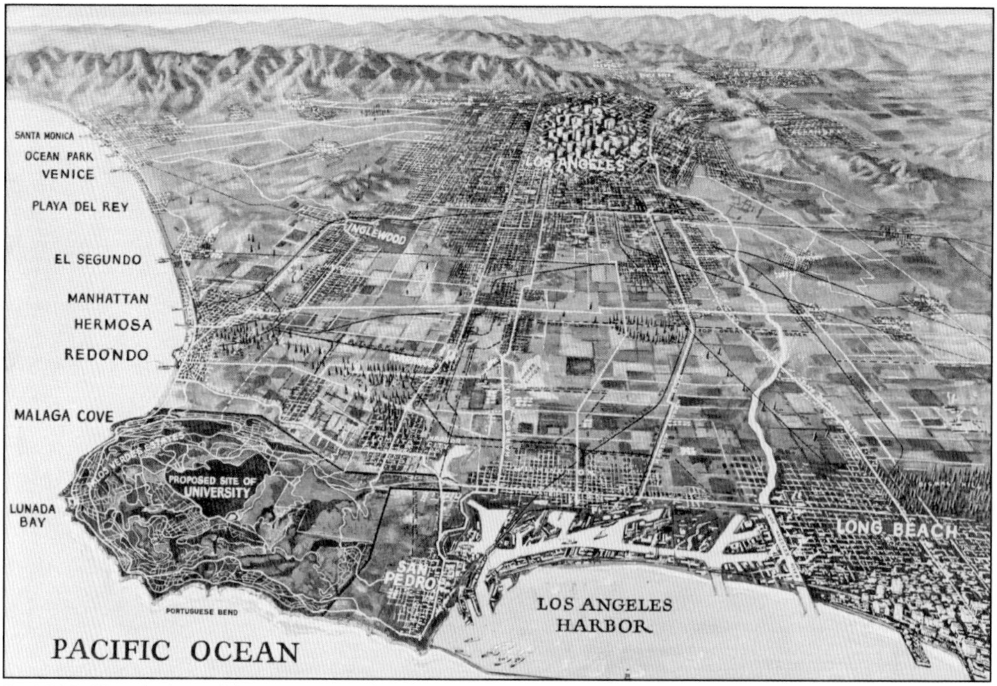

In 1923, Vanderlip sold 3,200 acres for the same price that he and his associates had paid for the whole peninsula. This became Palos Verdes Estates and Miraleste. In 1925, the University of California at Los Angeles, then on Vermont Avenue, considered Palos Verdes for its permanent home. However, according to Ralph Jester, the plans fell through and Janss Investment snagged the university for Westwood Village. (Courtesy Local History Collection, Palos Verdes Library.)

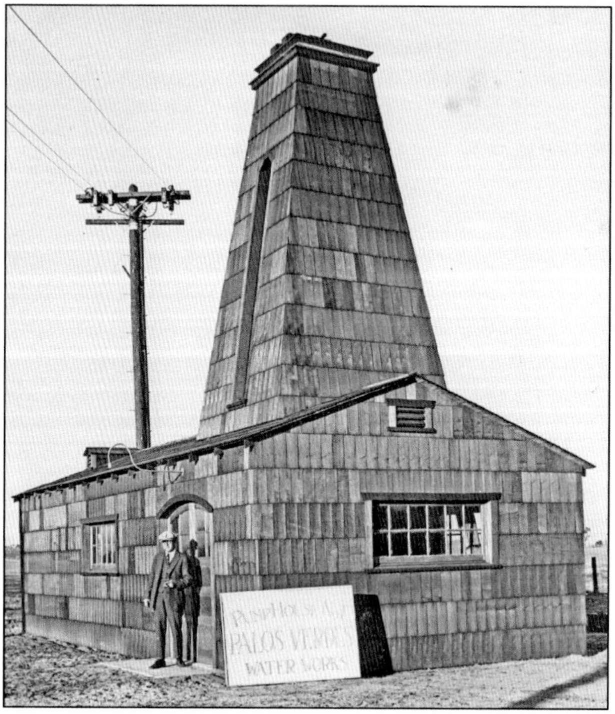

The Palos Verdes Water Company was formed in 1923 to bring water from the aquifer near Harbor Lake (formerly called Bixby Slough and earlier Laguna Machado) to the newly created town of Palos Verdes Estates. This 1925 photograph shows Pump House No. 1 near the lake, which drew the water and sent it around the north side of the hill. (Courtesy California Water Service Company and Point Vicente Interpretive Center.)

Los Angeles, Cal. Jan. 22, 1912.

Dear Sir:-

Pursuant to your request, on the 14th of January, I made a trip over the Palos Verdes Land with a view of making a study as to the possibility of irrigating them and also with the object of inquiring into the possible existance of a continguous water supply for this purpose.

I was already somewhat familiar with the topography and general composition of the Palos Verdes Hills and had always felt that at some future date the superlatively commanding view to be obtained from their slopes, together with the factors of soil and climate which there exist would, provided a water supply were obtained, make them not alone an attractive proposition to the investor, but a delightful site for homes for the wealthy settlers or sojourners whom Southern California attracts.

The time of my visit was particularly fortunate as it followed the period of one of the most disastrous frosts that has visited Southern California in many years, so that I was able to study the effect at first hand. I found a nursery of young tomato plants upon which no effort whatever had been made to protect them from the elements in full vigor and bloom at the ranch place to the southeast of Portuguese Bend on the property here under consideration.

However, as the purpose of my visit had particular reference to the water supply, I will not here attempt any reference to the character of the soil or the extent of the reclaimable areas, which is very considerable on the property.

I find that fortunately the property includes an easterly extension in the direction of Wilmington. It has for a long time been with me a fixed geological theory, which has for its foundation well marked and fully studied indications, that the deep seated fresh water gravels that afforded the copious water supplies of the Alamitos and Dominguez countries may be found bordering the northeast corner of the Palos Verdes Hills in the neighborhood of the Bixby Slough, and quite likely within the easterly extension of the property under discussion. Should this theory prove true, the mechanical difficulty of pumping water to supply the many fertile terraces extending around these hills below the 300 foot level would not prove prohibitive. In fact assuming, just as an instance, a supply of 200 miner's inches, following southerly along the

This first page of a two-page letter from William Mulholland, builder of the Los Angeles aqueduct, is dated right before Jotham Bixby sold the peninsula to Frank A. Vanderlip, so it is unclear to which of them it was addressed. Most interesting is Mulholland's enthusiastic aside on farming and his spot-on prediction of the aquifer's location. He never foresaw the population boom that would ultimately drain it. On page two, he goes on to say that "the proximity of this tract to the ocean gives reasonable assurance that the artificial demands of plant life would be relatively small." (Courtesy Donald B. Jensen and California Water Service Company.)

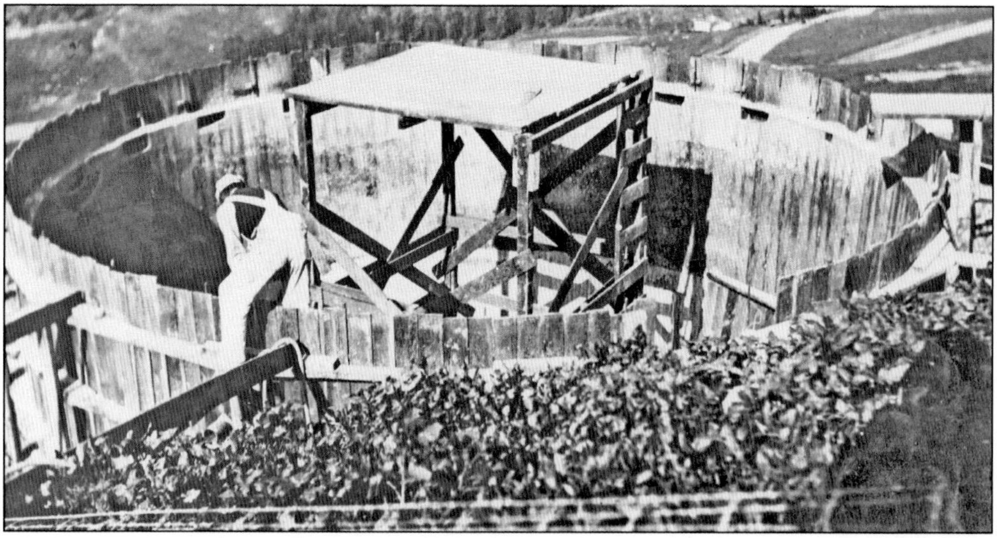

Pump House No. 1 also supplied water to Miraleste on the east side. Water was pumped up the hill in stages and gravity-fed to the houses below. The first pipes were redwood staves banded by iron, as was this early water storage tank shown here atop Miraleste. The pipes and tank were watertight since the wood expands when wet. (Courtesy California Water Service Company and Point Vicente Interpretive Center.)

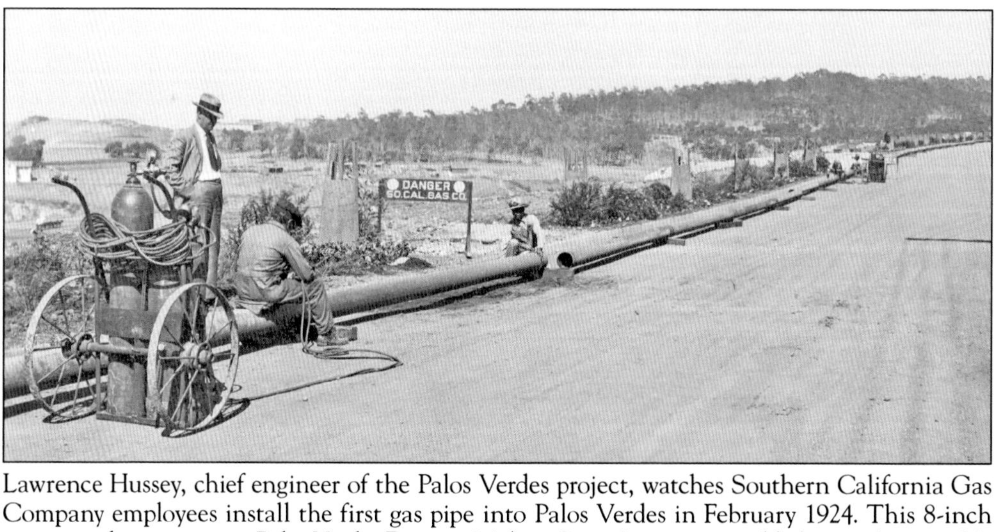

Lawrence Hussey, chief engineer of the Palos Verdes project, watches Southern California Gas Company employees install the first gas pipe into Palos Verdes in February 1924. This 8-inch unwrapped main runs up Palos Verdes Drive to Malaga Cove. Joints were welded using the portable acetylene gas welder on the left. This line was used for 80 years before being replaced. (Courtesy Southern California Gas Company and Point Vicente Interpretive Center.)

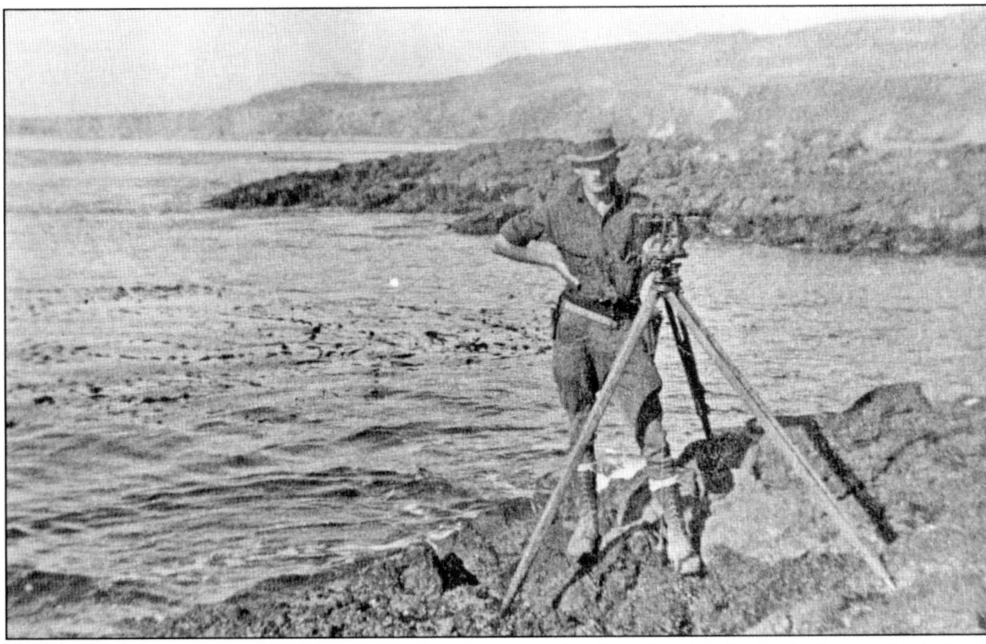

A road system was crucial to peninsula development. In October 1923, the hill over Bluff Cove was blasted with 60 tons of powder, to the great glee of 20,000 onlookers. Called the Douglas Cut, it flattened the Granvia La Costa grade. Work then began past it on the south side of the peninsula. Road surveyor H. Clinton Rapp stands near the road being built in 1925 near Abalone Cove. (Courtesy Local History Collection, Palos Verdes Library.)

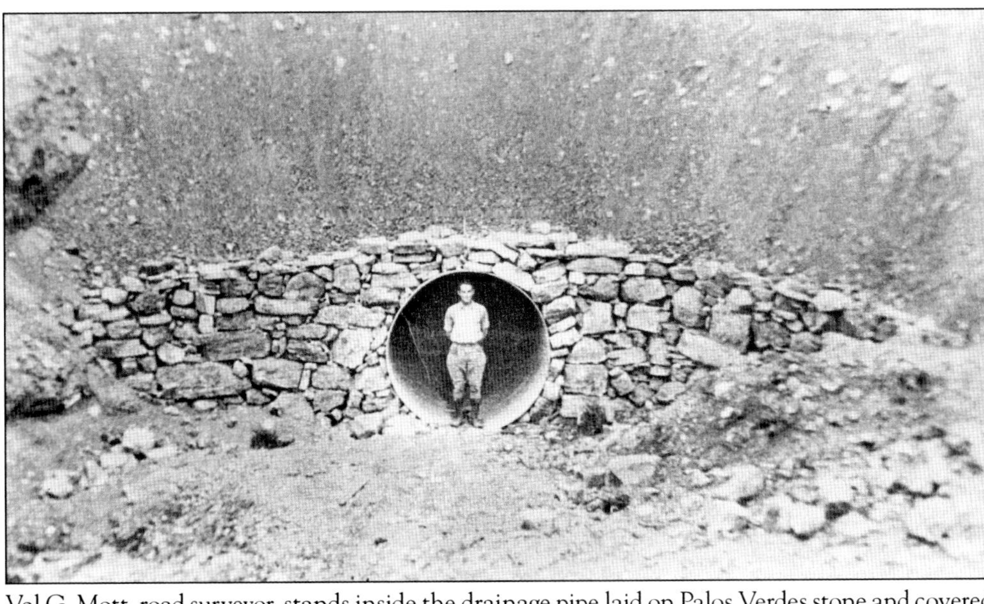

Val G. Mott, road surveyor, stands inside the drainage pipe laid on Palos Verdes stone and covered with dirt up to the roadbed. This process was repeated countless times as the New Coast Road was built over hills and coves along the south side bluffs toward Portuguese Bend and beyond. The road from Lunada Bay to Miraleste was built in one year. (Courtesy Local History Collection, Palos Verdes Library.)

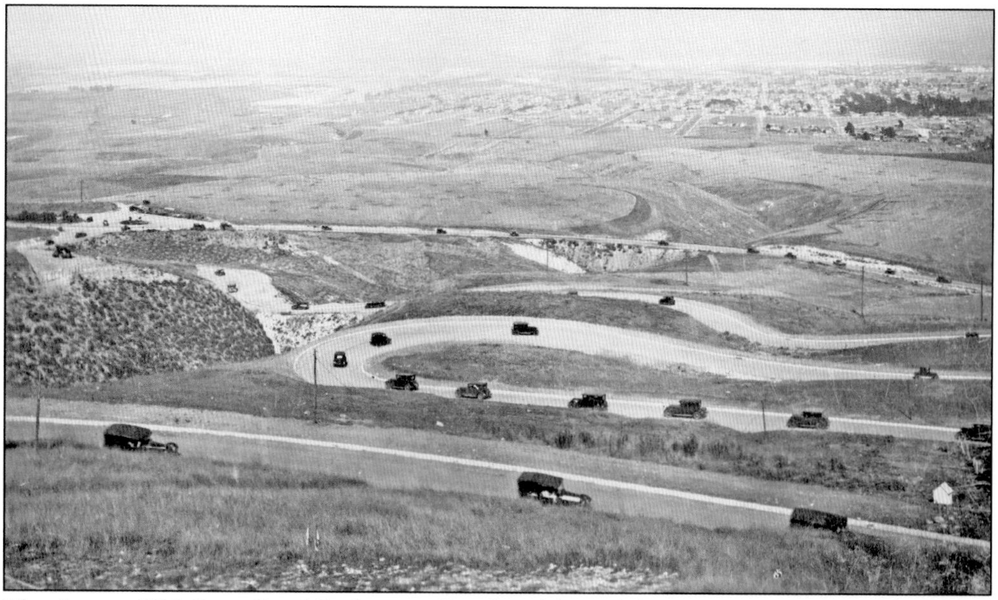

The August 1926 Coast Road Dedication Parade celebrated the completion of the 19-mile road from the Douglas Cut to Miraleste. A caravan of 300 cars paraded from Malaga Cove Plaza onto the New Coast Road (Palos Verdes Drive South) up the hill (Palos Verdes Drive East) toward Miraleste, then down the hill at Miraleste (pictured) to San Pedro. (Courtesy Local History Collection, Palos Verdes Library.)

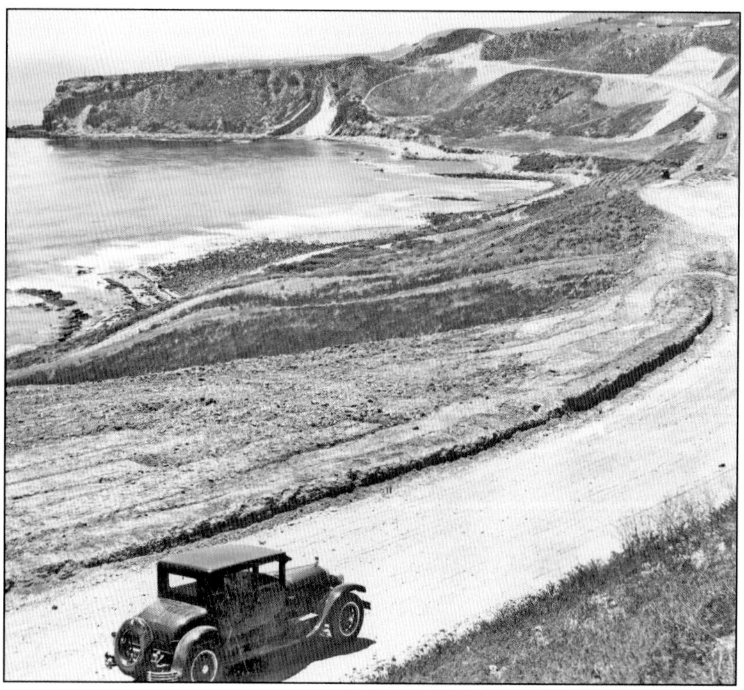

"I stood out where the Narcissa gate house is now, with one of these clocks to count the cars at the opening of the road," said Frank Vanderlip Jr. about the Road Dedication Parade. "I got up a little over a hundred. That pleased my father terribly." Vanderlip Sr. gave the road to the county, graded but unpaved. The county paved it eventually. (Courtesy Local History Collection, Palos Verdes Library.)

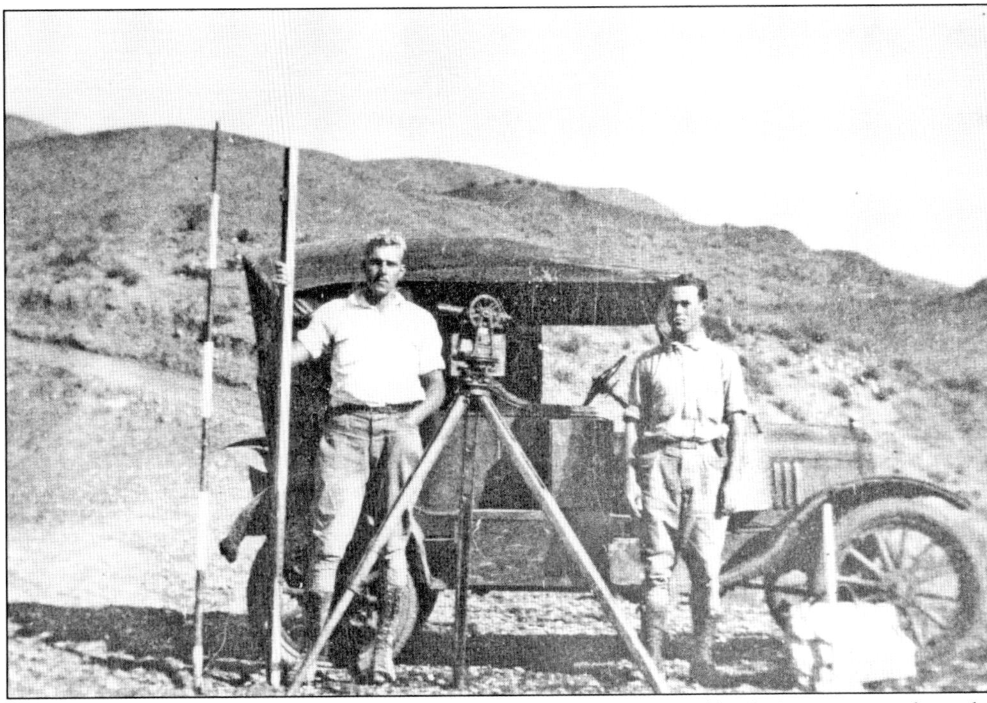

In 1931, the Palos Verdes Corporation contracted to have Crest Road built. It was to run from the New Coast Road at Point Vicente, up the hill, and over to Palos Verdes Drive East in Miraleste. Val G. Mott, the road surveyor (on the right), stands on the hill overlooking Point Vicente with Norm Marshmont, his rod and chain man. (Courtesy Local History Collection, Palos Verdes Library.)

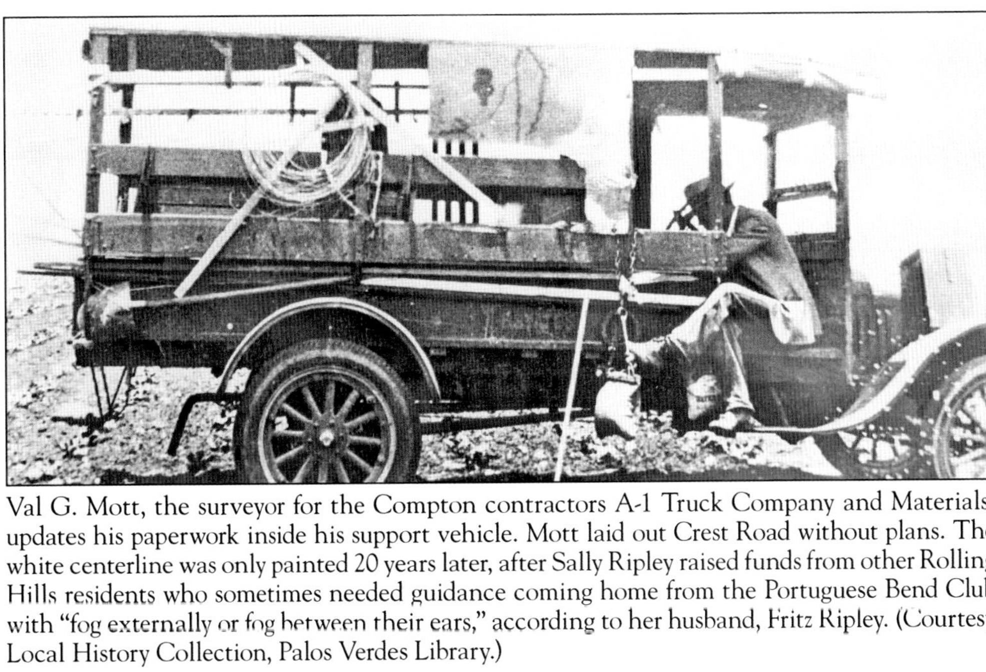

Val G. Mott, the surveyor for the Compton contractors A-1 Truck Company and Materials, updates his paperwork inside his support vehicle. Mott laid out Crest Road without plans. The white centerline was only painted 20 years later, after Sally Ripley raised funds from other Rolling Hills residents who sometimes needed guidance coming home from the Portuguese Bend Club with "fog externally or fog between their ears," according to her husband, Fritz Ripley. (Courtesy Local History Collection, Palos Verdes Library.)

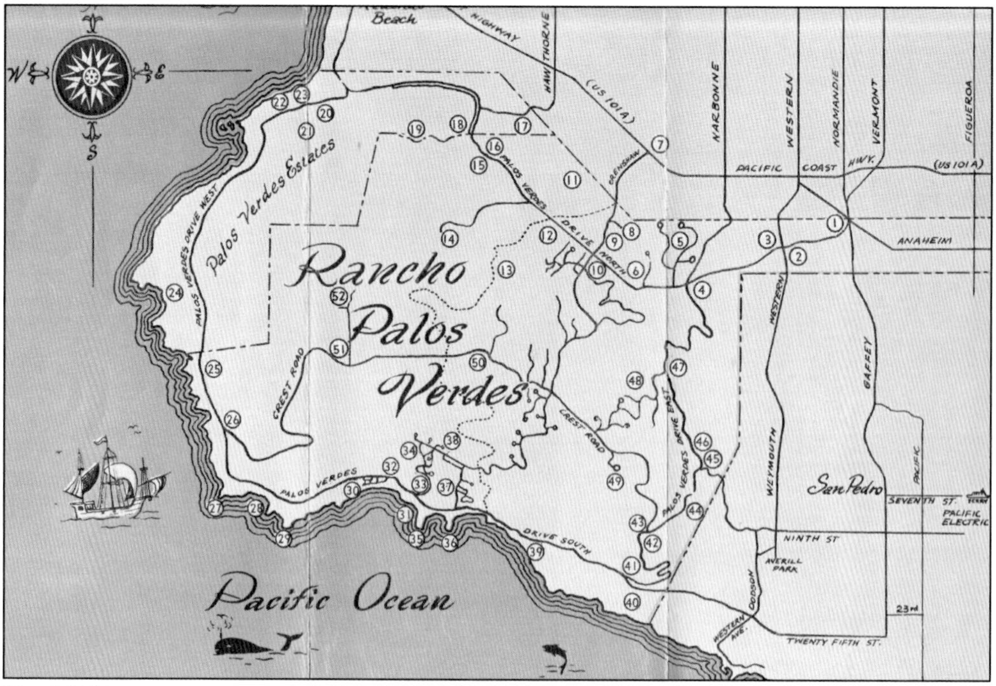

Until 1956, no new major roads were built. This map from a sales brochure of around 1949 shows Crest Road as Val G. Mott laid it out, going from Palos Verdes Drive South to Palos Verdes Drive East. Hawthorne Boulevard and Crenshaw Boulevard, the two roads that were to change the landscape and the future of the lovely Palos Verdes, had not yet been extended. (Courtesy Local History Collection, Palos Verdes Library.)

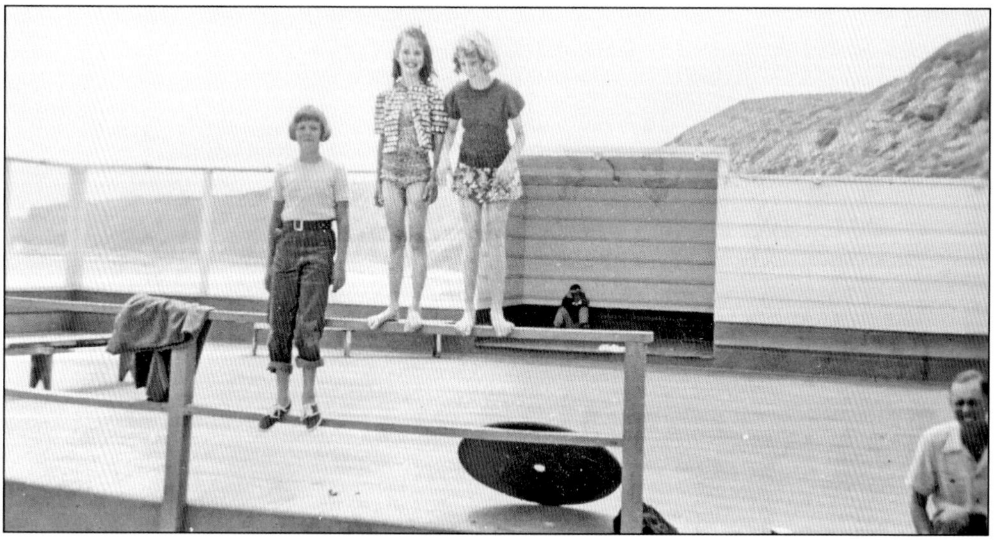

Chadwick School students are pictured at the Abalone Cove beach house in 1939. Diane Jurgens (left) of the Jurgens lotion family boarded at Chadwick while local residents Yvetta Townsend (center) and Nancy Cole commuted. Seated on the right is Yvetta's father, Ward Townsend. The boy in the back is unidentified. Chadwicks founded their Country Day and Boarding School in Palos Verdes from donations of land from the Vanderlips and money from the Roesslers, whose children attended. (Courtesy Yvetta Townsend Williams.)

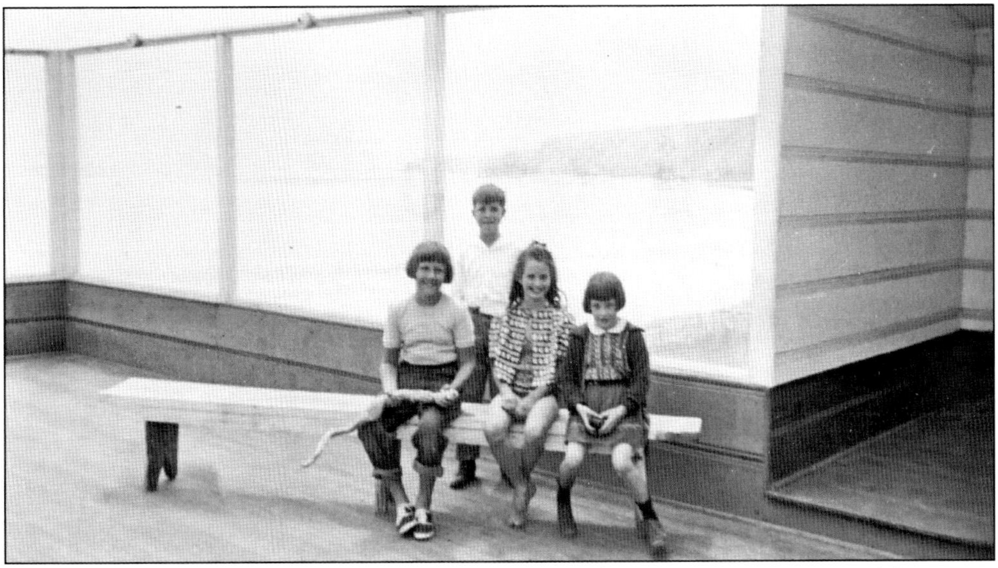

Abalone Cove was an ancient Tongva Indian kitchen midden. During construction of the private beach house, and when holes were dug to plant the two Canary Island date palms on either side of the house, pieces of abalone, the bones of small animals, and Tongva relics were found. Although white sand brought from Redondo Beach covered the cove, squirrels and children regularly dig out more relics. From left to right are Diane Jurgens, Yvetta Townsend, and Nancy Coke. (Courtesy Yvetta Townsend Williams.)

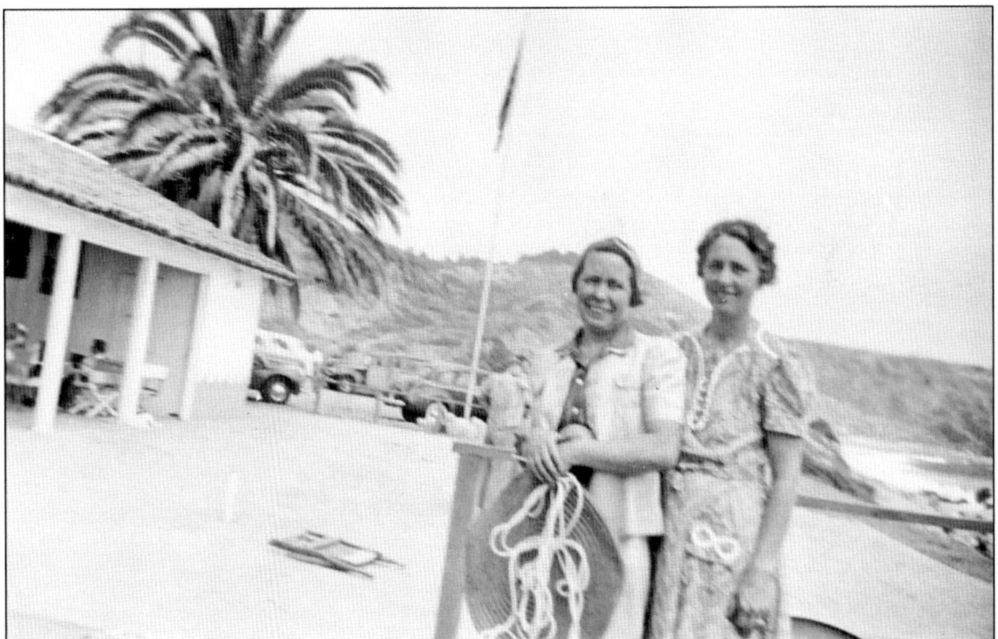

Architect Sumner Spaulding built this Abalone Cove beach house in the 1930s. Contracted by Archie Hanson for Rolling Hills residents, the white house with a red tile roof had a 2-foot wide blue dado painted like wavelets along the bottom few feet where mud might splash. To freshen, only the dado needed painting. Mrs. Ward (Anna C.) Townsend (right) is pictured with an unidentified Chadwick teacher beside her. (Courtesy Yvetta Townsend Williams.)

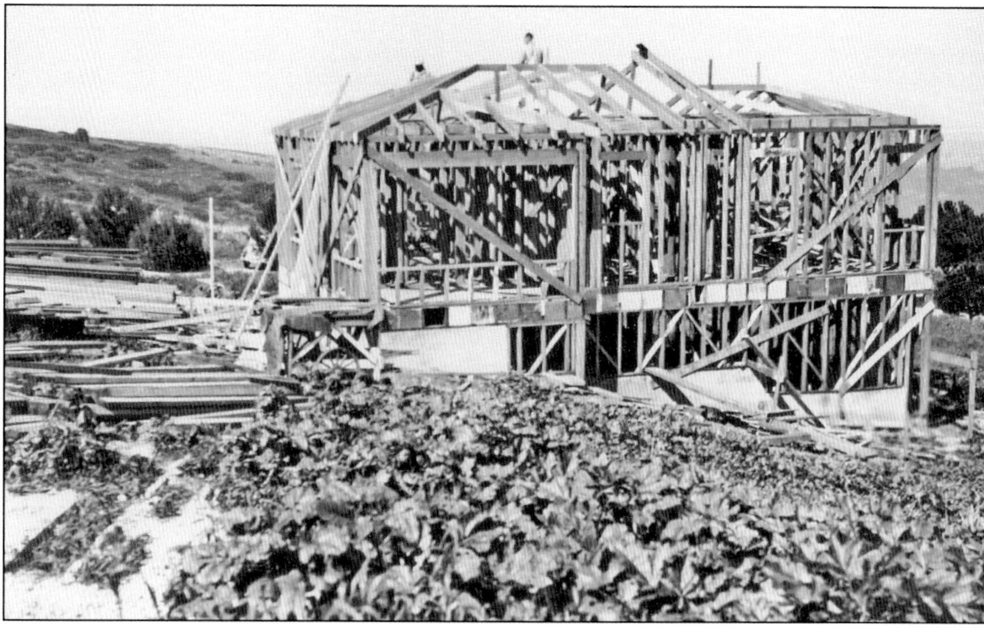

Miraleste (pronounced mir-a-lest-ay) is 300 acres of the Palos Verdes project that "look to the east," as the Spanish suggests. By 1930, eight homes had been built there. The Townsends bought their lot for $500 on Via Canada in 1942 and moved into their home in 1943. "My mother loved living out in the country," said Yvetta Townsend Williams, who was eight years old when the family moved in. (Courtesy Yvetta Townsend Williams.)

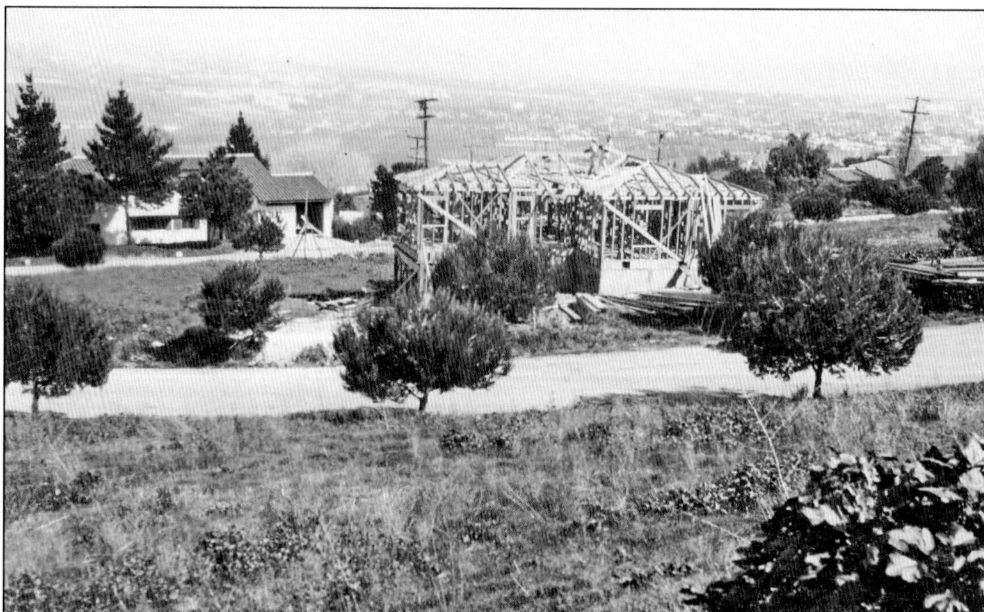

The Stone Pines (round trees) at the bottom of the hill were obtained in 1931 by the Miraleste Association Social Club. A nursery in Lunada Bay had been created and run at cost by landscape architect Frederick Law Olmsted Jr. for residents to beautify their homes, but the Depression put him out of business. Mrs. Arthur (Elsie) Ross, on Via Canada, asked for his stock of Stone Pines and got them. (Courtesy Yvetta Townsend Williams.)

Two

Those who Hug the Coast

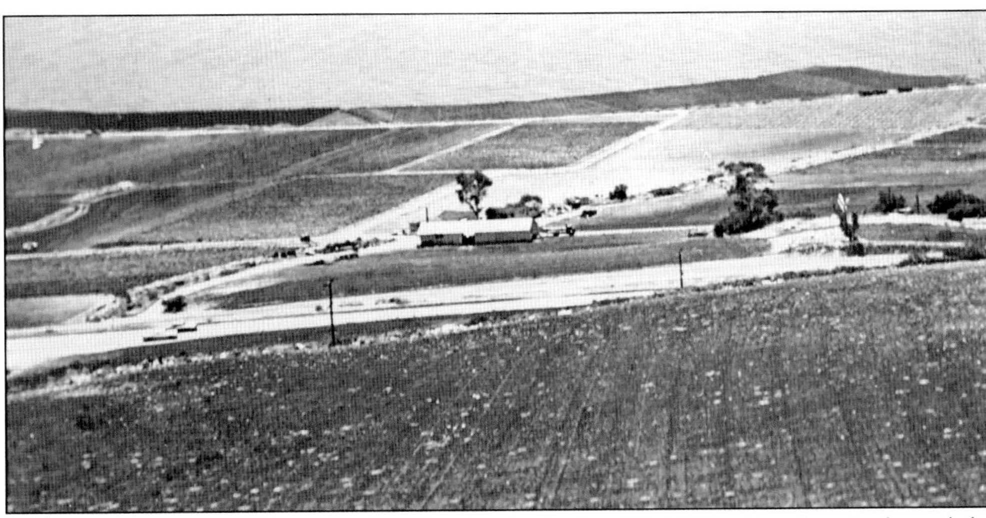

Mas and James Ishibashi brought their families back after World War II and again farmed the coast of Palos Verdes. James Ishibashi said, "It gripes me in my heart. We left everything. They gave us restitution—10 cents on a dollar. Nothing! Then the IRS made us pay income tax on that. They got 90 percent and they still wanted income tax. They were really hoggish about that." (Courtesy Point Vicente Interpretive Center.)

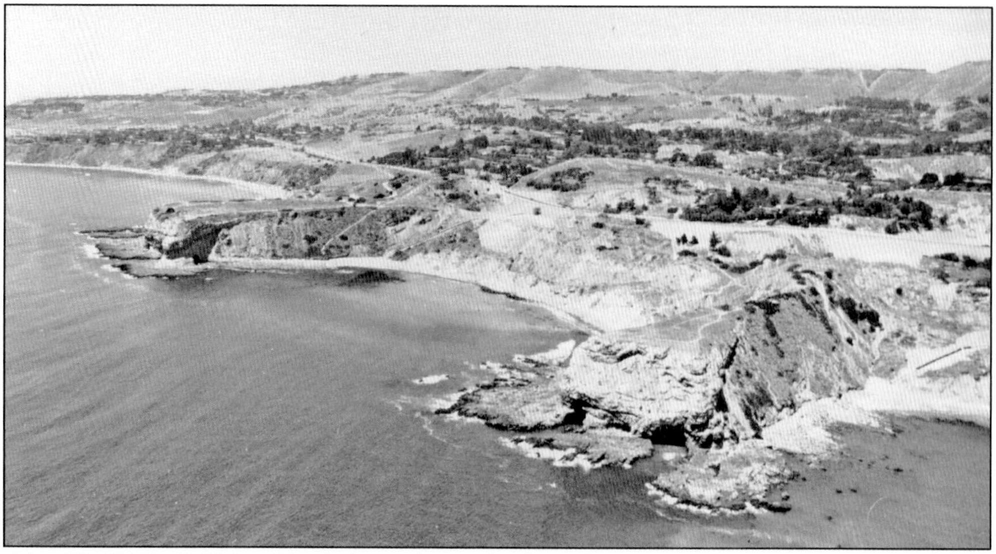

After World War II, Kelvin Vanderlip took over the family business, and for five years the peninsula saw development with gentle land use along the lines of his father Frank A. Vanderlip. Kelvin's most notable development was Portuguese Bend. Building flourished in Portuguese Bend and up the coast at Long Point, too. Shown here are Portuguese Point and Inspiration Point. (Courtesy Local History Collection, Palos Verdes Library.)

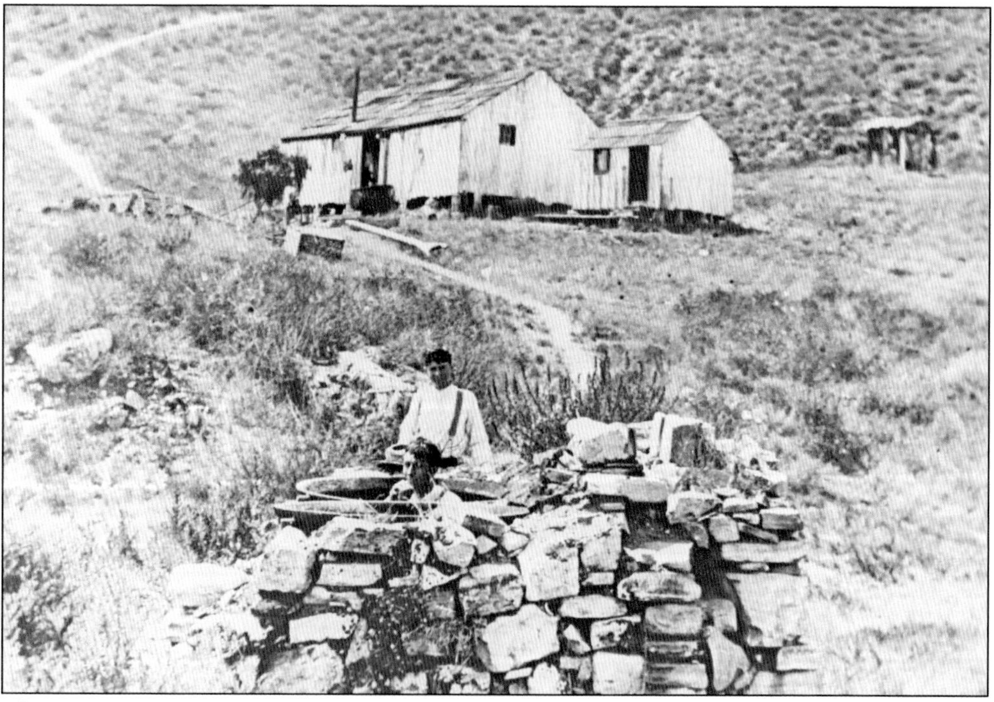

These cast iron try-pots were part of the seasonal Portuguese shore whaling camp, from 1864 to 1884. Migrating gray whales were spotted from a watchtower on Portuguese Point. Boats were rowed out with the spotter pointing the way. The whale was harpooned and dragged to the beach, where it was cut up and the blubber melted in these pots. One whale was worth a lot of money. (Courtesy Mike Fabian.)

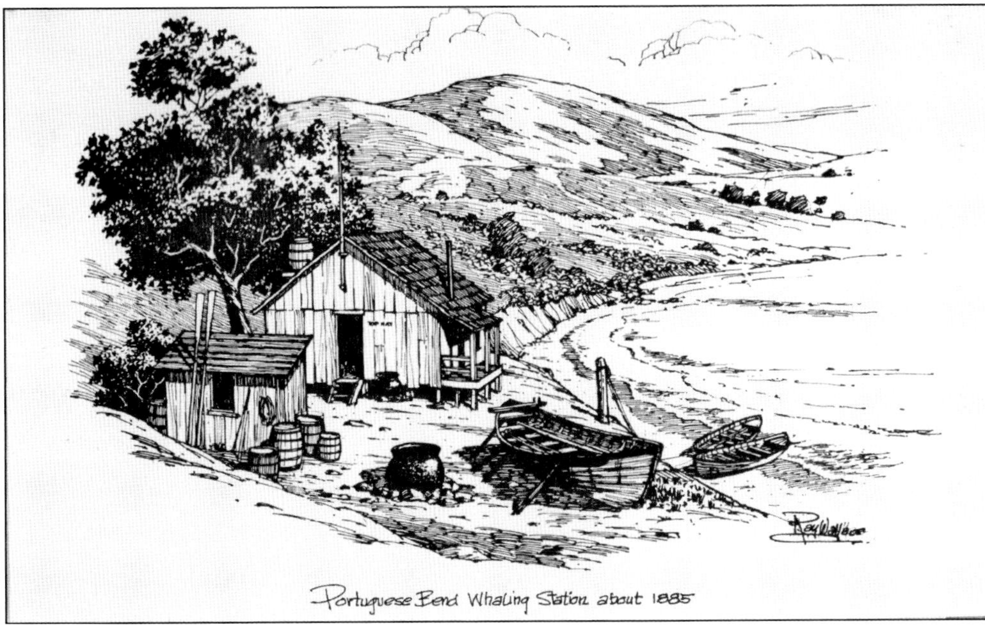

Maritime artist Ray Wallace researched all of his locations for accuracy before drawing them. He believed that these try-pots probably ended up in a café on Sterns Wharf in Santa Barbara. Wallace was also a marine architect, a designer of nautical-themed villages, designer of the ship *Columbia* at Disneyland, an historian, and a yachtsman who, when young, crewed the yacht *Resolute* for Spencer Tracey. (Courtesy Mike Fabian and Barbara Wallace.)

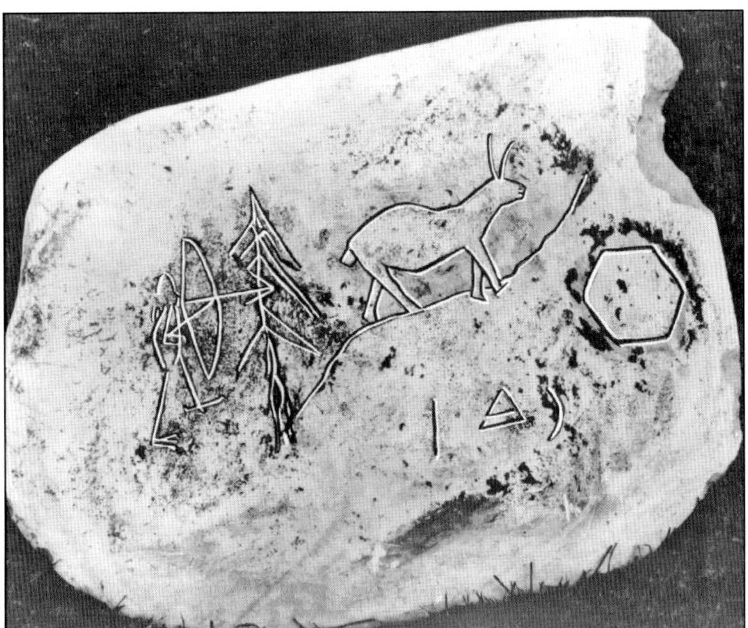

Before the shore whalers came to Portuguese Bend, the Tongva Indians had already discovered it and built a village nearby. This drawing carved on a stone was found in the Portuguese Bend hills and is reputed to be ancient. The photograph has been enhanced for clarity. (Courtesy Local History Collection, Palos Verdes Library.)

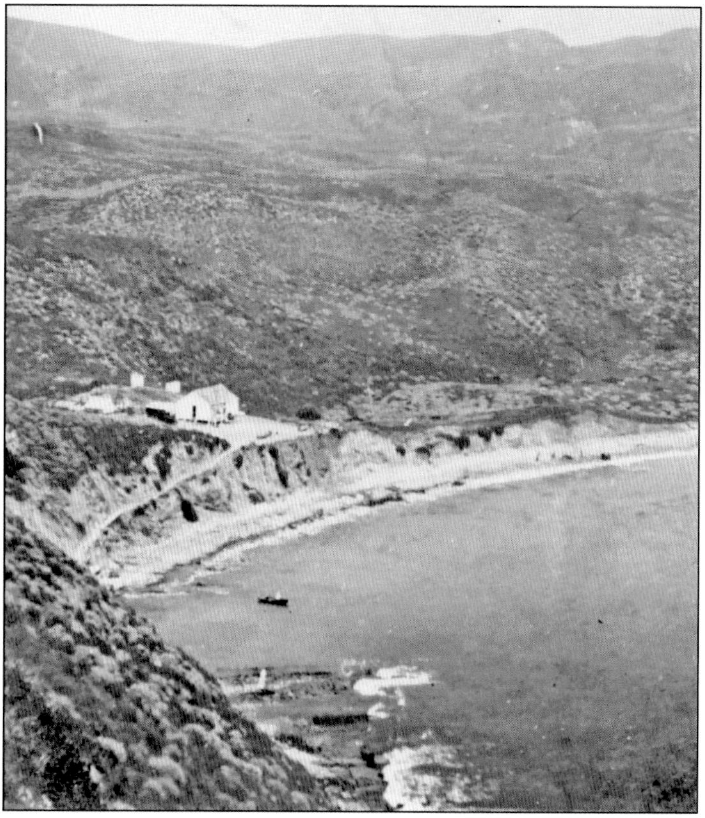

Around 1900, according to Portuguese Bend historian Connie Lufkin, a Scandinavian fisherman named Charles Lundquist moved into the cabin on the hill. Using the original iron try-pots, he prepared 25¢ fish dinners for yachtsmen and excursion boats that came from Long Beach and charged $1.50 for the round trip, including the dinner. Diners brought their own water. The photograph, dated 1909, is labeled "bachelor's house." (Courtesy Local History Collection, Palos Verdes Library.)

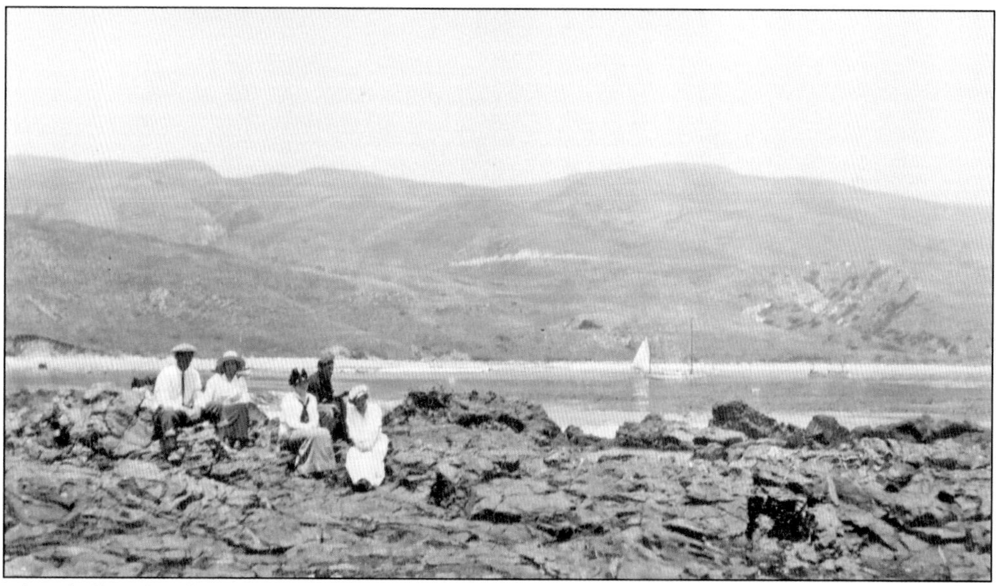

The Phillips family spends a day at Portuguese Bend. This 1914 photograph was taken at the base of Inspiration Point. The primitive road they might have traveled from their ranch can be seen as a line on the hillside. On the water is *Siwash*, a 1910 wooden yawl from the Los Angeles Yacht Club. The Howard Wright family still owns her 100 years later. (Courtesy Local History Collection, Palos Verdes Library.)

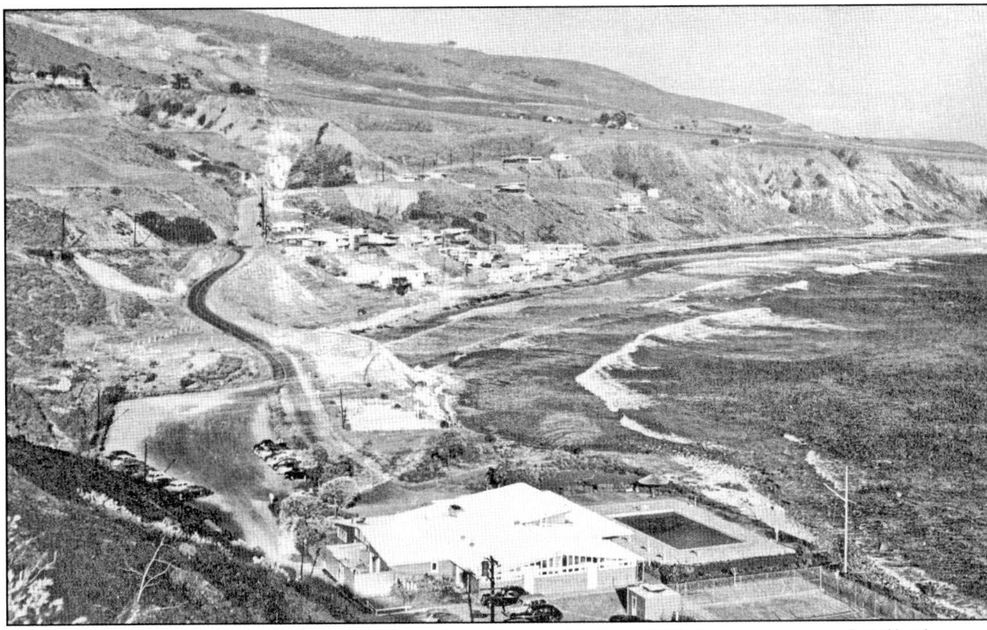

In 1946, six friends—including Fritz Ripley, George Fisher, Bill Severence, and Bill Slater—organized a sailing club at Portuguese Bend. Kelvin Vanderlip, who was developing 1,100 acres in the Portuguese Bend hill area, enthusiastically adopted the idea. By 1948, his Palos Verdes Corporation had created a separate financial entity to build a pier, pool (lower right), and the beachside Portuguese Bend Club. (Courtesy Dennis Jaconi.)

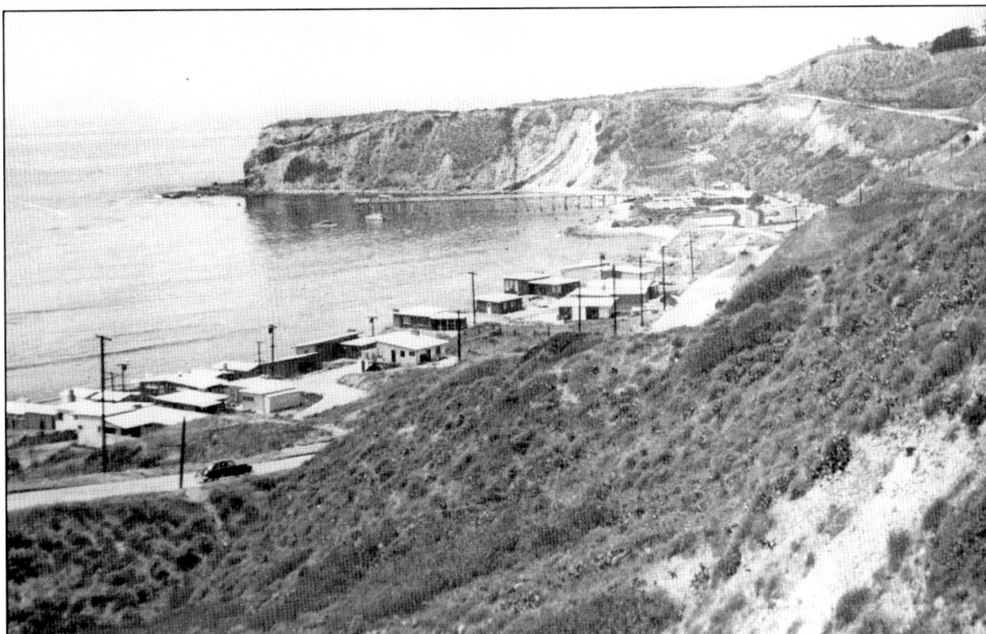

The new Portuguese Bend Club became a social hub for Portuguese Bend parents and children. Along the beach near the club, small lots were leased and homes built. Directly above the pier, that patch of white limestone that identifies Portuguese Bend cove was, according to a reliable source, great for sliding down. (Courtesy Mike Fabian.)

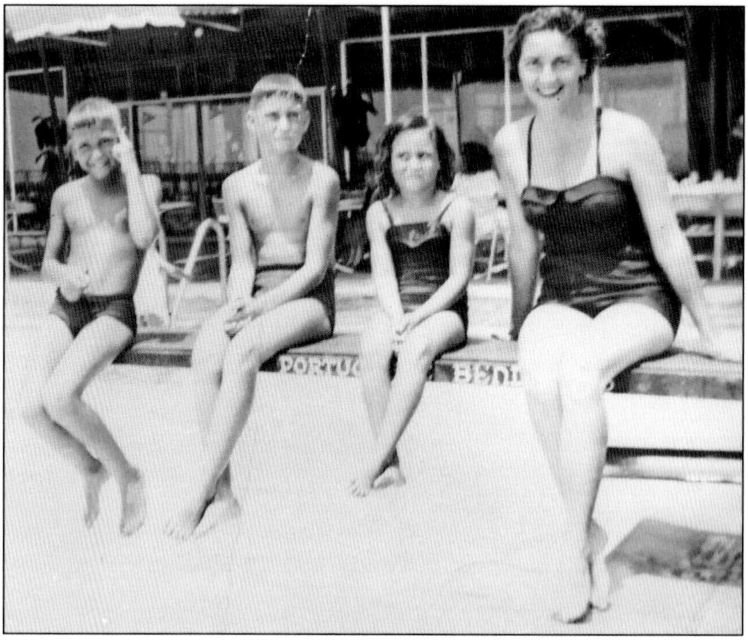

Many of the children took swimming lessons in the club pool from instructor Adrian Beauchamp. Here, in this undated photograph at the pool, is the Jaconi family (from left), Dennin, Marty Junior, Suzy, and their mother Sally Jaconi. Their father, Marty Jaconi, represented the Bank of America's interests with the club. (Courtesy Mike Fabian.)

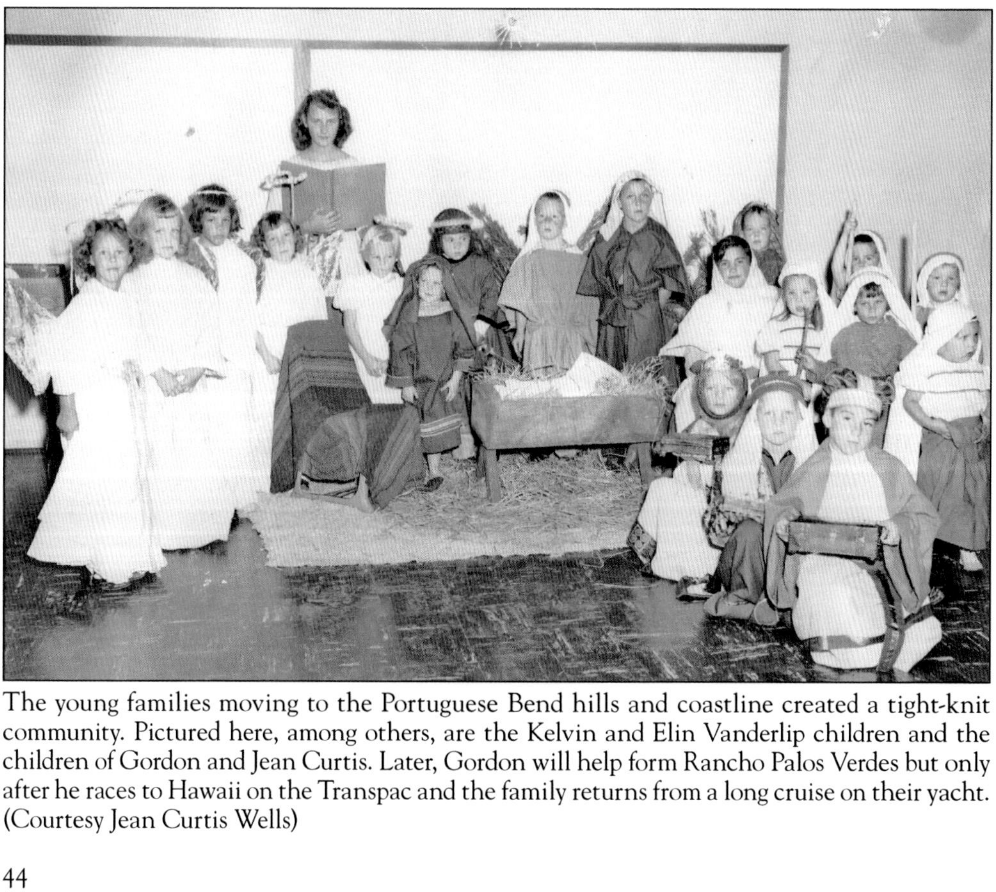

The young families moving to the Portuguese Bend hills and coastline created a tight-knit community. Pictured here, among others, are the Kelvin and Elin Vanderlip children and the children of Gordon and Jean Curtis. Later, Gordon will help form Rancho Palos Verdes but only after he races to Hawaii on the Transpac and the family returns from a long cruise on their yacht. (Courtesy Jean Curtis Wells)

The Club's Fourth of July celebrations were packed with Portuguese Bend neighbors. There were picnics during the day and fireworks at night. Well-known naval architect Hugh Angleman was creating a line of small sailboats called Bendys, and one year he offered the Bendy as a raffle prize. Sally and Marty Jaconi won the boat (pictured). They owned and sailed it for years. (Courtesy Dennis Jaconi.)

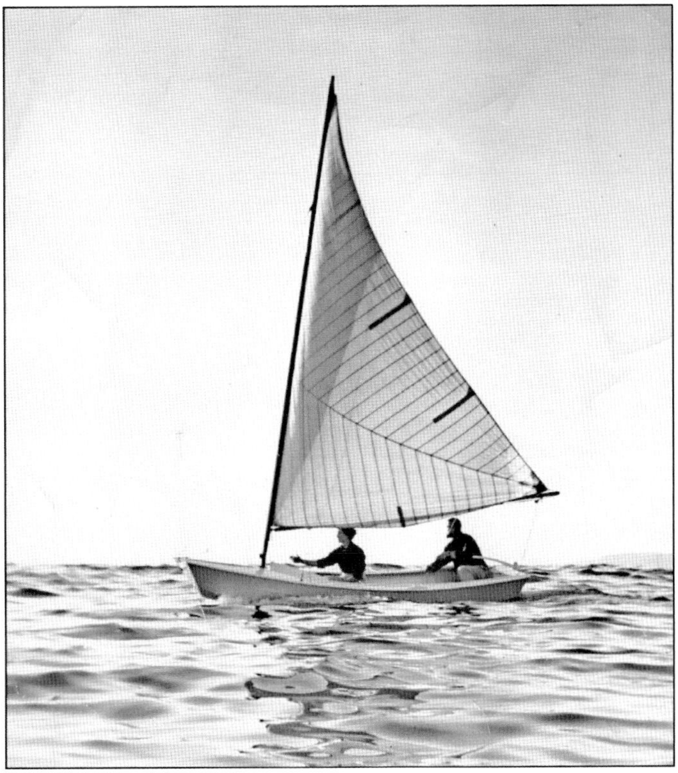

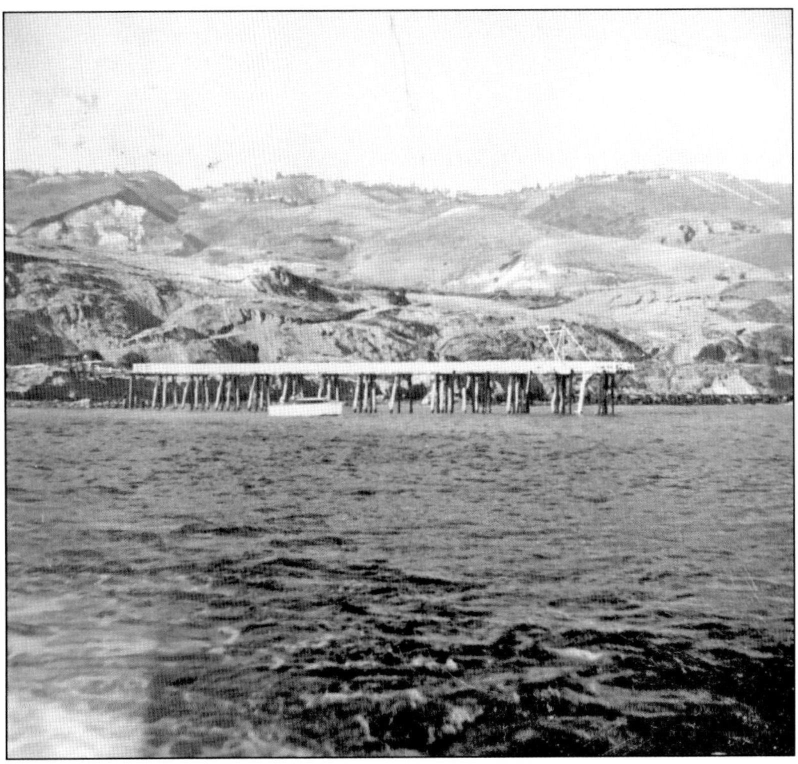

The club provided sailing dinghies for its members to go explore the coastline or, as in the case of at least one young member, an opportunity to learn more about the ocean by going out too far and having to struggle to get back in. The dinghies were launched by the boat hoist shown here at the end of the pier. (Courtesy Dennis Jaconi.)

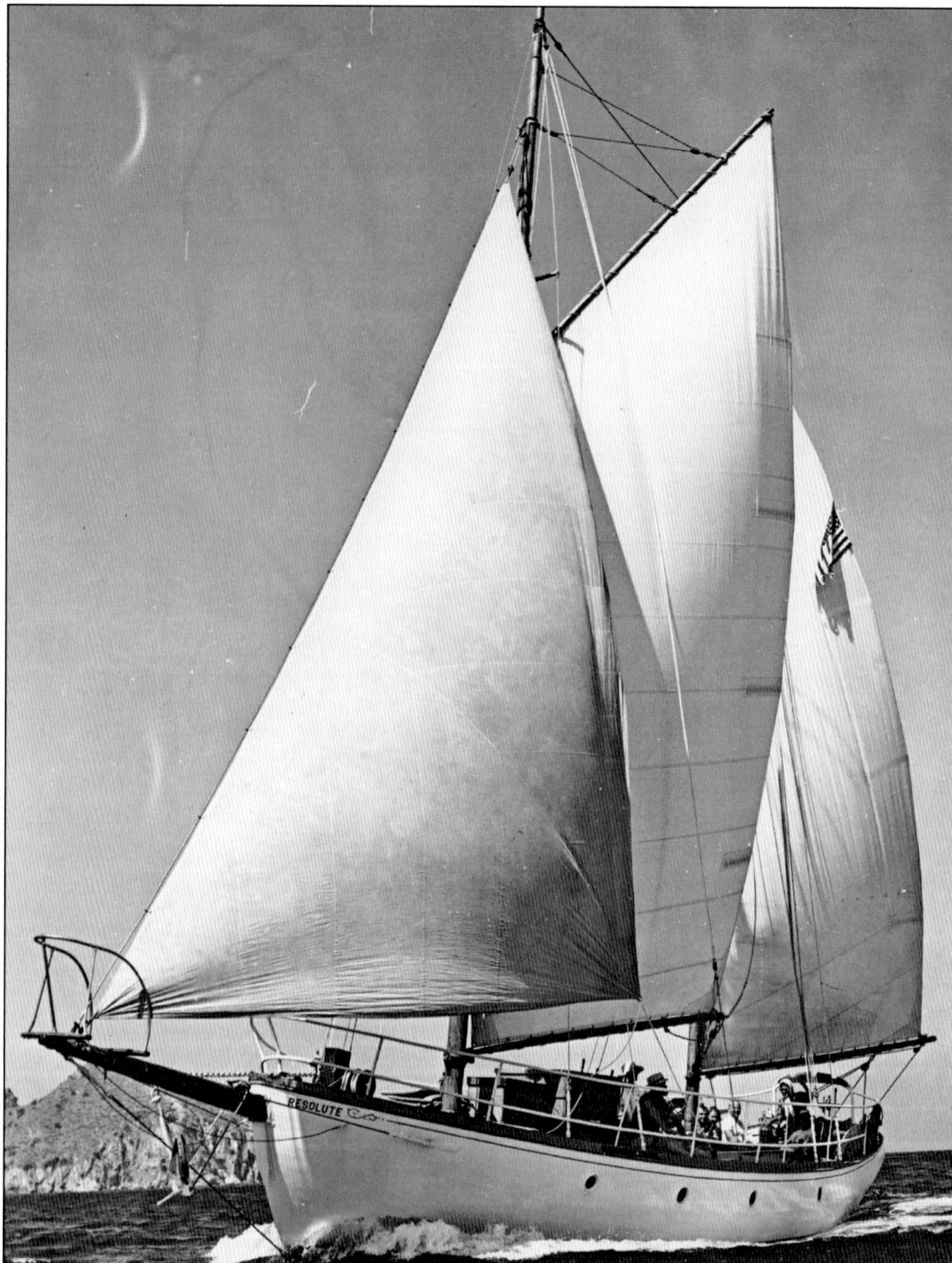

The *Resolute*, a 42-foot ketch, was built by the renowned Hugh Angleman in 1934. She was commissioned with "the works" by a buyer who went bankrupt. Spencer Tracey bought her and hired a captain and a deckhand. The deckhand was Ray Wallace, the painter of the old Portuguese whalers' camp. (Courtesy Capt. Mike Fabian.)

Huntington Hartford bought *Resolute* in the early 1940s. Hartford met Capt. Ed Fabian during the war and offered Fabian the *Resolute* if he should survive. Both survived the war, but Captain Fabian got the boat. He entered the 1947 Transpac race to Hawaii and came in third in class, crewing it with his non-sailing surfing buddies on the apparently correct premise that "if you can surf, you can sail." (Courtesy Capt. Mike Fabian.)

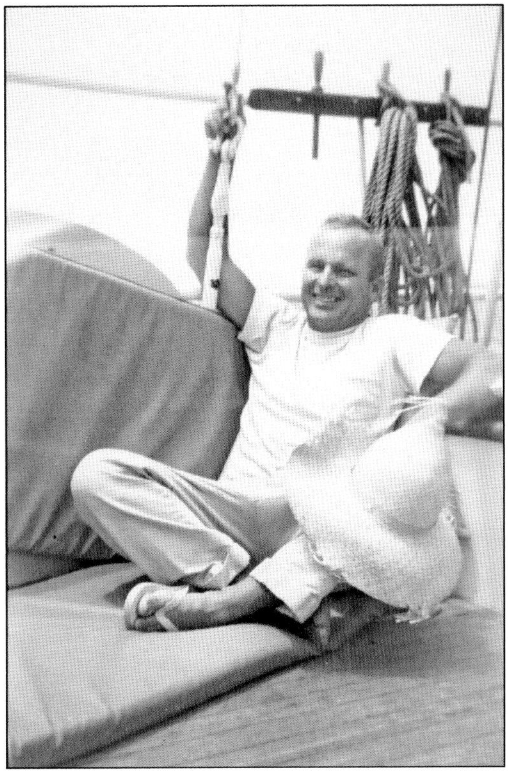

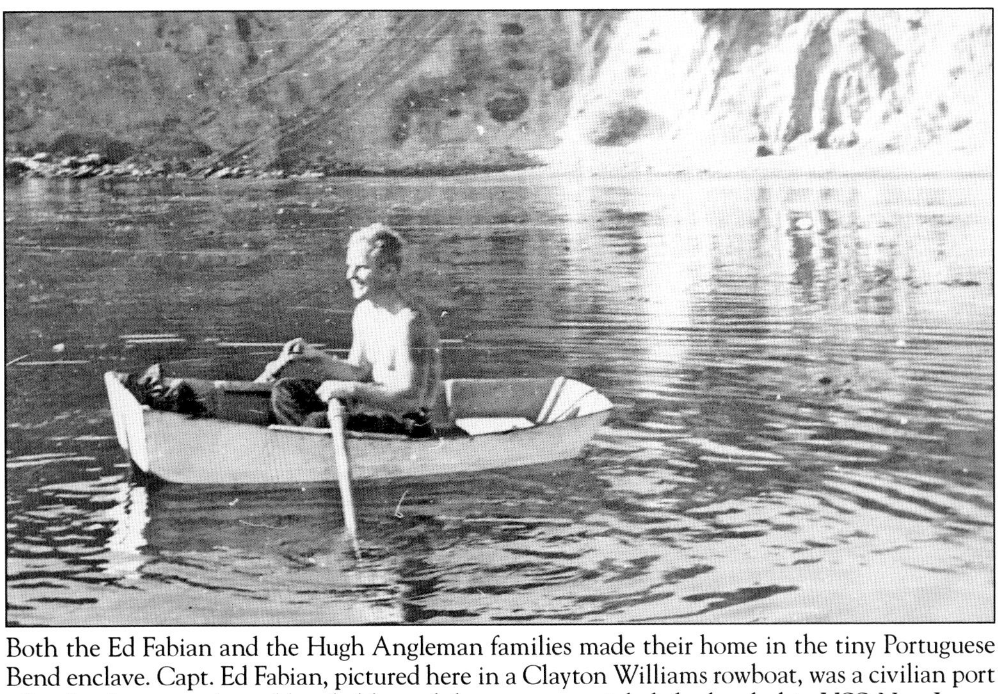

Both the Ed Fabian and the Hugh Angleman families made their home in the tiny Portuguese Bend enclave. Capt. Ed Fabian, pictured here in a Clayton Williams rowboat, was a civilian port pilot for the navy. A cool-headed legend, he once sea-trialed the battleship USS *New Jersey*, refurbished with updated electronics, with a group of worried navy brass by touring them past his old surfing spots to put them at their ease. (Courtesy Capt. Mike Fabian.)

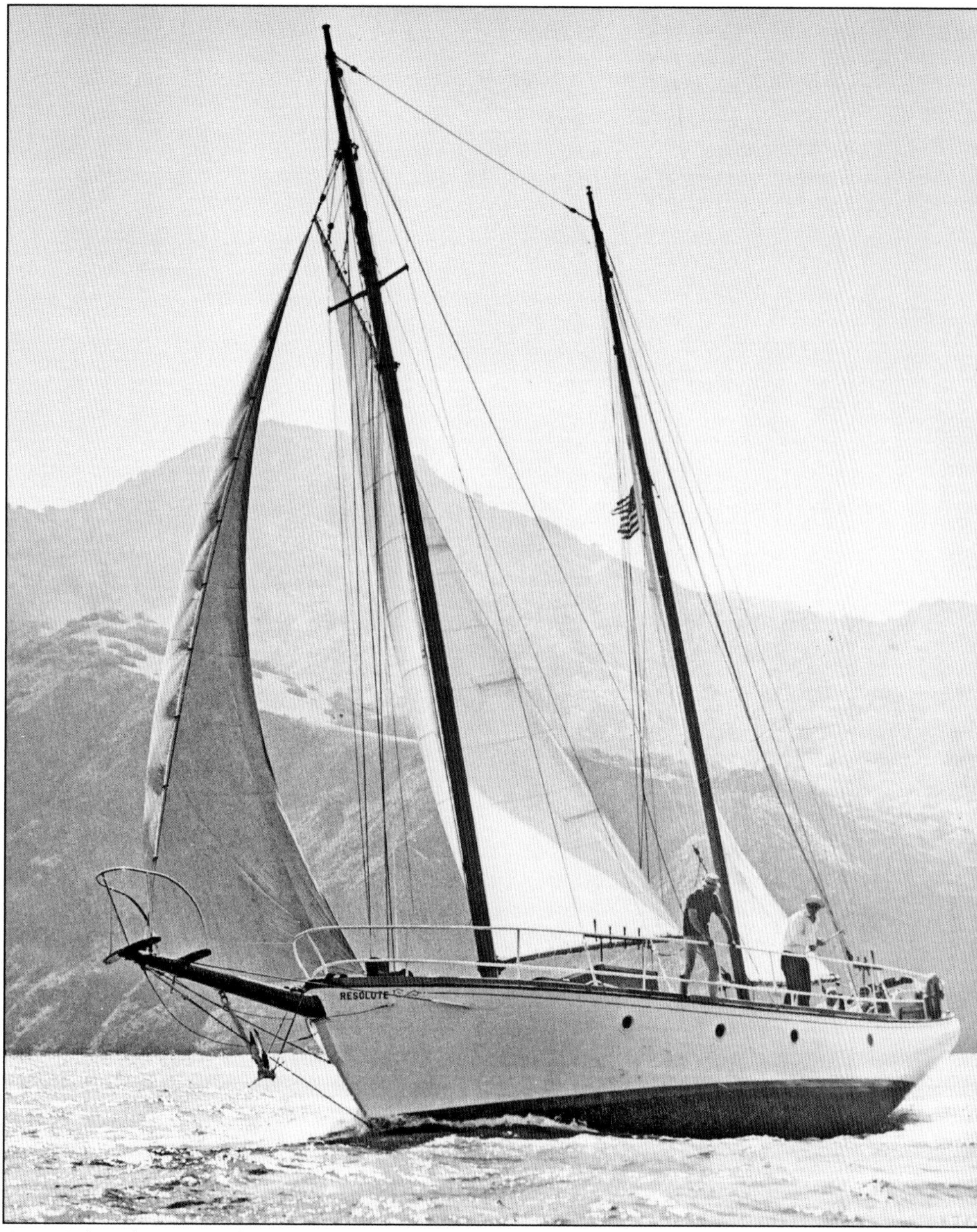

Capt. Ed and Dottie Fabian chartered *Resolute,* and generations of Sea Scouts learned to sail on her. Occasionally, though, the Fabians raced *Resolute.* On the inaugural San Diego to Acapulco race in 1953, a teenaged Bungy Hedley crewed and in her book, *View From the Top of the Mast,* tells of making a peanut butter sandwich during a heavy storm for the Fabian's happy little daughter, Lili—as unflappable as her parents. Captain Fabian loved to teach sailing. During World War II, he piloted an LST landing craft onto the beaches in Europe. In between battles, he would teach the guys how to sail. When you see photographs of the LSTs, look for the one with the skiff lashed to it; that was Captain Fabian's. (Courtesy Capt. Mike Fabian.)

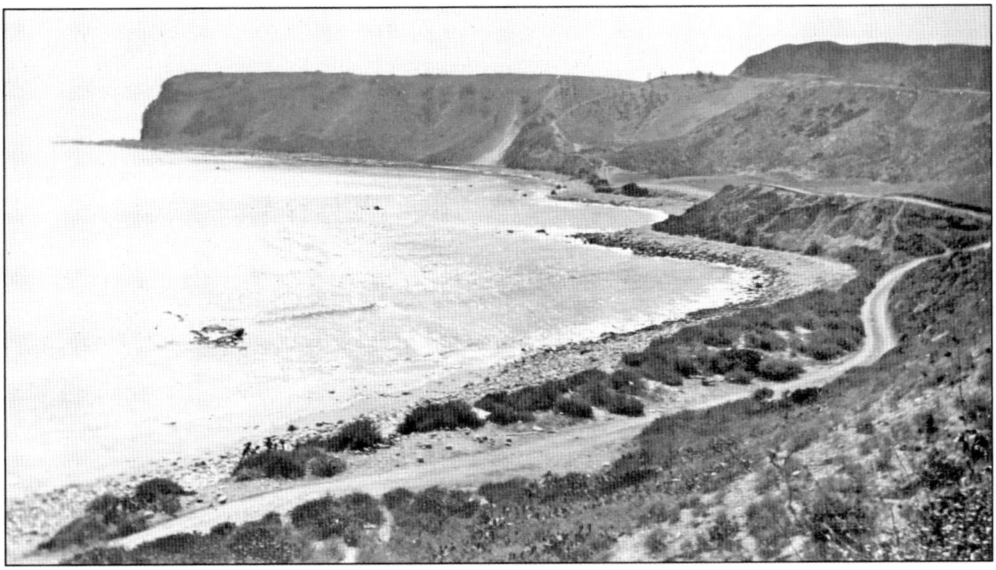

In 1928, at the time this photograph was taken, Elizabeth Schellenberg had begun campaigning to build a chapel for dusty, tired travelers. After the war, Ralph Jester contacted Lloyd Wright who, discouraged by his wartime public works projects, was delighted to design a sunny, welcoming homage to the traveler featuring the great, overarching redwoods he had seen and loved on a trip up the California coast. (Courtesy Yvetta Williams.)

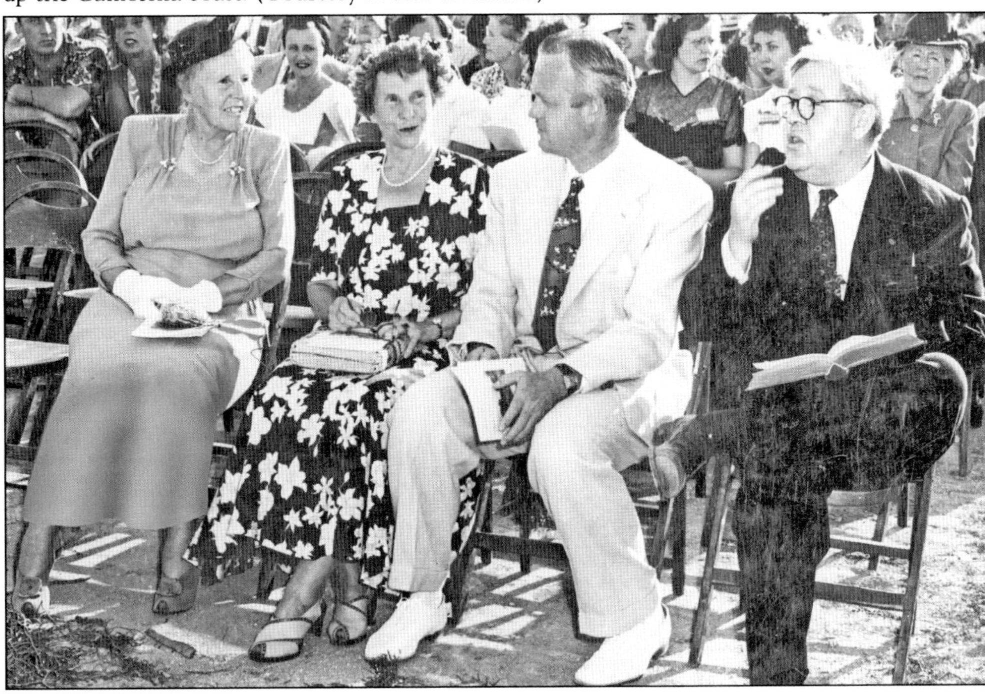

The ground for the Wayfarers' Chapel was consecrated and the cornerstone laid on Saturday, July 16, 1949. From left to right are Mrs. Elizabeth Schellenberg of Palos Verdes Estates, who drove the plan to completion; Mrs. Narcissa Vanderlip who, with her husband, Frank, donated the land; son Kelvin Vanderlip, the president of the Palos Verdes Corporation; and Charles Laughton, a Portuguese Bend resident. (Courtesy Local History Collection, Palos Verdes Library.)

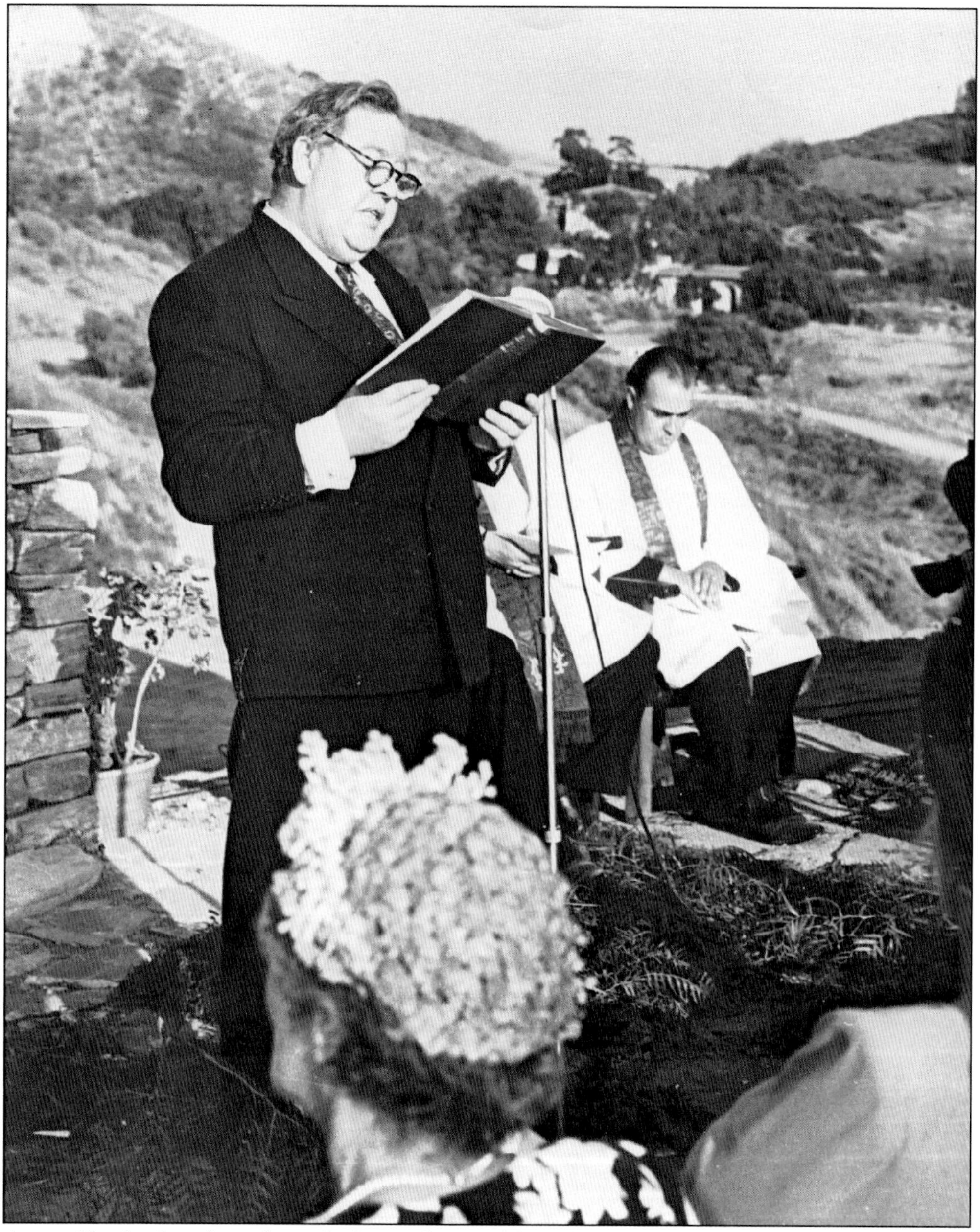

Actor Charles Laughton brought his unforgettable style and voice to the cornerstone-laying ceremony of the Wayfarers' Chapel. Here he reads the 107th psalm, verses 1–30, which say, in part, "He bringeth them unto their desired haven." Laughton had earlier used his Bible to rap an inattentive child on the head—the nephew of the presiding Reverend Tafel. (Courtesy Wayfarers' Chapel.)

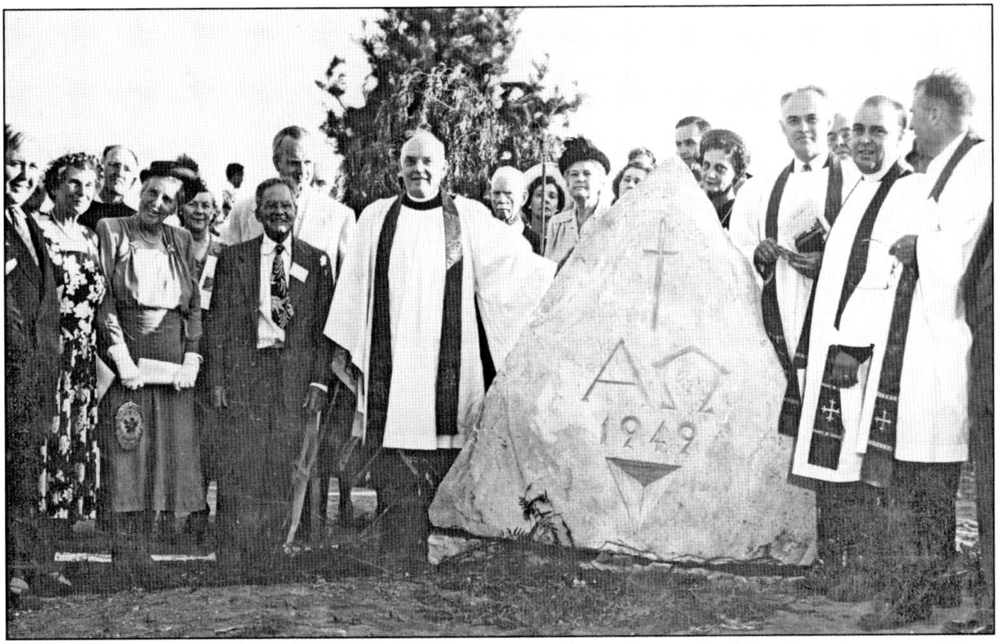

This formal photograph includes many of the principal people involved in planning, organizing, and creating Wayfarers' Chapel. In the center is Rev. Leonard Tafel, who presided over the ceremonies. His nephew, now Rev. Harvey Tafel, was the inattentive eight year old who Charles Laughton rapped on the head for not moving when asked. Young Tafel returned in 1972 as chapel minister. He had grown up to look exactly like his uncle. (Courtesy Wayfarers' Chapel.)

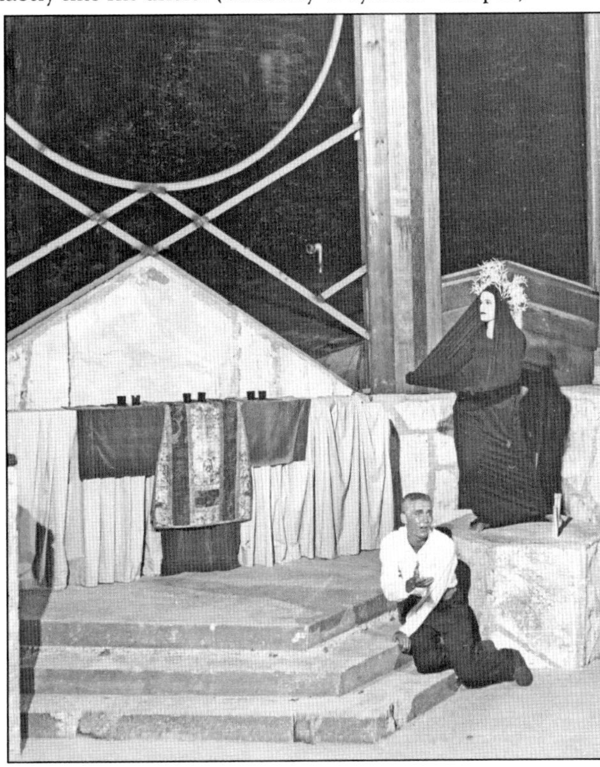

In 1950, during the chapel's construction, an acting class from Palos Verdes College used it to stage an old English morality play called *Everyman*. They were possibly allowed to use the unfinished chapel because Ralph Jester was also a professor at the college. This student actor is Burton Kessenick, who lived in Hollywood Riviera. The chapel seated 60 people along the walls, and admission was $1.20. (Courtesy Jean Curtis Wells.)

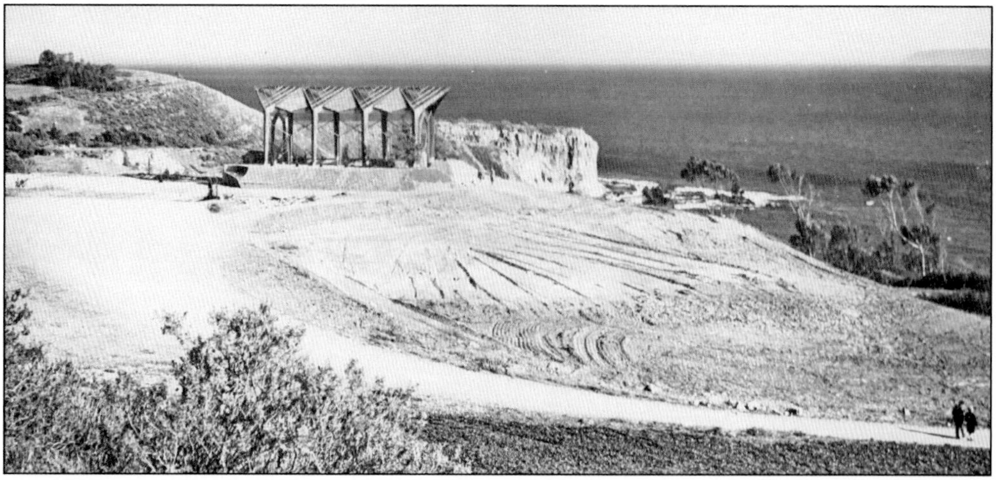

The Wayfarers' Chapel finally opened in 1951 after 25 years of planning. The widowed Narcissa Vanderlip, a Swedenborgian, had donated the three acres of land, and church members from around the country had raised the funds for completion of this national memorial to their founder, Emanuel Swedenborg. (Courtesy Wayfarers' Chapel.)

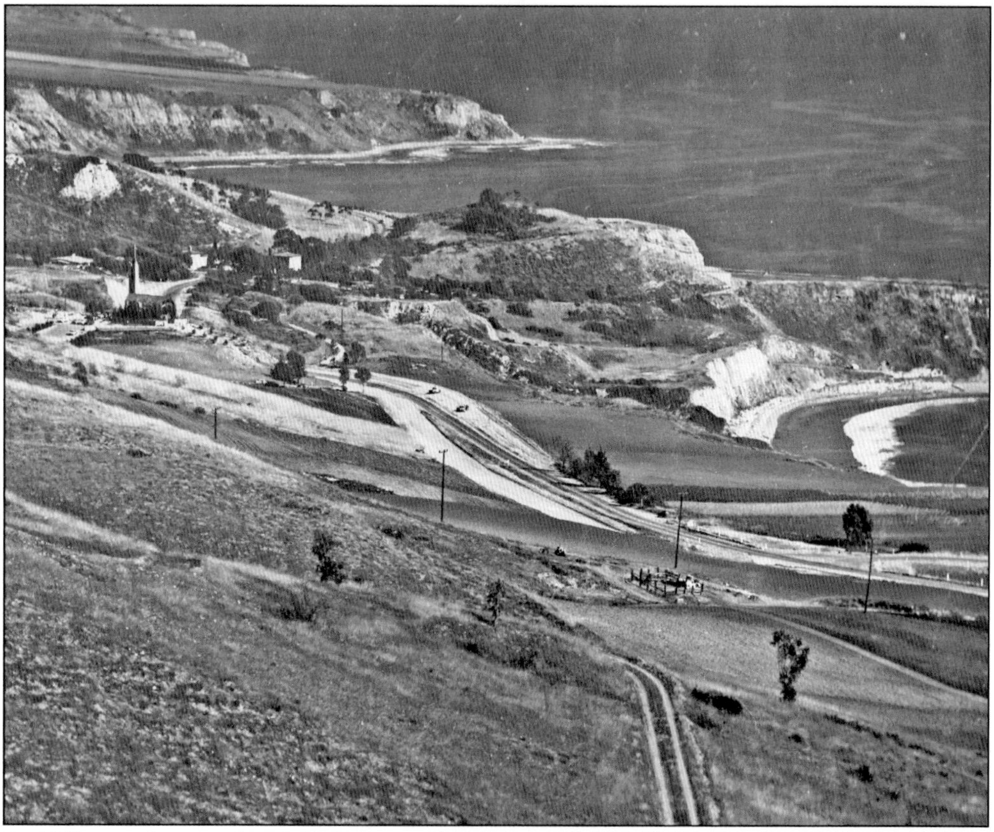

By 1952, travelers wending halfway around the peninsula found the Wayfarers' Chapel (far left) on the Pacific Ocean and surrounded by farms. The landscaping is beginning to grow under the stewardship of the chapel's gardener, Jess Fernandez, who retired in 1981 after 30 years. (Courtesy Point Vicente Interpretive Center.)

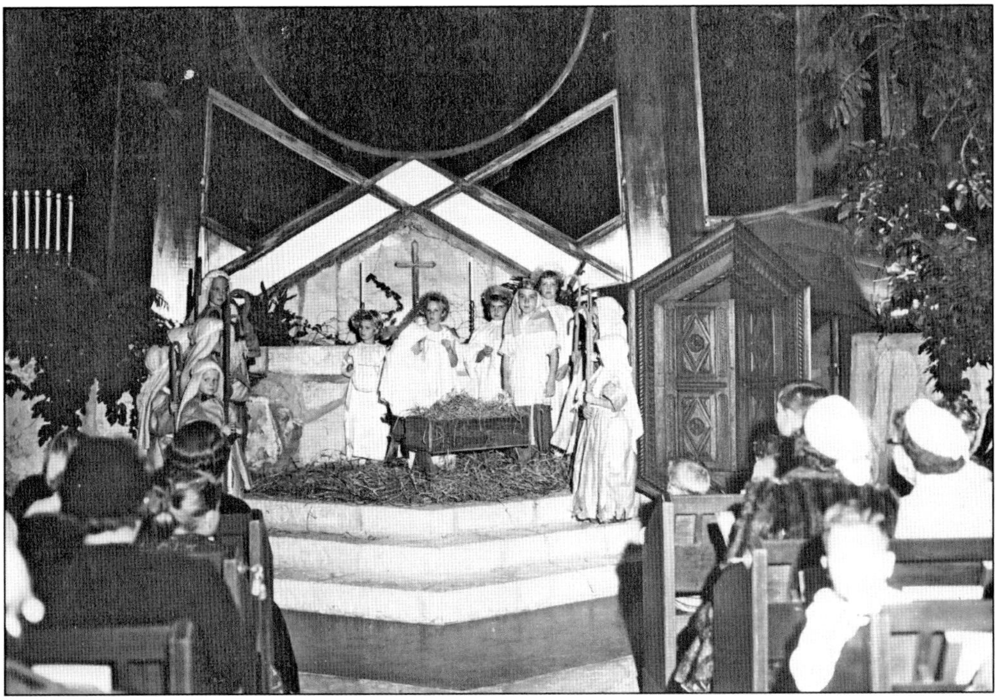

The first baby to be christened at Wayfarers' Chapel was Narcissa Cox Vanderlip, granddaughter of Narcissa and the late Frank A. Vanderlip and daughter of Kelvin and his wife, Elin. In this 1953 photograph, the tightly knit Portuguese Bend neighborhood had moved its Christmas pageants to the Wayfarers' Chapel. (Courtesy Jean Curtis Wells.)

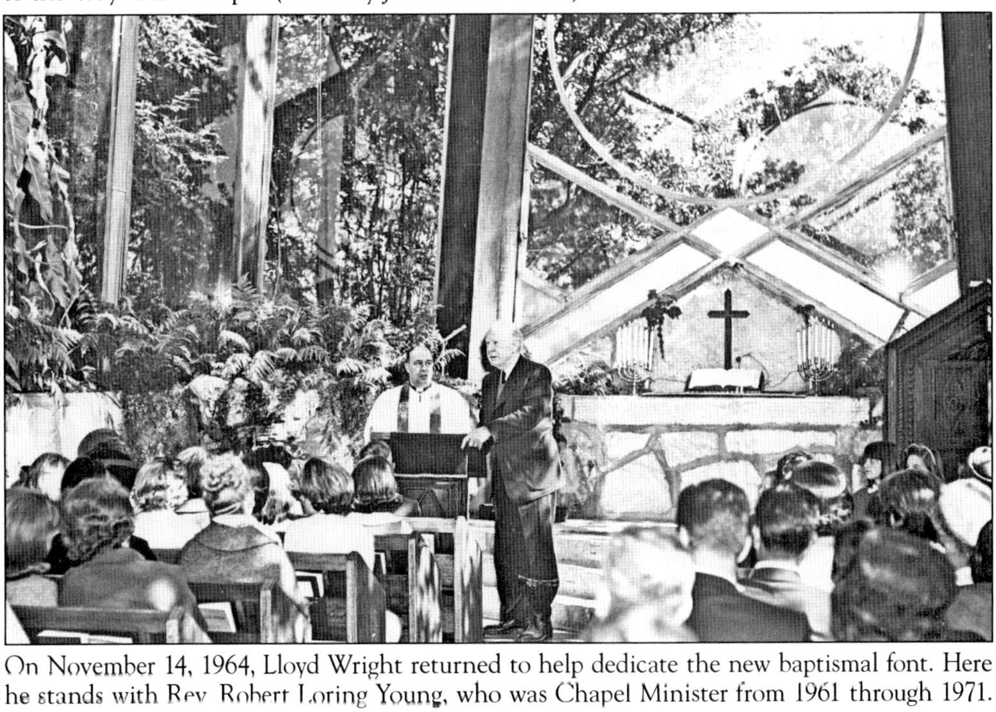

On November 14, 1964, Lloyd Wright returned to help dedicate the new baptismal font. Here he stands with Rev. Robert Loring Young, who was Chapel Minister from 1961 through 1971. (Courtesy Wayfarers' Chapel.)

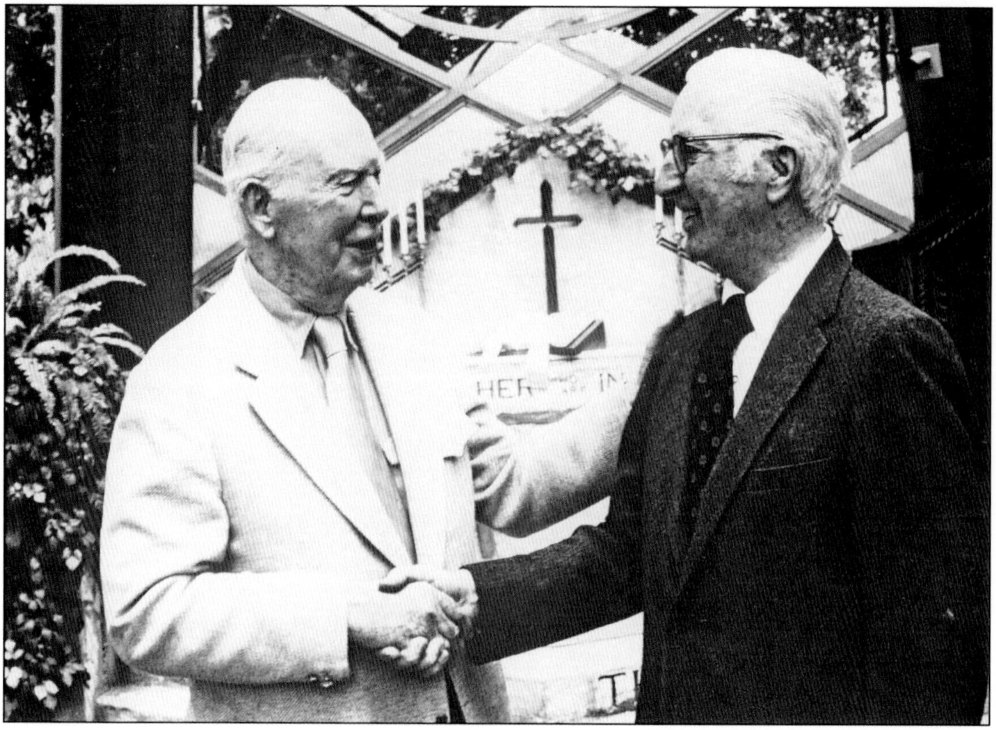

Good friends and associates Lloyd Wright (left) and Ralph Jester celebrate their friendship and collaboration in this undated photograph possibly taken in 1964 when Wright returned to dedicate the new baptismal font. Both Wright and Jester are listed on the original architectural drawings of the chapel, as architect and associate respectively. Those originals, dated April 15, 1947, are framed and hung in the chapel's administration offices. (Courtesy Wayfarers' Chapel.)

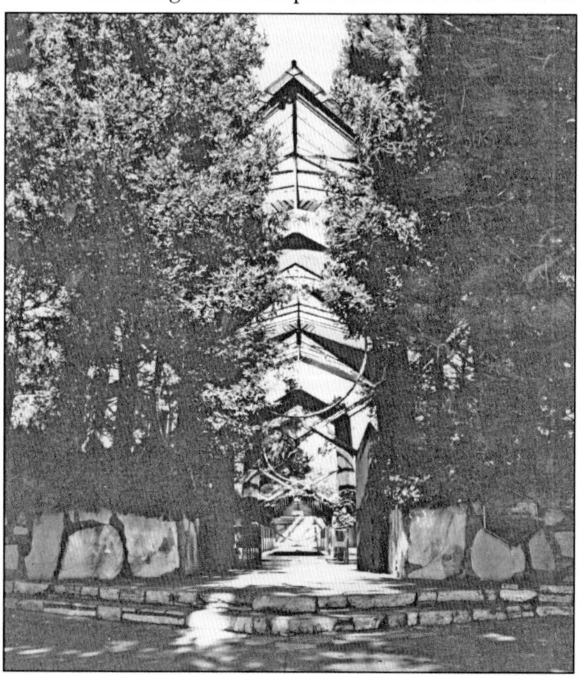

The Wayfarers' Chapel has grown into what Lloyd Wright and Ralph Jester envisioned. Wright called it "a living center of a tree grove in which the branches arched over and sheltered the congregation—one of the earliest types of church." To this end, Wright had used, in his words, "organic materials that would lend themselves to warm human correlation." (Courtesy Wayfarers' Chapel.)

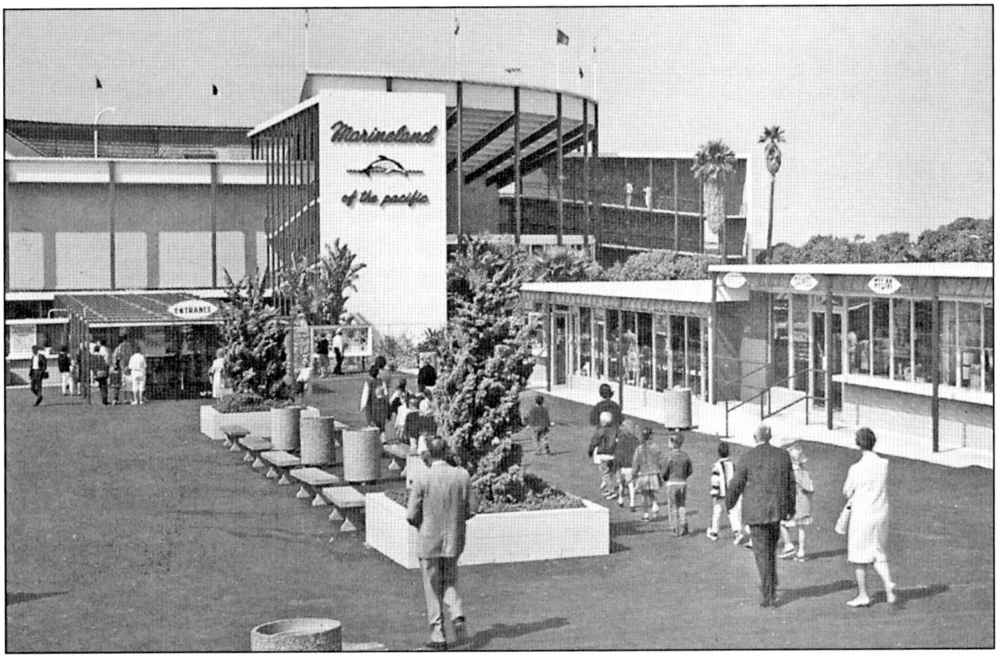

On August 28, 1954, Marineland of the Pacific opened on Long Point as a sister oceanarium to Marine Studios in Florida. Ilya Tolstoy, grandson of writer Leo, chose the site for its proximity to the public, its climate, and the purity of its seawater. Thus began a 33-year-long love affair between Marineland and the people of Palos Verdes. (Courtesy Point Vicente Interpretive Center.)

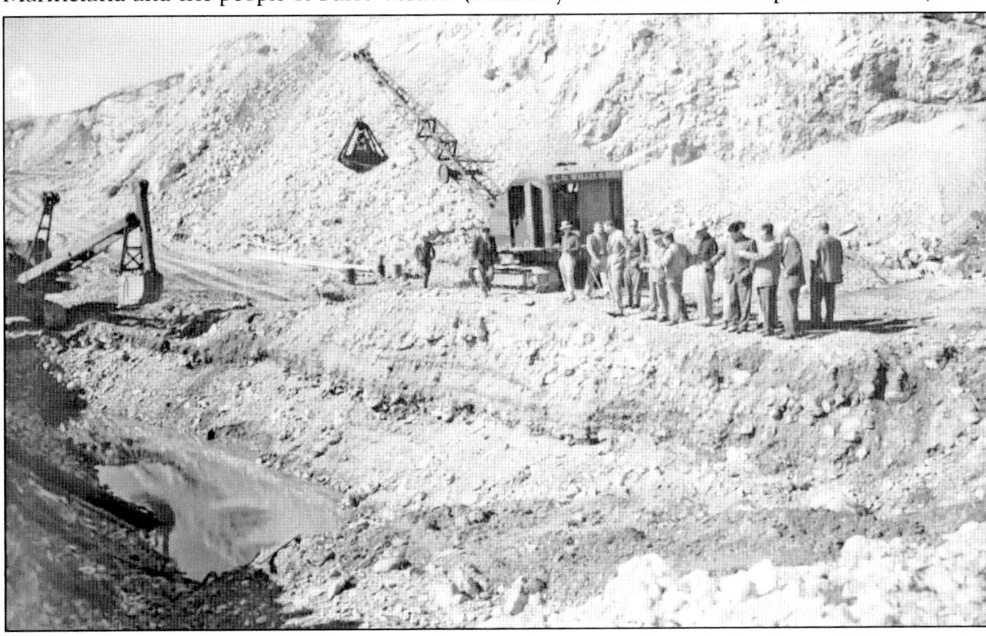

Marine Studios in Florida was built in 1938 by Vanderbilt heir C. V. "Sonny" Whitney, his cousin Sherman Pratt, and Ilya Tolstoy to film marine life. Its public popularity was a surprise. In response, they and Wall Street broker Henry Upham Harris financed a Marineland on the West Coast for research and tourism. In 1953, as soon as the Korean War was over, they began building the pier. (Courtesy Point Vicente Interpretive Center.)

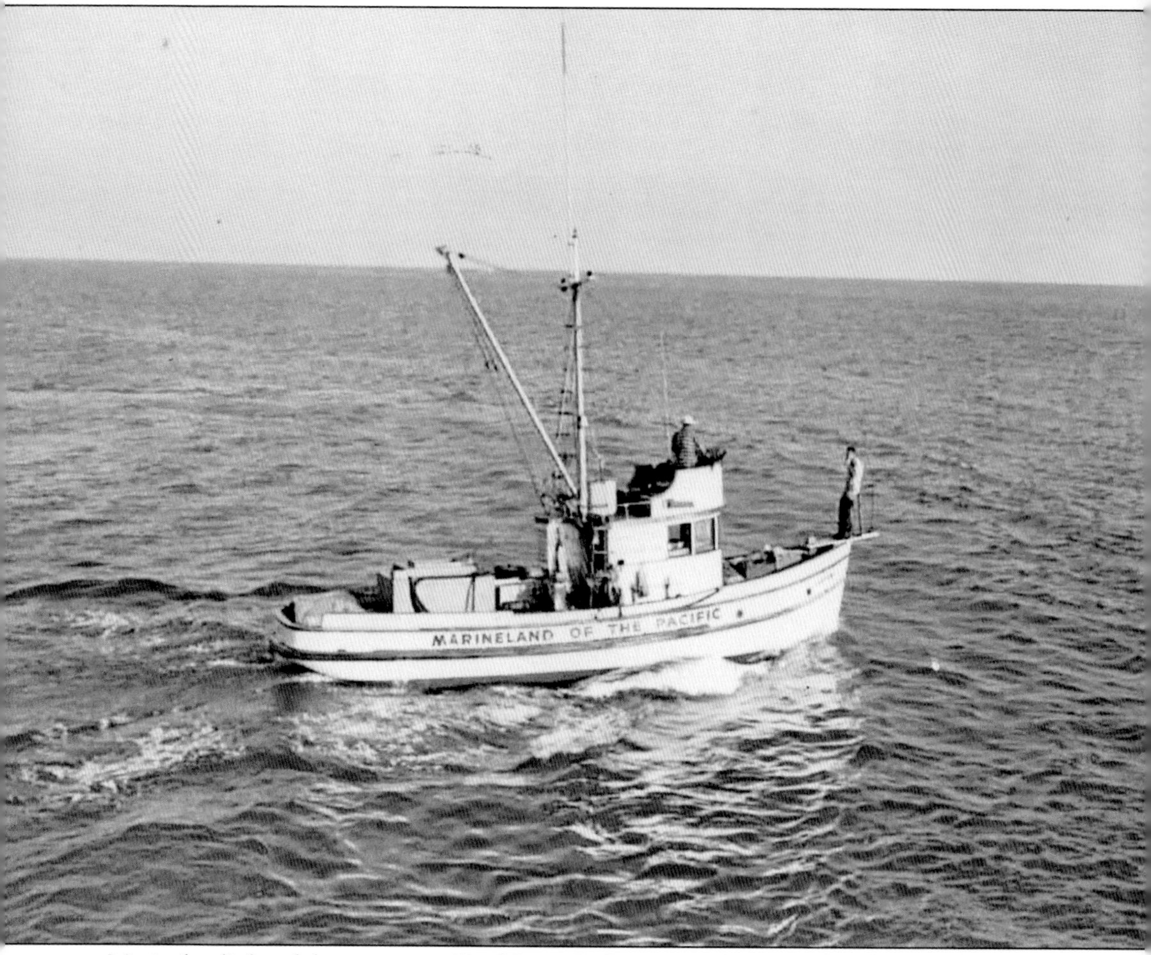

Marineland's first fish curator was Ken Norris. In January 1954, Norris hired San Pedro fisherman Frank Brocato, widely admired for being able to find and outwit whatever fish he was after. Brocato turned his 37-foot gillnet boat *Geronimo* into a collection vessel, and the chase was on to stock the oceanarium with sea animals. Norris later said that Brocato was the most remarkable man he had ever met. (Courtesy Point Vicente Interpretive Center.)

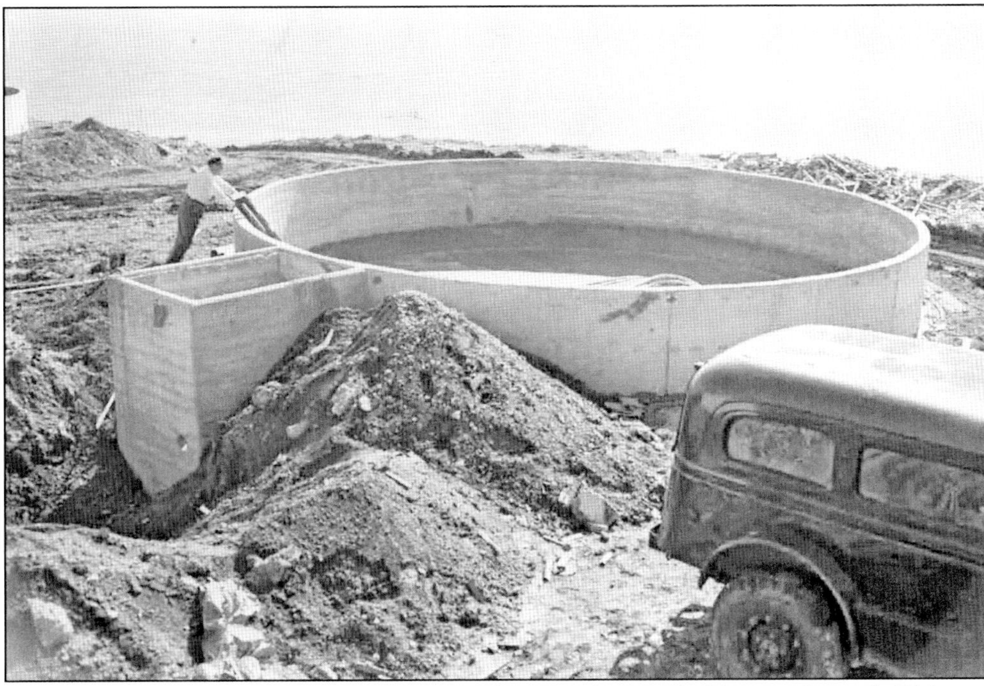

The construction superintendent had promised Norris that two holding tanks, each 35 feet in diameter, would be built on the old coast guard gun emplacements on the cliff above the pier. They would be large enough to hold the entire catch. Opening day was scheduled for May 15. It was already March and there were no holding tanks for the *Geronimo* to deliver to. (Courtesy Point Vicente Interpretive Center.)

Norris rented an old, rusty, algae-covered, abandoned aquarium in Avalon on Santa Catalina Island to hold the animals as they were caught. The group cleaned it, got it running, and filled it with sheepshead, bass, rockfish, perch, and more. But a series of mishaps killed the entire catch, and in mid-April, they had to begin again. Frank's godson, Boots Calandrino (pictured), joined the collecting team. (Courtesy Point Vicente Interpretive Center.)

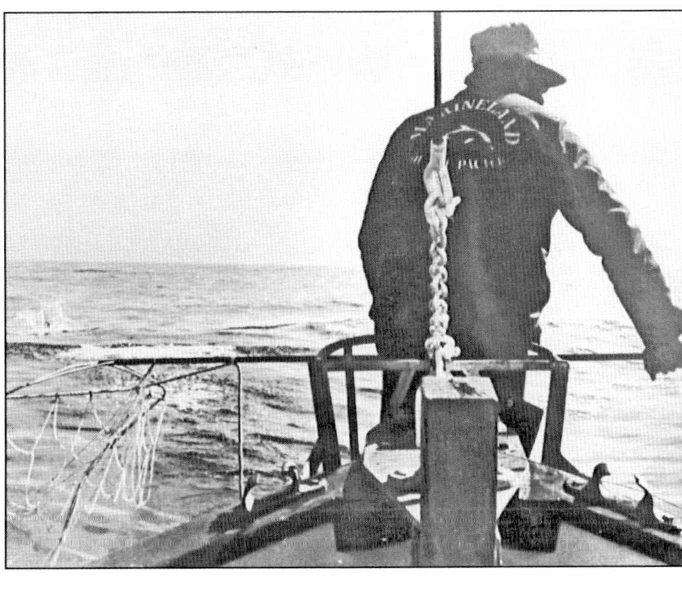

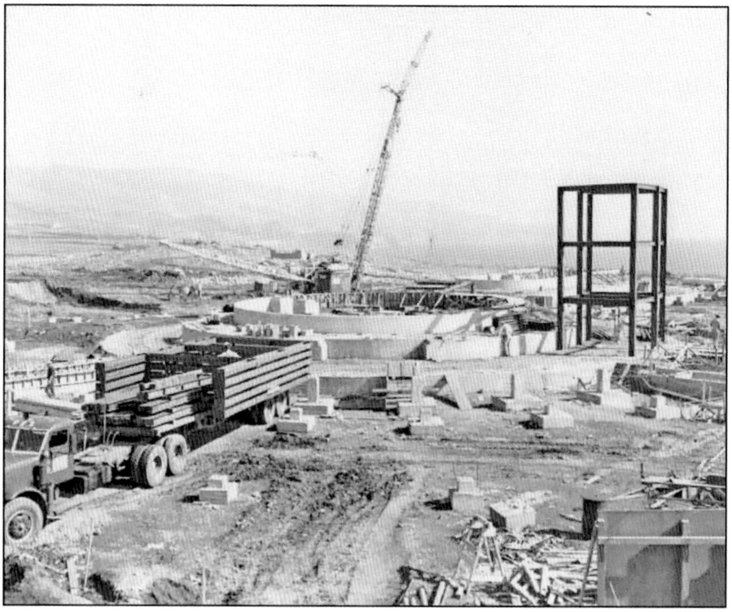

The display tanks at Marineland had building problems. A fill pipe transporting ocean water was seated in its trench without pea gravel and the surrounding rocks punched holes in it. The pipe had to be dug up and done right. Later, when they filled the dolphin tank, a window gave way, flooding the facility. Opening day was delayed for three months. (Courtesy Point Vicente Interpretive Center.)

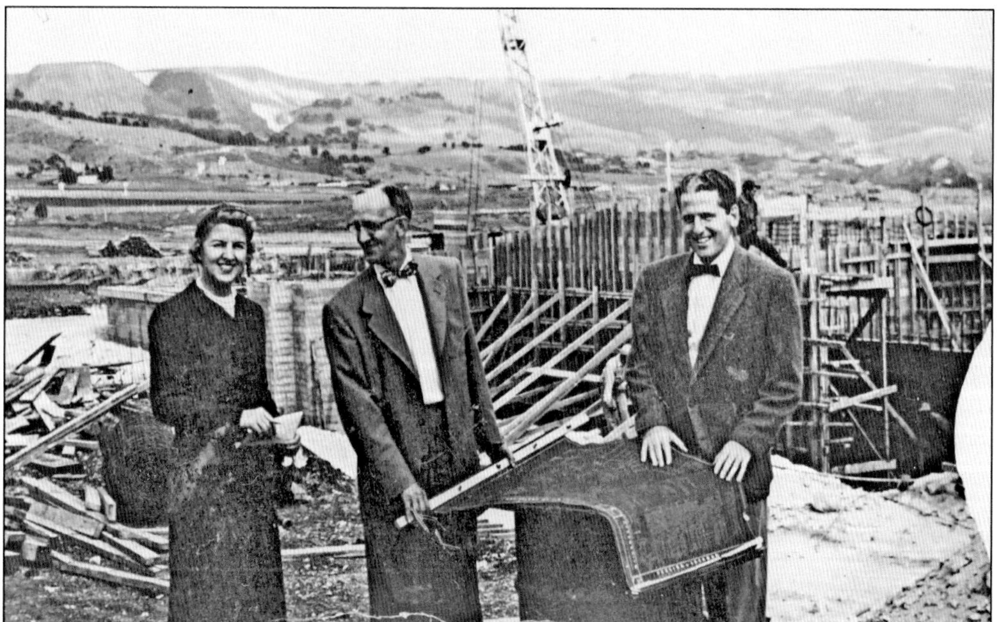

Oceanarium, Inc., had purchased the land on Long Point from the Vanderlips, paying them with company stock instead of money. Other stockholders included the original owners of the Florida oceanarium. They hired Ray W. Smith as vice president and general manager. Going over the plans are, from left to right, Helen Ryan Smith, director of public relations; Ray Smith; and John Frederick Bradshaw, engineer. (Courtesy Christina de Meglio and Point Vicente Interpretive Center.)

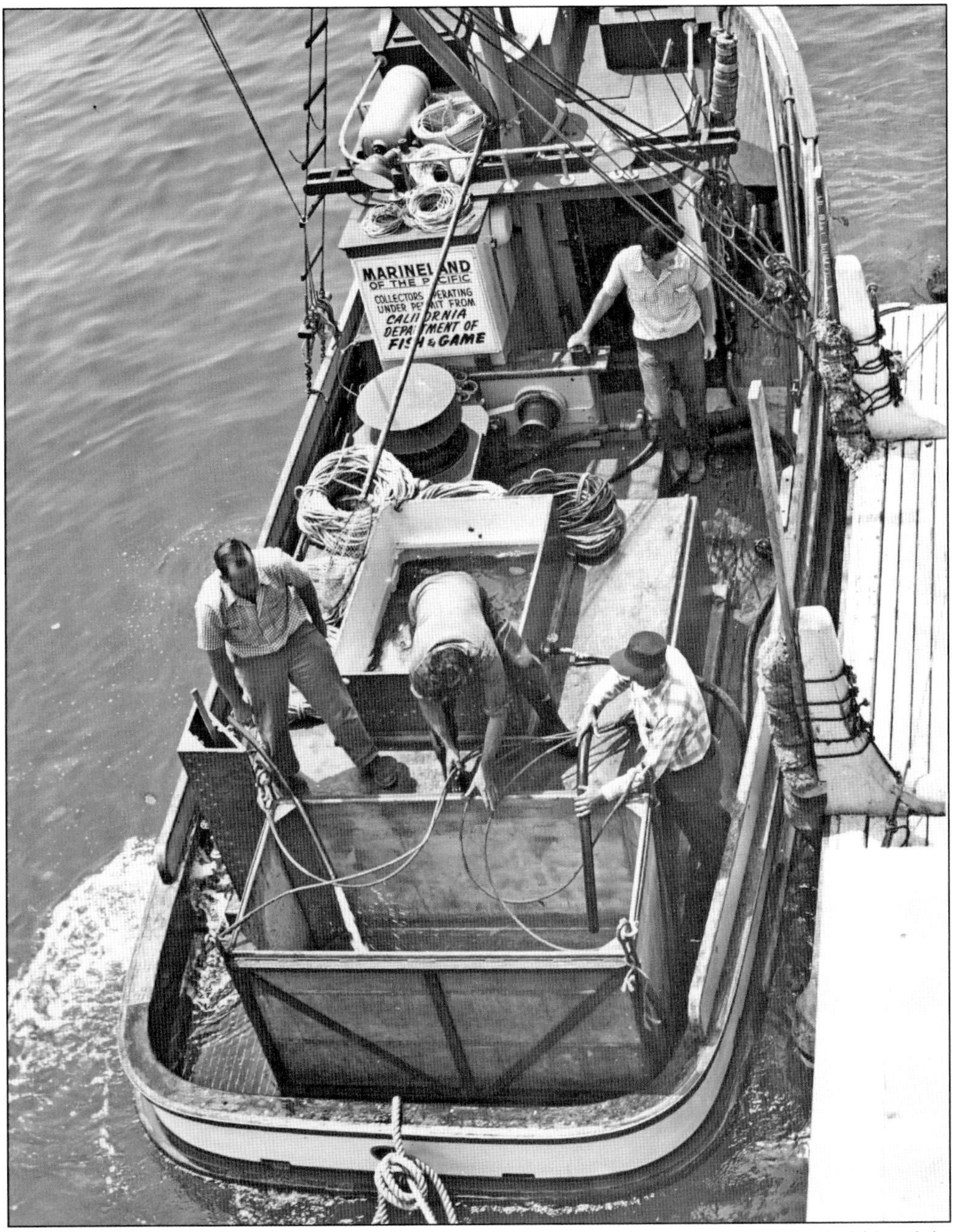

The holding tanks were built but leaked badly, so Norris found creative places to hold his fish. Here *Geronimo* is tied to the Marineland pier after dumping the catch into old steel sardine transport tanks on the beach near the pier. Norris also used slatted underwater boxes, stashing fish all over nearby waters but losing some of them to fishing by small boys and eagles. (Courtesy Point Vicente Interpretive Center.)

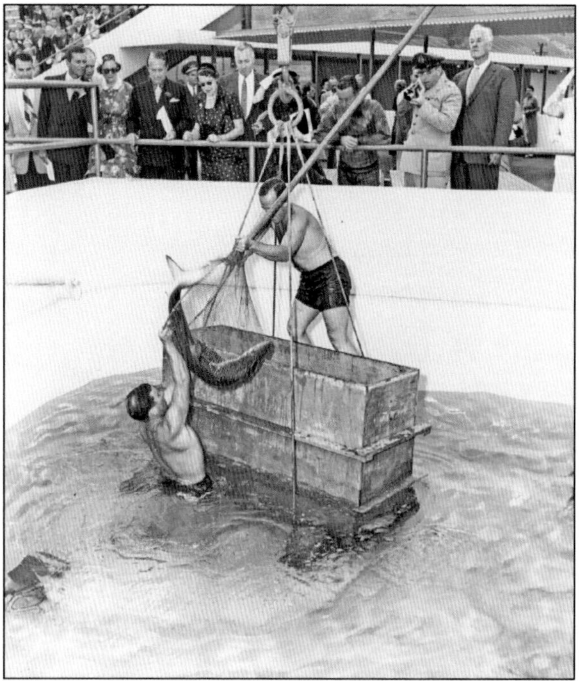

Three days before opening day, the construction company finally successfully filled the viewing tanks. Ken Norris and his crew had decorated them earlier with huge boulders and underwater artifacts. Frank Brocato and Boots Calandrino in the *Geronimo* and a hired bait boat with crew shuttled back and forth across the San Pedro Channel hauling sea animals from their stashes and winching them into the tanks. (Courtesy Point Vicente Interpretive Center.)

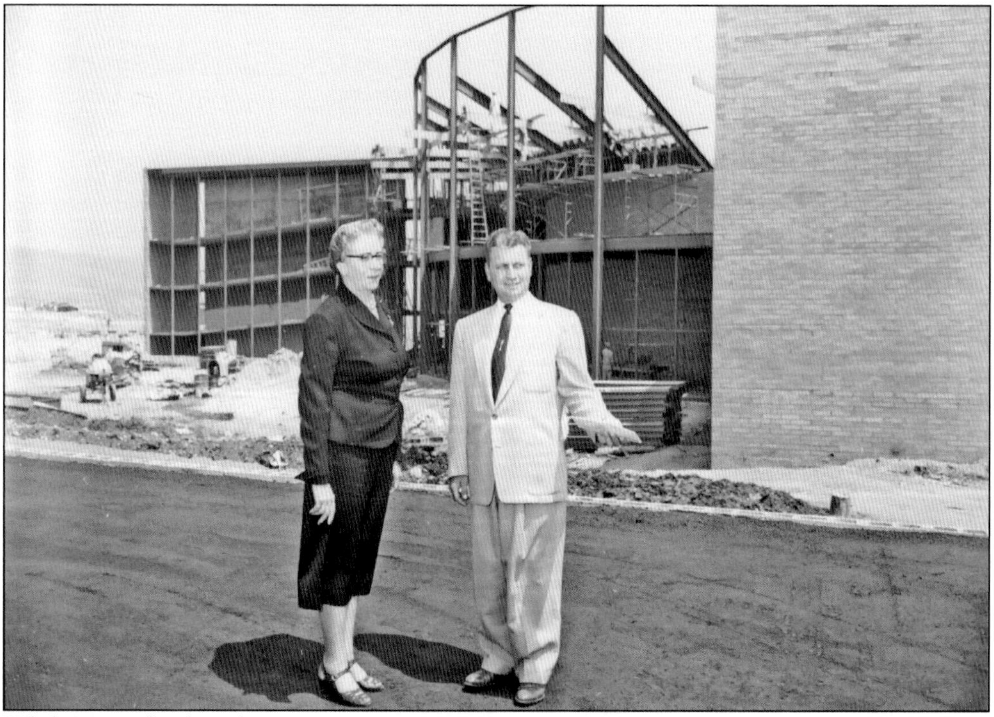

While Marineland was becoming an oceanarium, it was also becoming a community. Here Lillian Throne, postmaster of Palos Verdes Estates, stands with Leon Dwight, former postmaster of San Pedro. Marineland was given its own post office. Although Frank Vanderlip Jr., a stockholder, requested a Palos Verdes Estates address, the city said no and the address became Marineland, Palos Verdes Peninsula. (Courtesy Point Vicente Interpretive Center.)

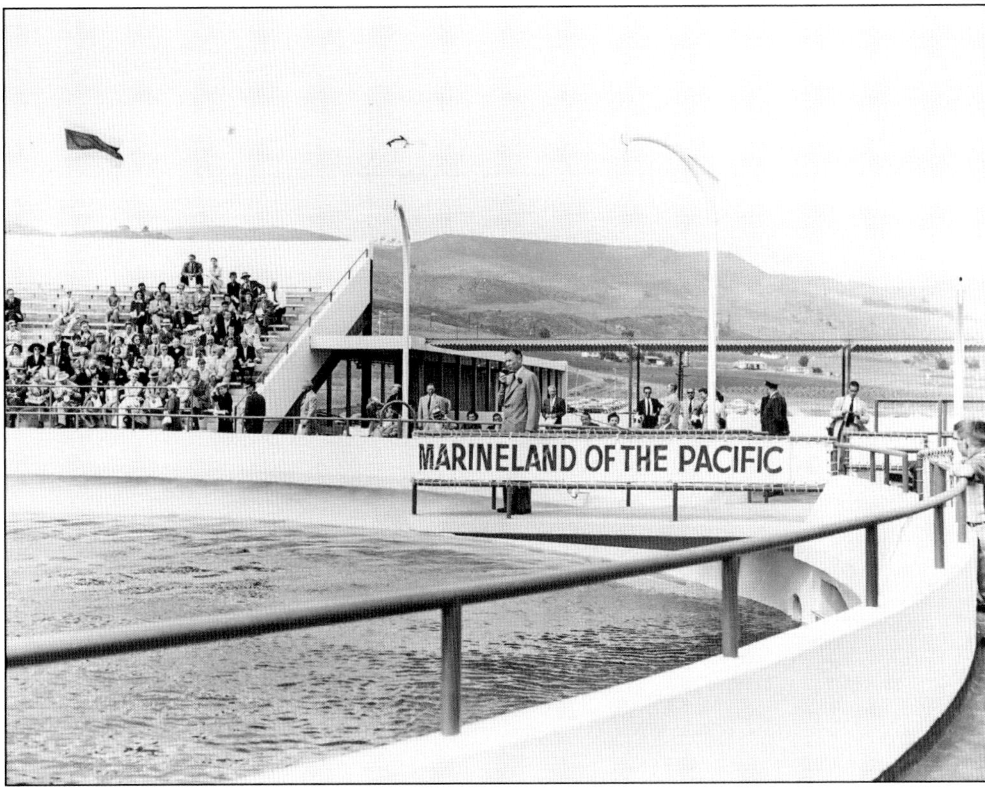

Marineland of the Pacific opening day on August 28, 1954, went off without a noticeable hitch. It involved a net-cutting ceremony and a welcoming speech by Ray Smith (center), the general manager, speaking here on the earlier press day. Marineland, the second oceanarium in the United States and the largest, greeted 14,850 guests that day, all of whom drove past miles of empty farm fields to see the fish. (Courtesy Point Vicente Interpretive Center.)

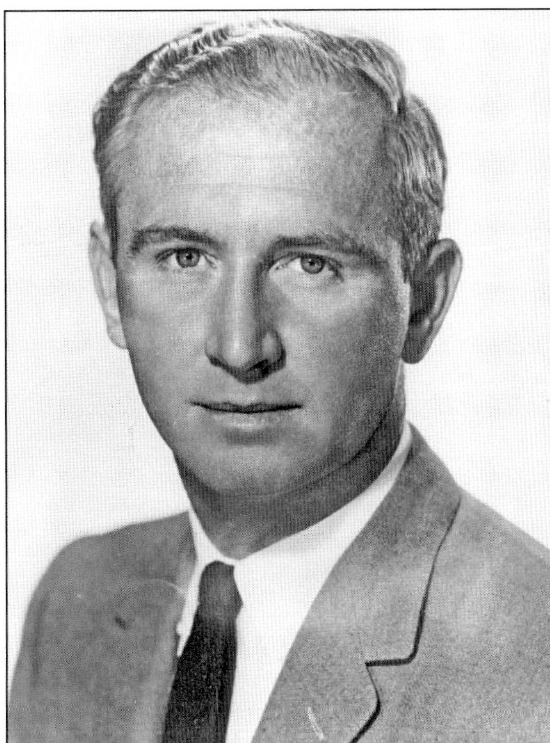

In 1956, with Marineland struggling financially, Henry Harris brought in William Monahan to be general manager. Under Monahan's direction, Marineland became profitable again and expanded, emphasizing entertainment to draw the crowds but still maintaining the research studies. Marineland became family to all who worked there. (Courtesy Point Vicente Interpretive Center.)

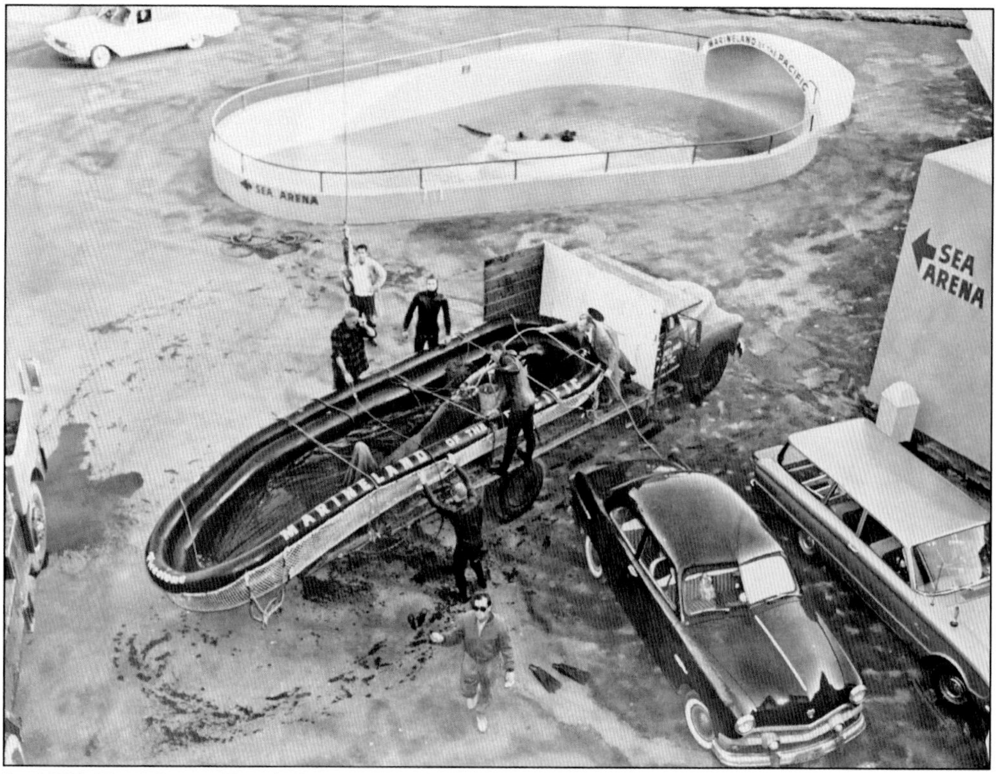

In 1957, Ken Norris, Frank Brocato, and Boots Calandrino caught a pilot whale off Catalina Island. They discussed it with her half the night as she sounded, surfaced, then sounded again. At midnight, she was finally brought alongside the *Geronimo*. They tucked a rubber raft under her, inflated the tubes around her, and gently towed her in. She was 12 feet long and weighed 1,500 pounds. (Courtesy Point Vicente Interpretive Center)

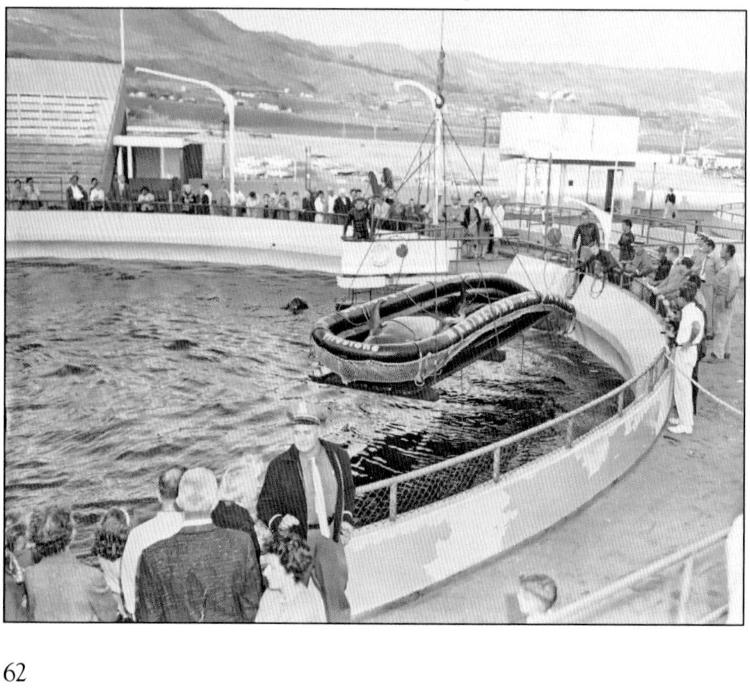

The little pilot whale and her raft were trucked up from the Marineland pier and winched into a holding pool, then into the larger giant fish tank when the holding pool proved too small. Curator David Brown finally convinced her to start eating her 100 pounds of squid a day, and she began training with the porpoises. (Courtesy Point Vicente Interpretive Center.)

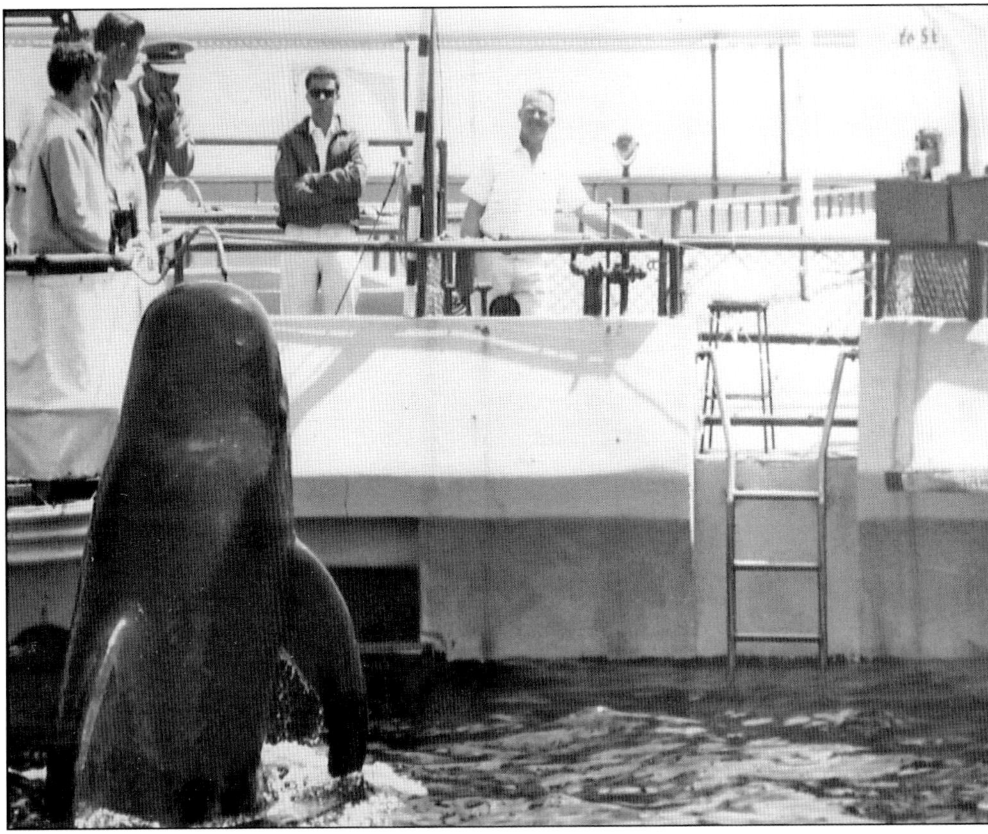

Word spread of the amazing catch. The community adored the cute little pilot whale, and the children named her Bubbles. Marineland's annual attendance reached one million, much to the delight of Bill Monahan. Although other pilot whales were eventually caught, Bubbles was a first love. She became Marineland's symbol, and a statue of her with a couple of white-sided dolphins greeted visitors at the entrance. (Courtesy Point Vicente Interpretive Center.)

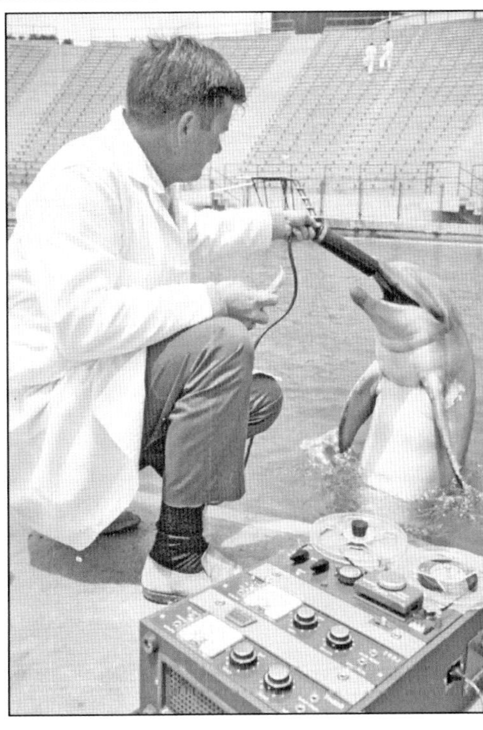

In 1959, Ken Norris and assistant curator John Prescott conducted a series of experiments with Kathy, an Atlantic bottlenose dolphin. By blindfolding her, they confirmed that a dolphin navigates by echolocation: emitting clicks from its forehead and listening to them bounce back. This photograph may be from an episode about Kathy on the popular CBS science series *Conquest*. It was good publicity for the oceanarium. (Courtesy Point Vicente Interpretive Center.)

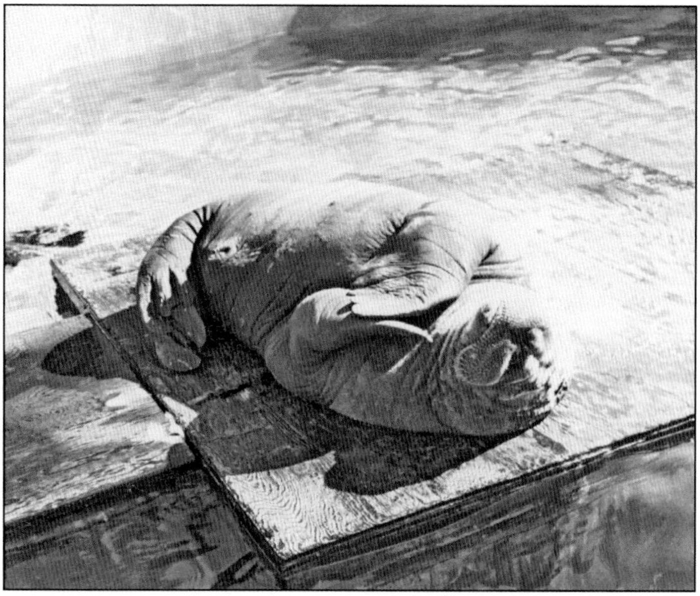

Marineland's next big first was the acquisition and successful raising of four 80-pound, two-week-old Arctic Walruses that the Marineland collection team took from St Lawrence Island off Alaska in 1961. Farouk, Woofy, Petula, and Priscilla were raised on sugarless whipping cream, minced claims, brewers yeast, and vitamins. This baby, named Blue, was a more recent rescue from Alaska. (Courtesy Point Vicente Interpretive Center.)

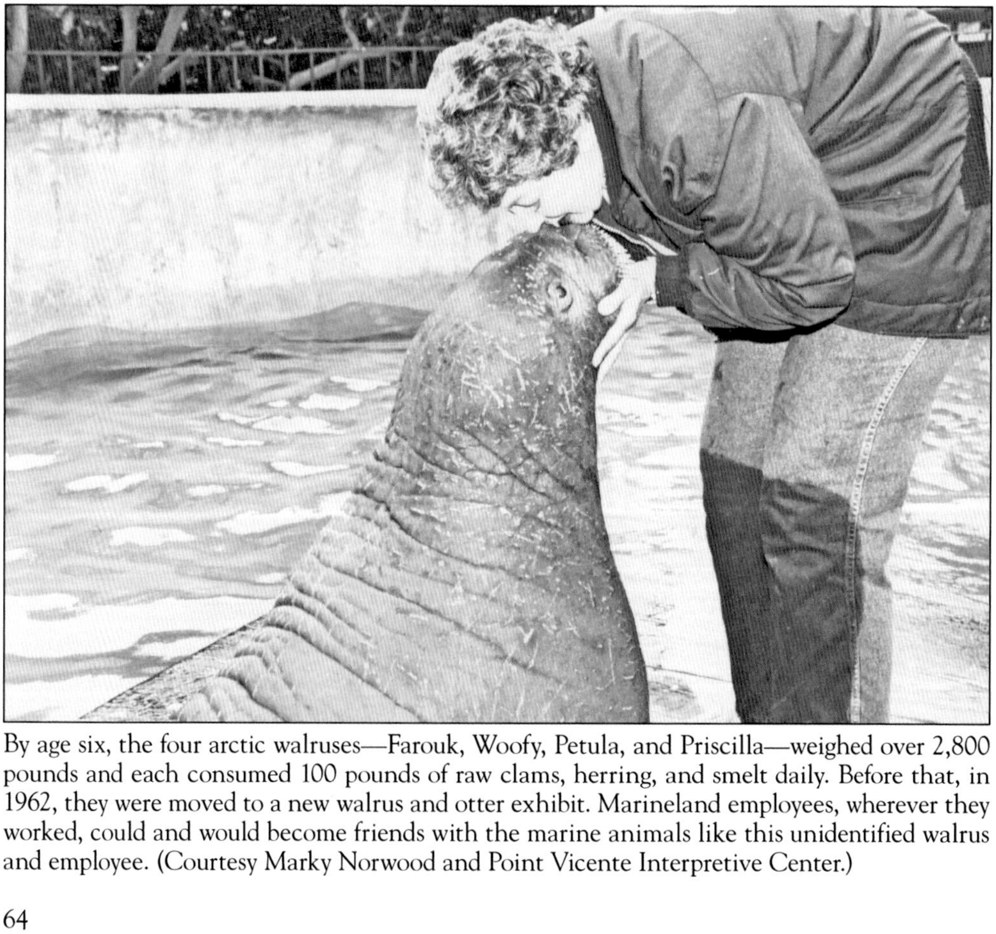

By age six, the four arctic walruses—Farouk, Woofy, Petula, and Priscilla—weighed over 2,800 pounds and each consumed 100 pounds of raw clams, herring, and smelt daily. Before that, in 1962, they were moved to a new walrus and otter exhibit. Marineland employees, wherever they worked, could and would become friends with the marine animals like this unidentified walrus and employee. (Courtesy Marky Norwood and Point Vicente Interpretive Center.)

In 1963, Frank Brocato in *Geronimo* caught a rare false killer whale (*Pseudorca crassidens*) for Marineland. Swifty was unusually intelligent and easily trained. Jim Patryla, in his *Marineland* book, said he would arrive in the early morning and run to the whale stadium to play follow the leader with Swifty and then pet her. He called her "playful and gentle." (Courtesy Point Vicente Interpretive Center.)

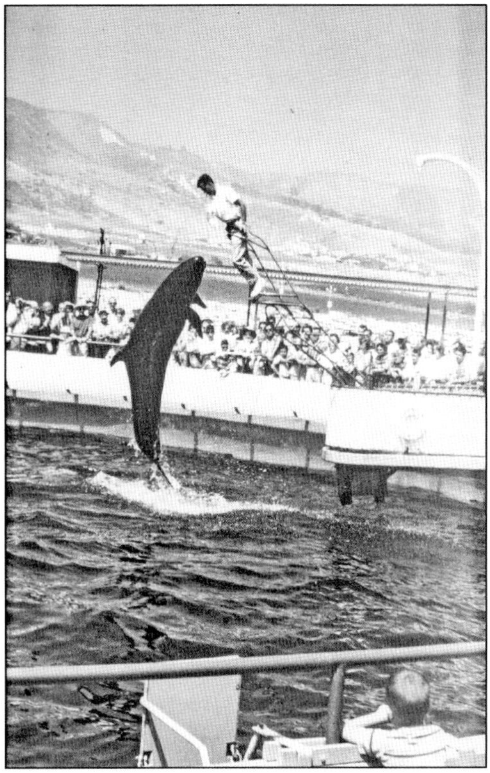

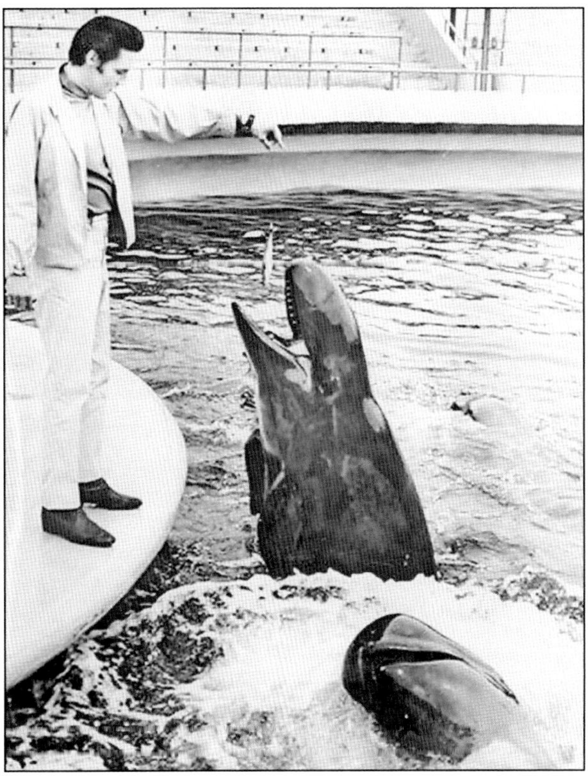

Marineland had its share of famous visitors. Here Swifty, the false killer whale, is happily receiving her fish from a young Elvis Presley while one of the pilot whales waits her turn nearby. False killer whales and pilot whales are two of the largest members of the dolphin family. (Courtesy Point Vicente Interpretive Center.)

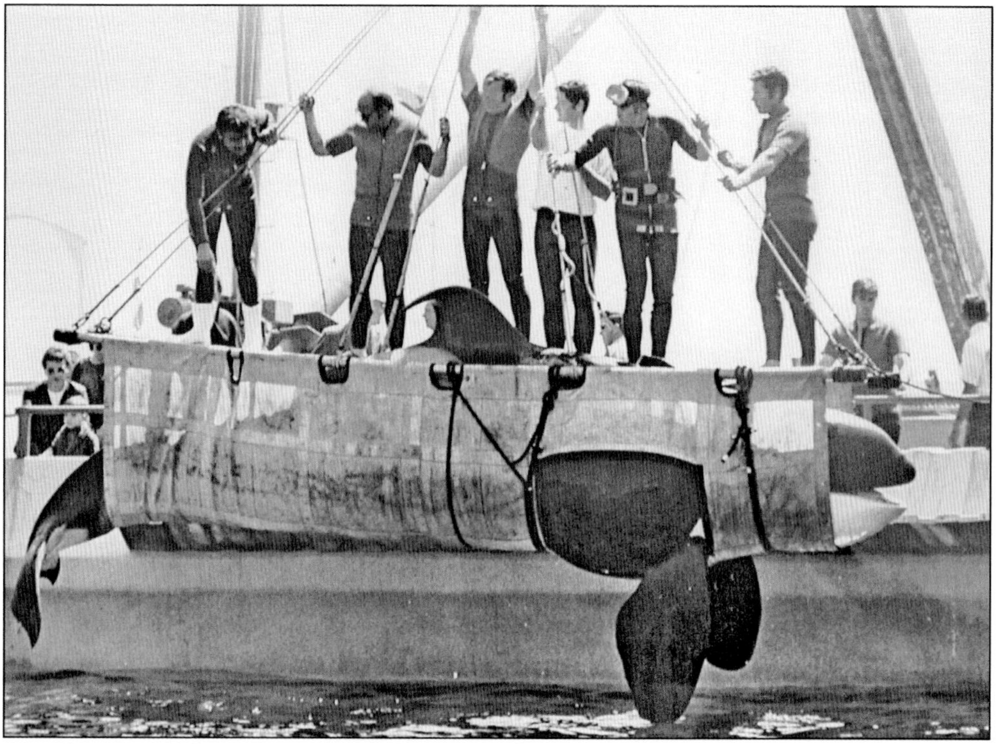

In 1967, curator John Prescott, general manager William Monahan, and Marineland staff went to British Columbia to retrieve a killer whale that had been caught in a net. Orky was shipped back in a DC-6 in this hammock-like device accompanied by the Marineland group. Despite the arduous journey, he was soon eating his daily 250 pounds of mackerel. (Courtesy Point Vicente Interpretive Center.)

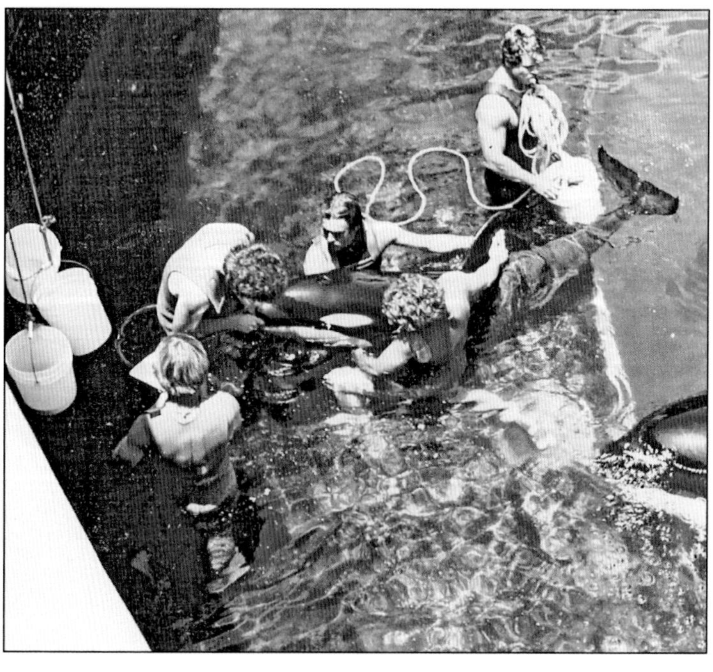

Orky was soon joined by Corky. Between 1977 and 1986, Corky conceived six times. Only four calves survived after birth, but she failed to nurse any of them, despite the staff's efforts during her fourth pregnancy to teach her to bond and nurse using a fiberglass reproduction of a baby. Here the staff is tube-feeding the baby in the shallow part of the tank while Corky anxiously waits nearby (lower right). (Courtesy Point Vicente Interpretive Center.)

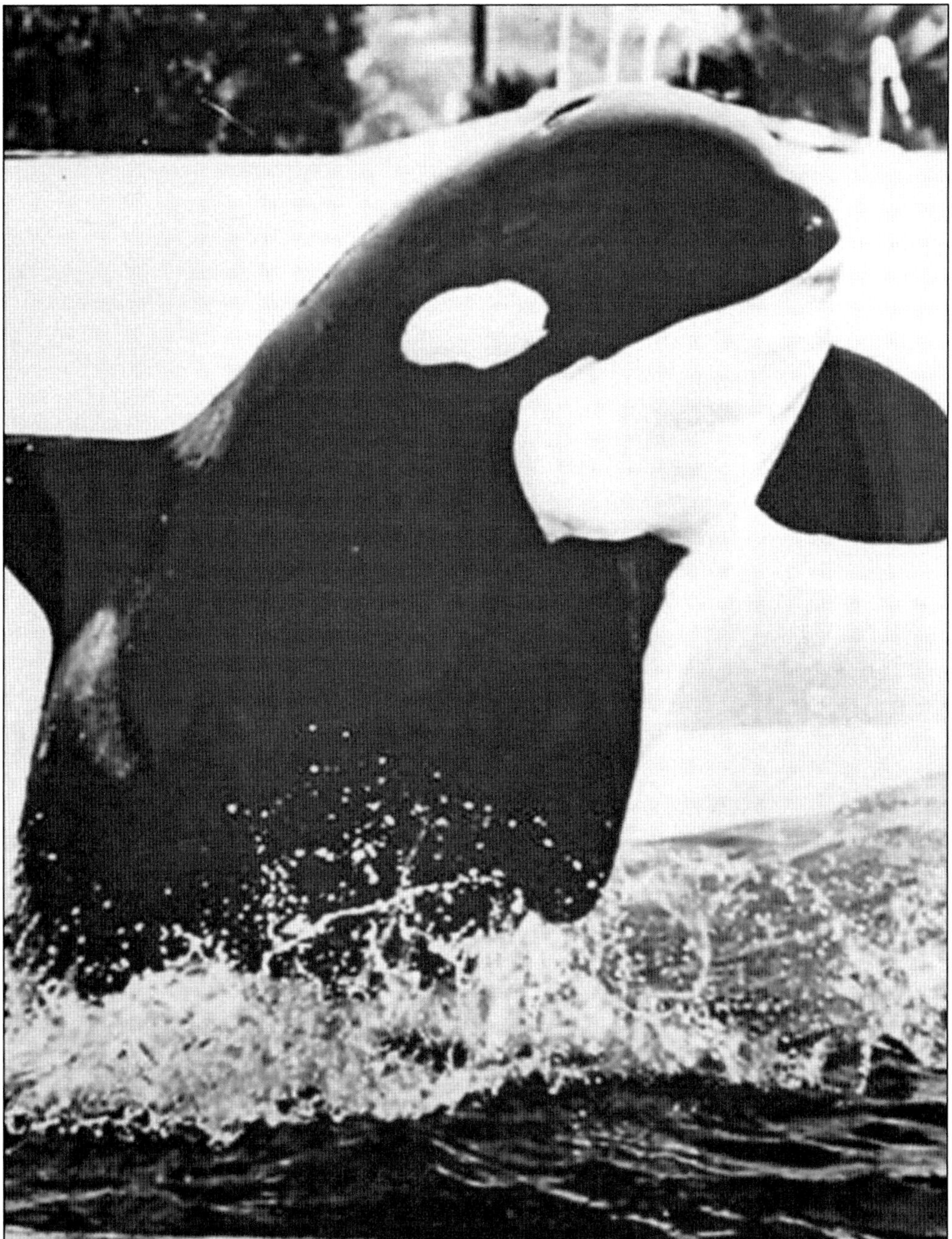

Corky, the other killer whale, or *Orcinus orca*, was captured in 1969, also from British Columbia. Killer whales are large members of the dolphin family as are pilot whales such as Bubbles. Corky and Orky became a breeding pair. In 1977, much to the surprise of the Marineland staff who didn't even know that she was pregnant, Corky gave birth. (Courtesy Point Vicente Interpretive Center.)

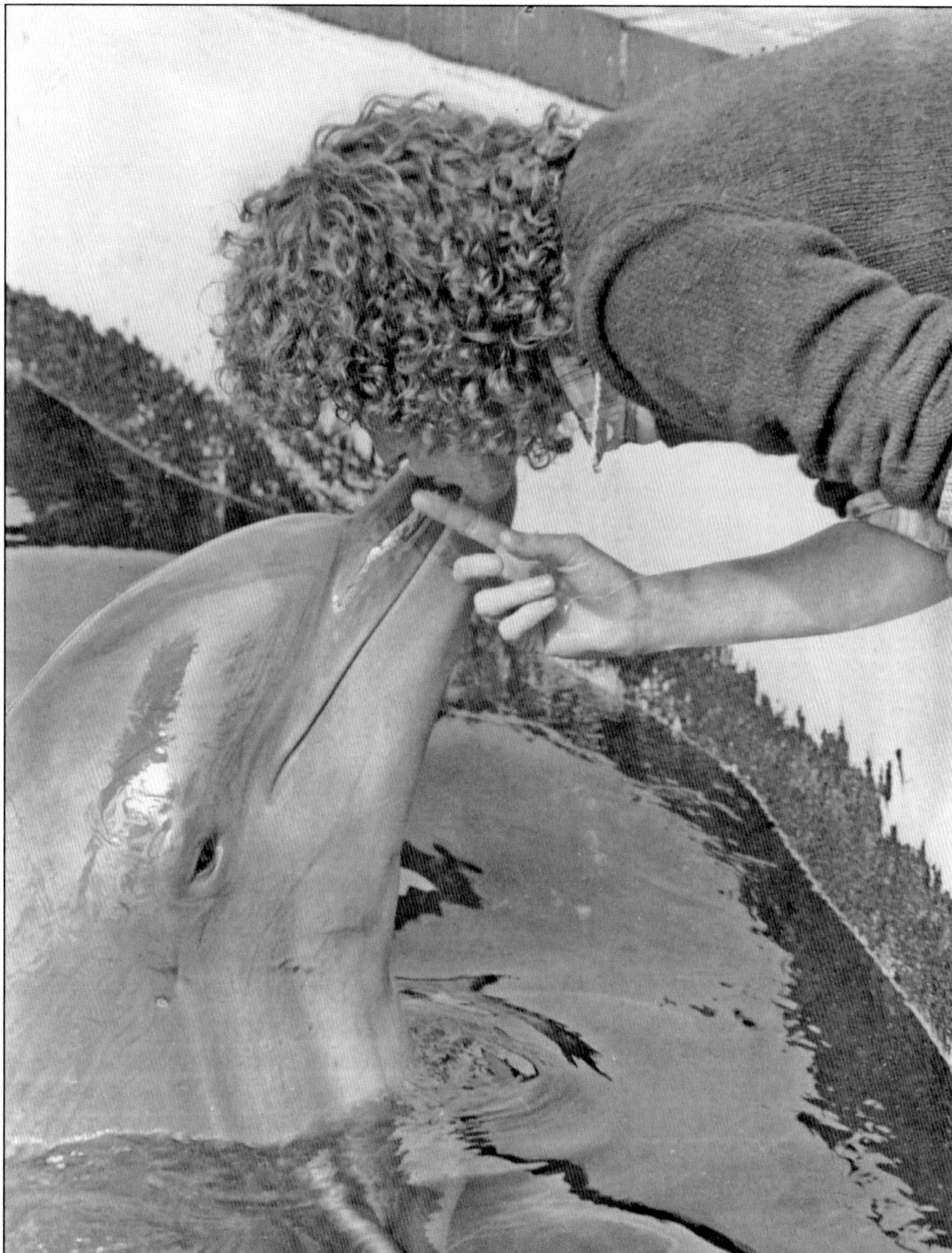

Employee Leslie Hutton plays with a bottlenose dolphin. Working at Marineland changed the lives of innumerable young people. Some met there and married. For instance, of five volunteer Explorer Scouts who scrubbed tanks and worked odd jobs, four became MDs and one a PhD. One of them, emergency physician Charles Rennie, also became adjunct curator of vertebrate zoology at the Santa Barbara Museum of Natural History, and Marineland curator Brad Andrews became corporate vice president of zoological operations for the multipark Busch Entertainment Corporation. (Courtesy Point Vicente Interpretive Center.)

Three

It All Came from the Land

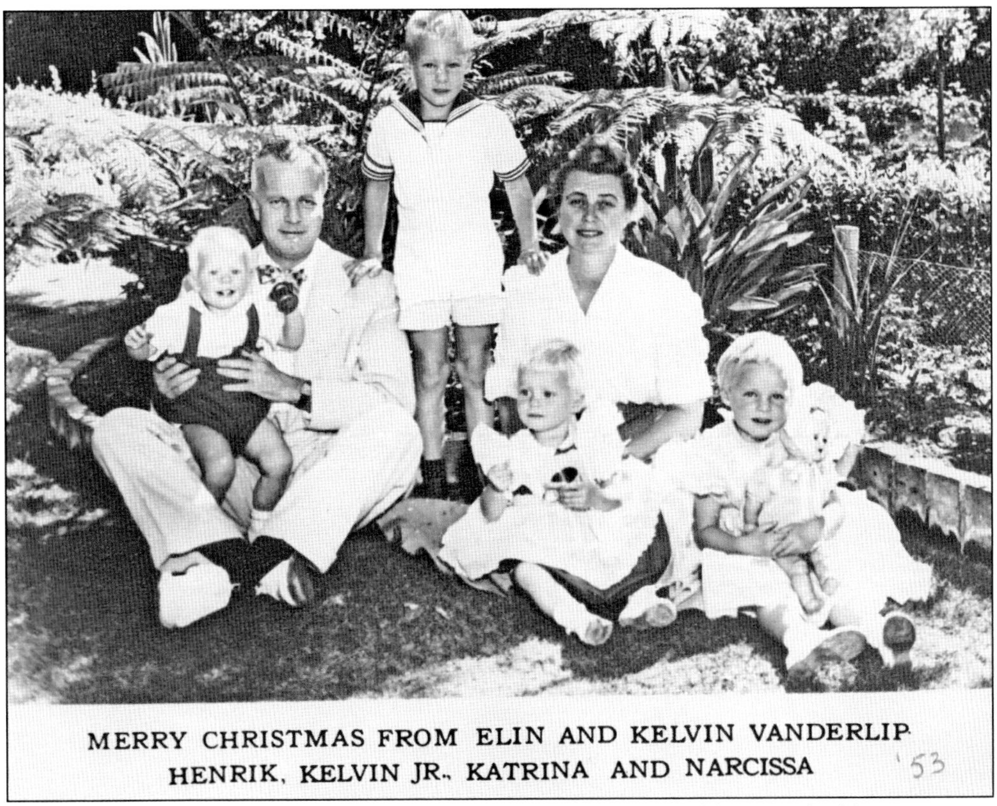

Kelvin Vanderlip became president of the family business in 1945 and began to build communities in the Palos Verdes hills. He developed and sold four tree-filled neighborhoods—Dapplegray, Eastfield, Westfield, and Southfield. For the most part, the hills inland were being used but not developed. Here in a Christmas card, he sits with his young family: his wife, Elin, and four children. (Courtesy Jean Curtis Wells.)

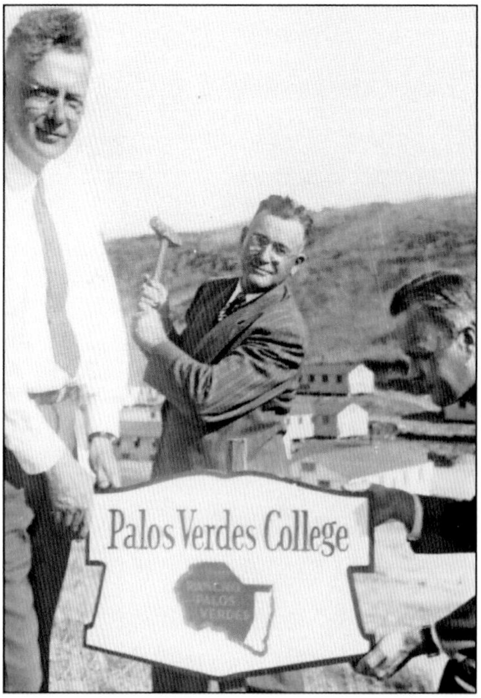

When Dr. and Mrs. Richard Saunders approached Kelvin Vanderlip about opening a college in Palos Verdes, Vanderlip happily donated land in a swale near Crest Road and Crenshaw, just as his father had earlier donated land to create the Chadwick school. Palos Verdes College, a two-year, coeducational liberal arts college, opened in 1947 after some vigorous fund-raising. From left to right are Dr. Saunders, Mr. ? Rash, and Kelvin Vanderlip. (Courtesy Local History Collection, Palos Verdes Library.)

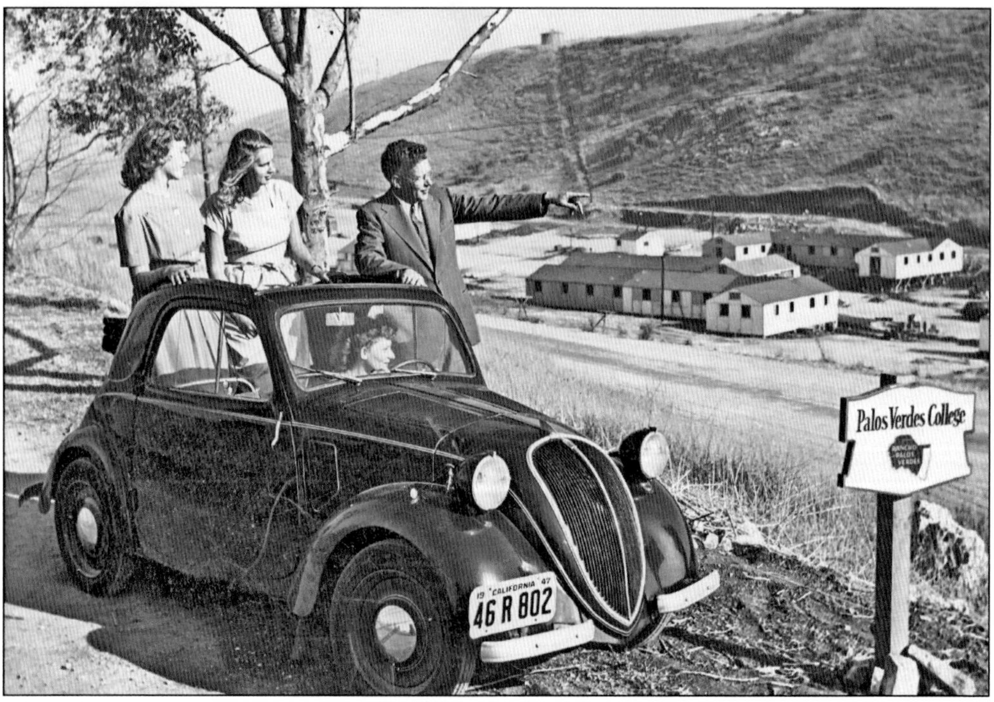

The college was lodged in temporary buildings that had been an army air force installation during the war. The prefabs were rearranged to create classrooms, dormitories, a library, and a dining room. Incoming students Ruth Lissauer, seated in the little Simca; Coralie Howard; and Barbara Lois Verket are shown the campus by Dr. Saunders. (Courtesy Local History Collection, Palos Verdes Library.)

Mabel Cory, shown here, a 30-year veteran of the San Pedro High School library, came out of retirement to set up the college library. Given only one month before the college opened, she and Elin Shaffer, a rare book specialist, sorted, catalogued, and shelved 3,000 books. A "Send Your Books to College" community campaign netted 2,000 more volumes and the Vanderlips donated many first editions. (Courtesy Local History Collection, Palos Verdes Library.)

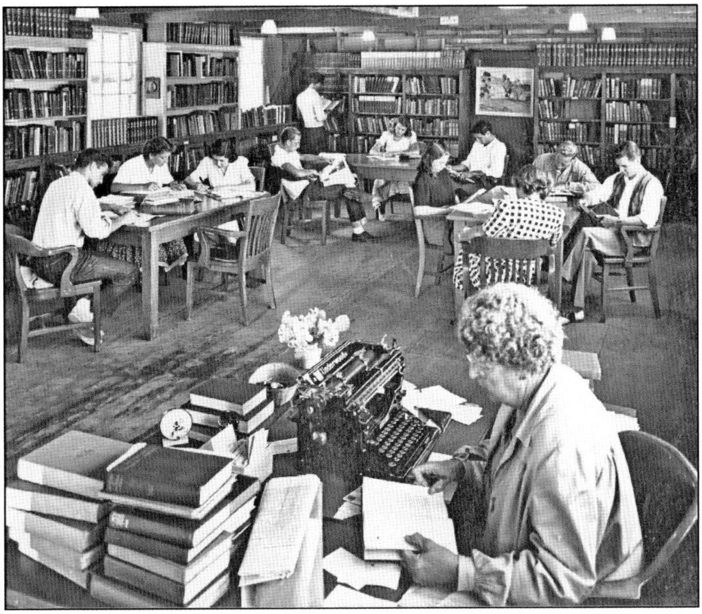

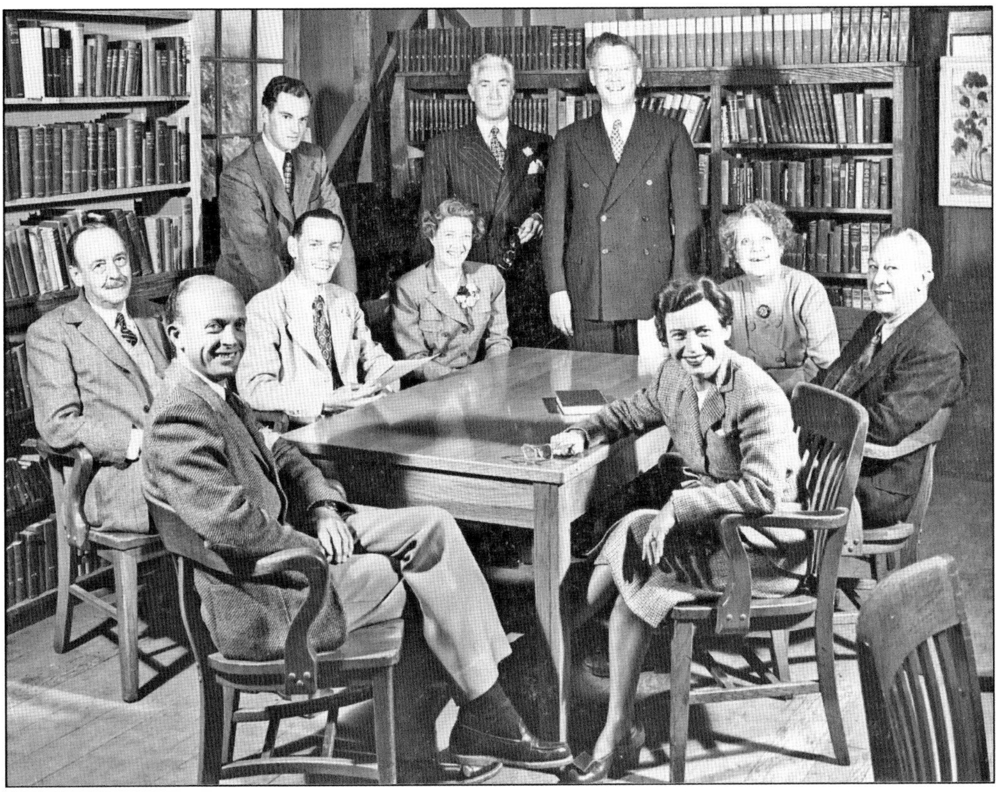

The first faculty members, in 1947, from left to right are Mr. ? Wheaton, Frank Braye, Hinton Miller, John Howard (standing), Charlotte Vanderlip Conway, Ralph Jester, Dr. Richard Saunders, Miss ? Cory, Captain Schneider, and Elizabeth Jacobs. By 1951, the college could not afford to pay Dr. Saunders so John Howard, independently wealthy, took over, becoming the youngest college president in the country. (Courtesy Local History Collection, Palos Verdes Library.)

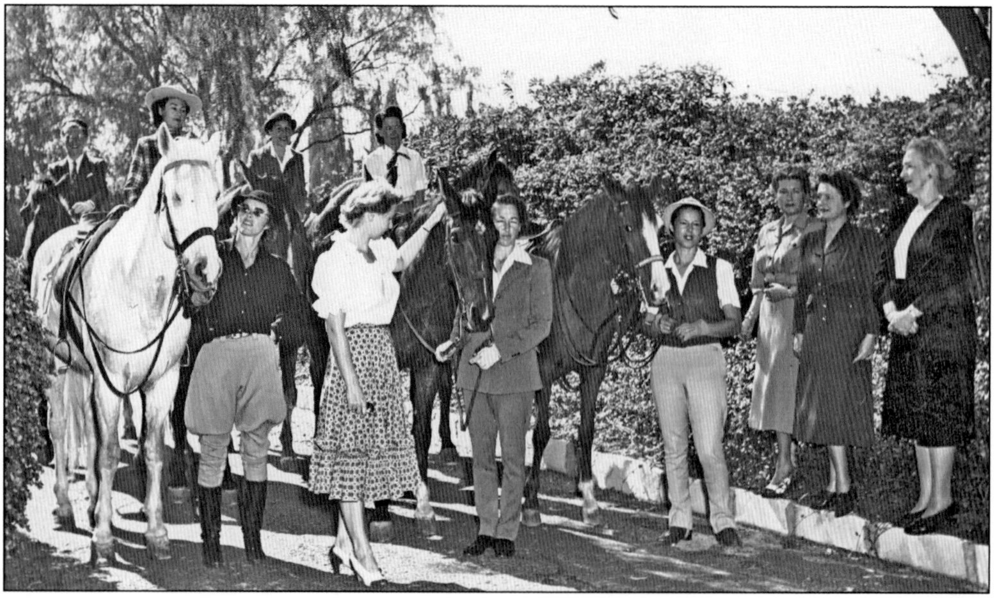

Mrs. Kelvin Vanderlip hosts one of the innumerable fund-raising events in support of the cash-strapped college. In this photograph dated 1948, standing in riding togs are Evelyn Burns, Elin Vanderlip, and Roberta Shaw. Riders behind them are an unidentified man, Maybel Ripley, Mary Ann Hix, and an unidentified woman. Watching on the side are Lucille Houghton, Grace Armstrong, and Agnes Robertson. (Courtesy Local History Collection, Palos Verdes Library.)

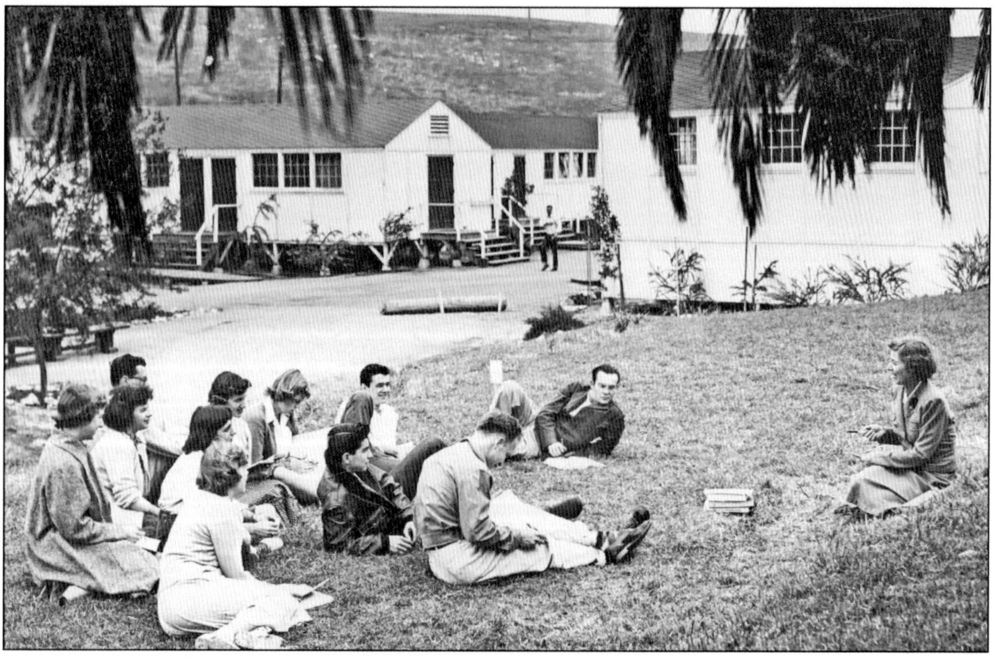

Charlotte Vanderlip Conway is teaching anthropology on the grass outside her classroom on a January day in 1949. She is Kelvin's sister, and she introduced him to his future wife, Elin. Marilyn Hedley, in her book *How Daddy Became a Beachcomber*, said, "She is my favorite Vanderlip . . . she has a passionate interest in the (welfare of the) un-white man of the world and she teaches us a great deal." (Courtesy Local History Collection, Palos Verdes Library.)

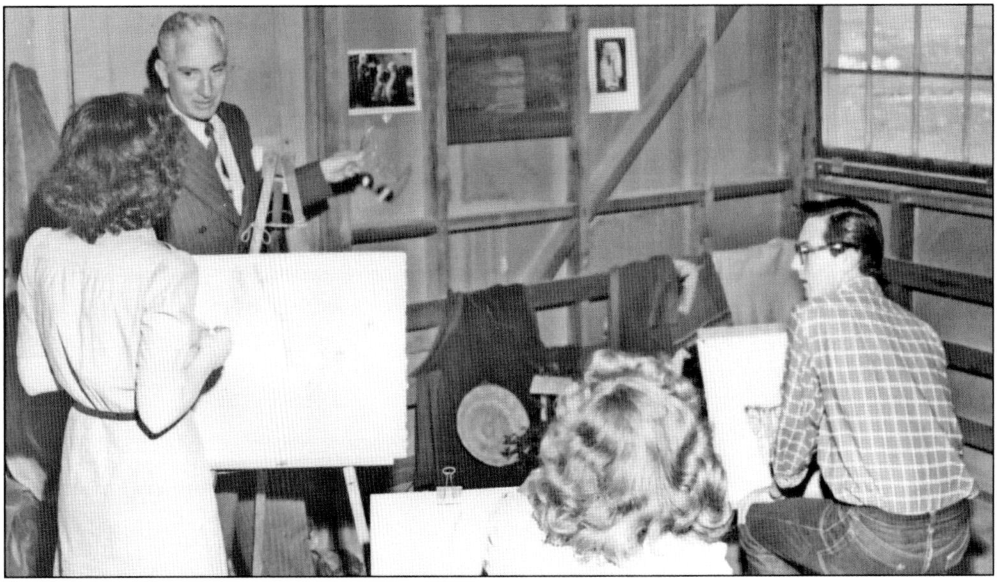

Ralph Jester worked for Cecil B. DeMille as a costume designer and taught part time at the college. At least two of his students, Flo Ann and Marilyn Hedley, went on to design sets and costumes for the Players Ring Theatre in Hollywood with director Raymond Burr. The women were daughters of Eli Hedley, whose artistic creations from beachcombing finds were prized by Hollywood stars. (Courtesy Local History Collection, Palos Verdes Library.)

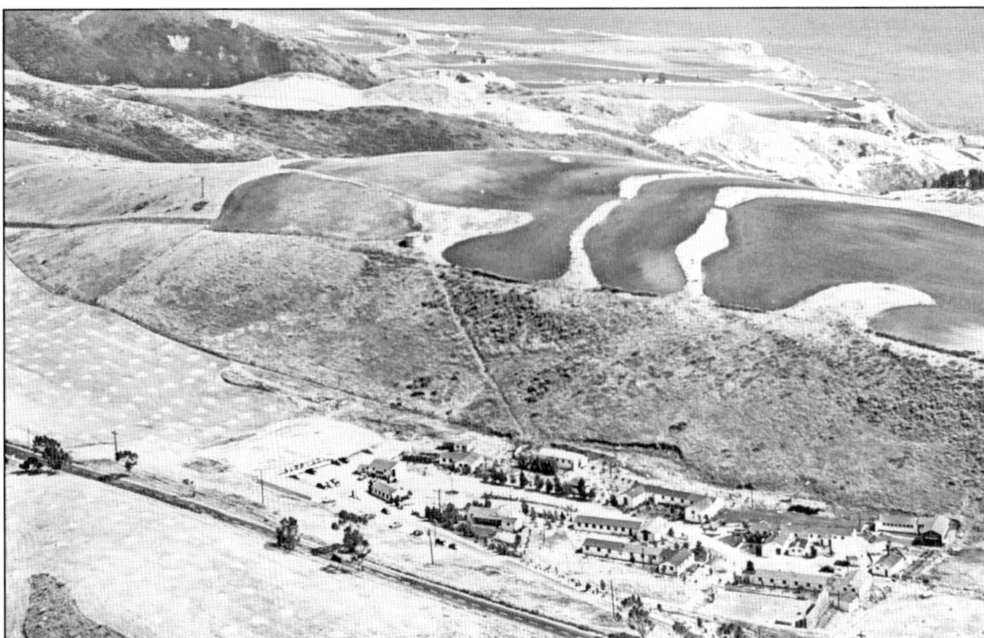

Here in the swale is the temporary college. The top of the hill is where they planned to site the permanent college with a view of Portuguese Bend and the ocean. Ralph Jester was chairman of the architectural committee to draw up plans for its development. He worked with two architectural firms. Although plans were drawn, they were never implemented. (Photograph by Peter Gowland; courtesy Local History Collection, Palos Verdes Library.)

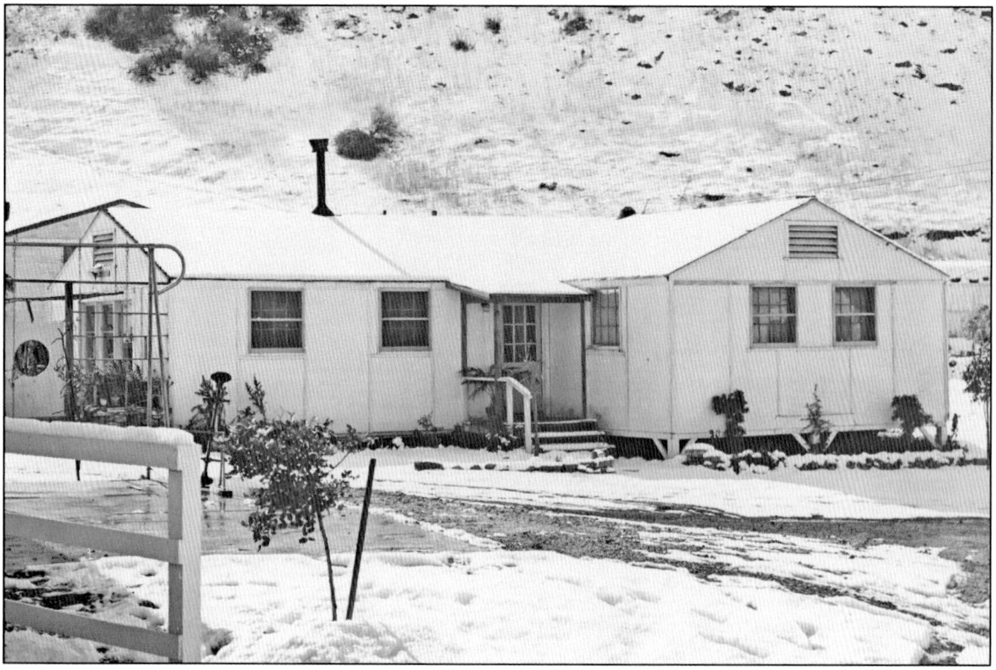

On January 12, 1949, everyone on the peninsula woke to snow on the ground. The campus was no exception. Getting to school that Wednesday morning was no problem for the students who were living on campus. There is no record of whether the off-site students could make it to classes. (Courtesy Local History Collection, Palos Verdes Library.)

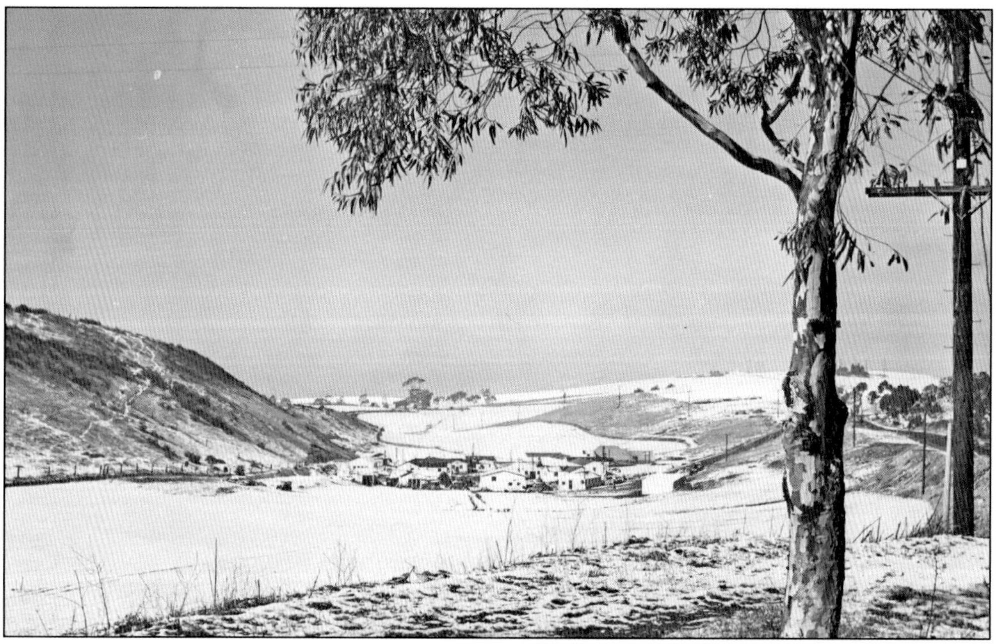

The winter of 1949 brought the first real snow Los Angeles had gotten in well over 100 years, and it was exciting. Although it was only .3 inches at the Los Angeles civic center, it blanketed the Palos Verdes hills and sent the students out to make snowmen and snow angels, too busy to photograph the fun. (Courtesy Local History Collection, Palos Verdes Library.)

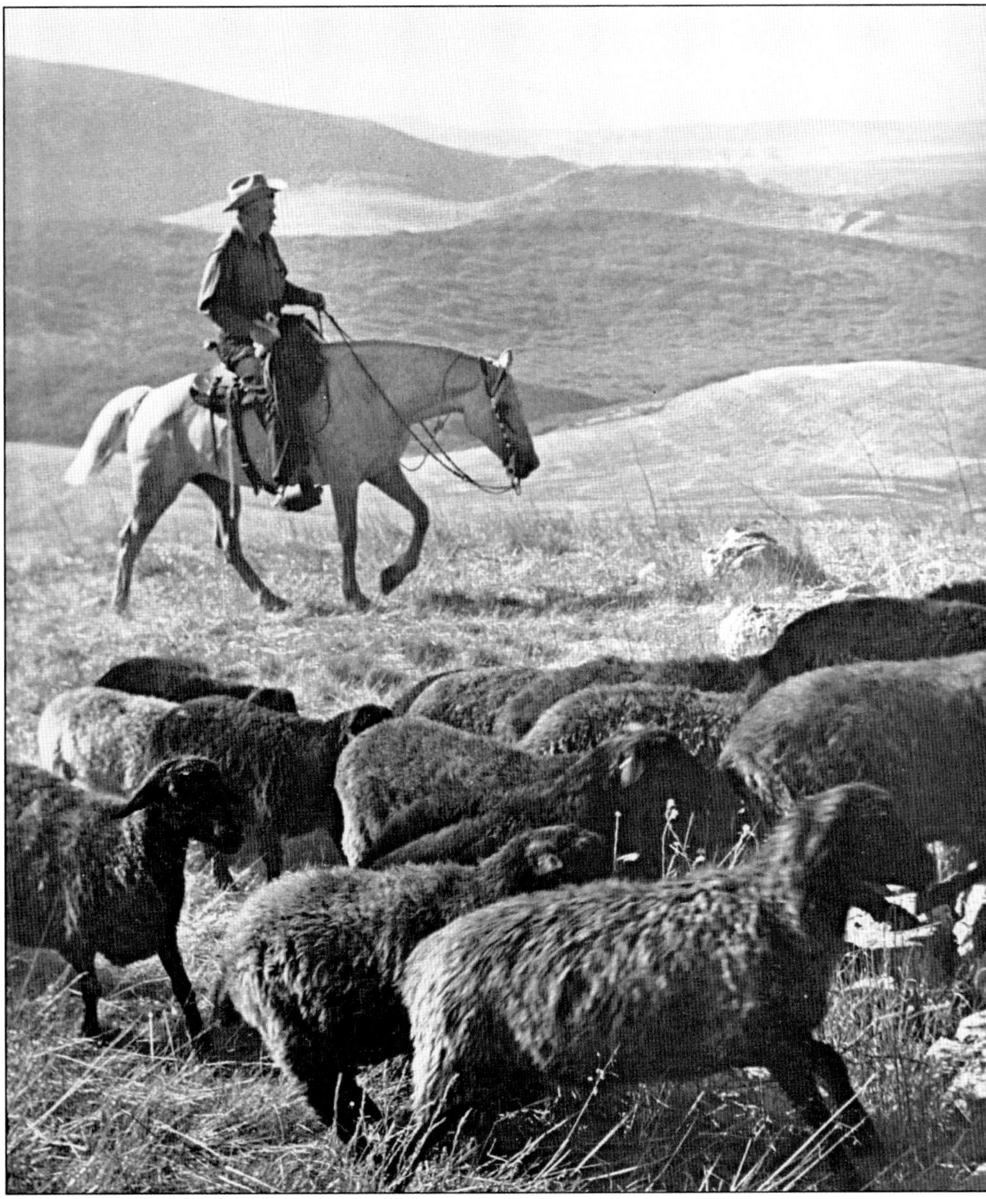

Around 1949, Bob Boyd arranged with Kelvin Vanderlip to bring in 700 black karakul sheep for weed control. Boyd had camps on the Pacific side and in Miraleste. His winter camp was in the Peninsula Center area. "He was always kind of apologetic that he was in the sheep business. He had been an old cowhand from Montana," said Rolling Hills rancher Gordon Schultz. (Courtesy Local History Collection, Palos Verdes Library.)

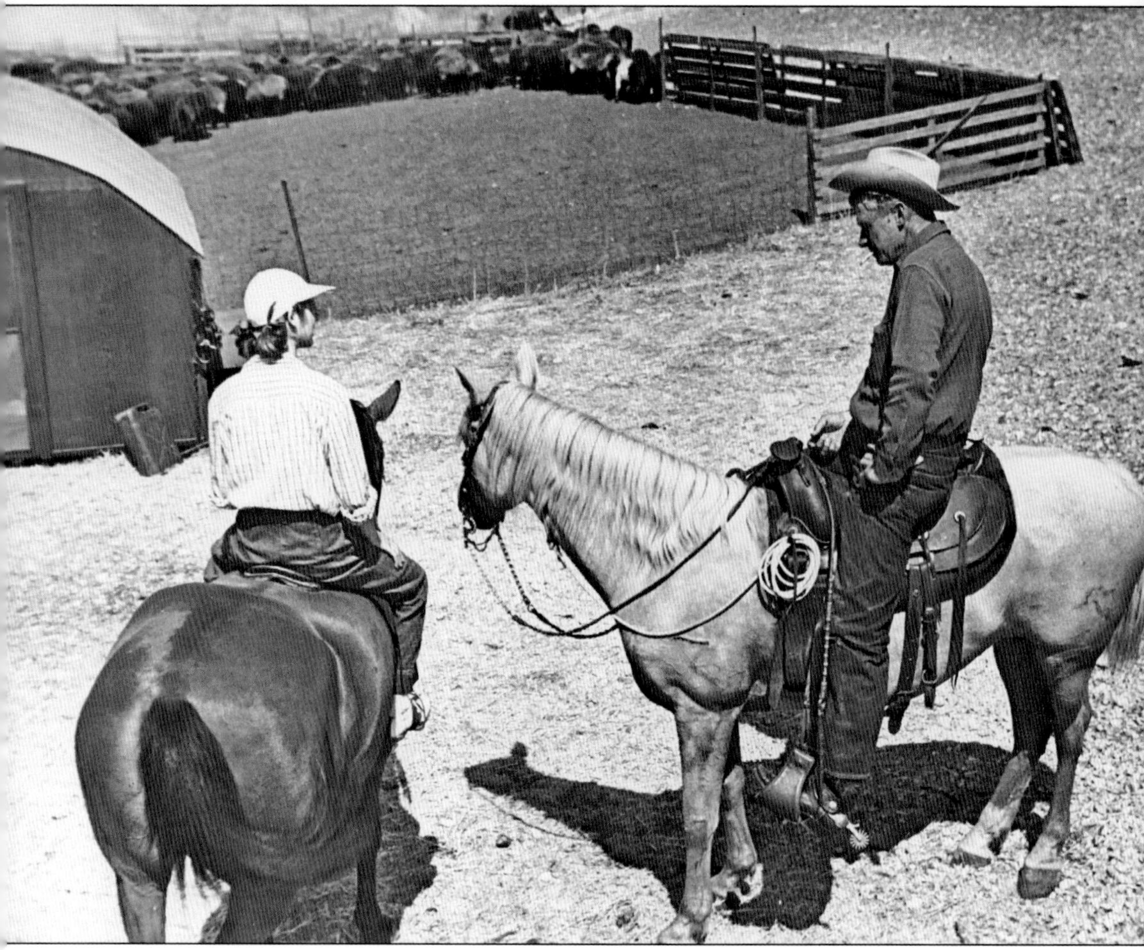

This is Janet Sweet, a University of Southern California coed from Miraleste. Bob Boyd sold her the horse she is riding. He liked people who liked horses, and they often stopped by for conversation. He was a huge man, about 6 feet 6 inches and about 240 pounds. According to rancher Gordon Schulz, Boyd "set a horse very well. He just was a wonderful chap." (Courtesy Local History Collection, Palos Verdes Library.)

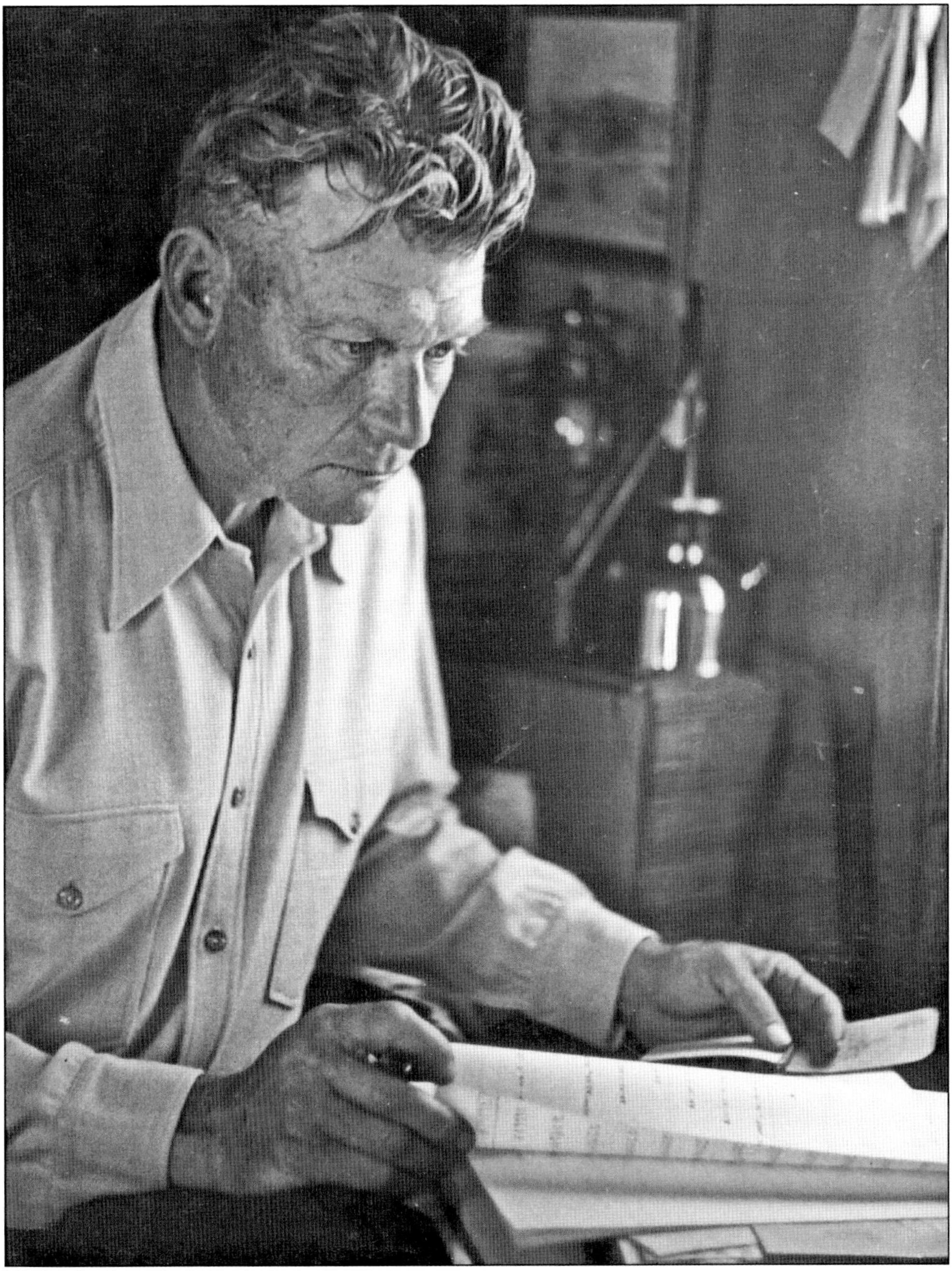

Being a one-man karakul breeder and herder also meant being a bookkeeper. At night in his snug trailer, Boyd goes over his books, which include financial figures and carefully kept breeding figures because of the close registry of all karakuls. All American karakul bloodlines stem from 25 ewes and 26 rams imported after special diplomatic action by Pres. Theodore Roosevelt in 1909. Karakul sheep come from Central Asia. (Courtesy Local History Collection, Palos Verdes Library.)

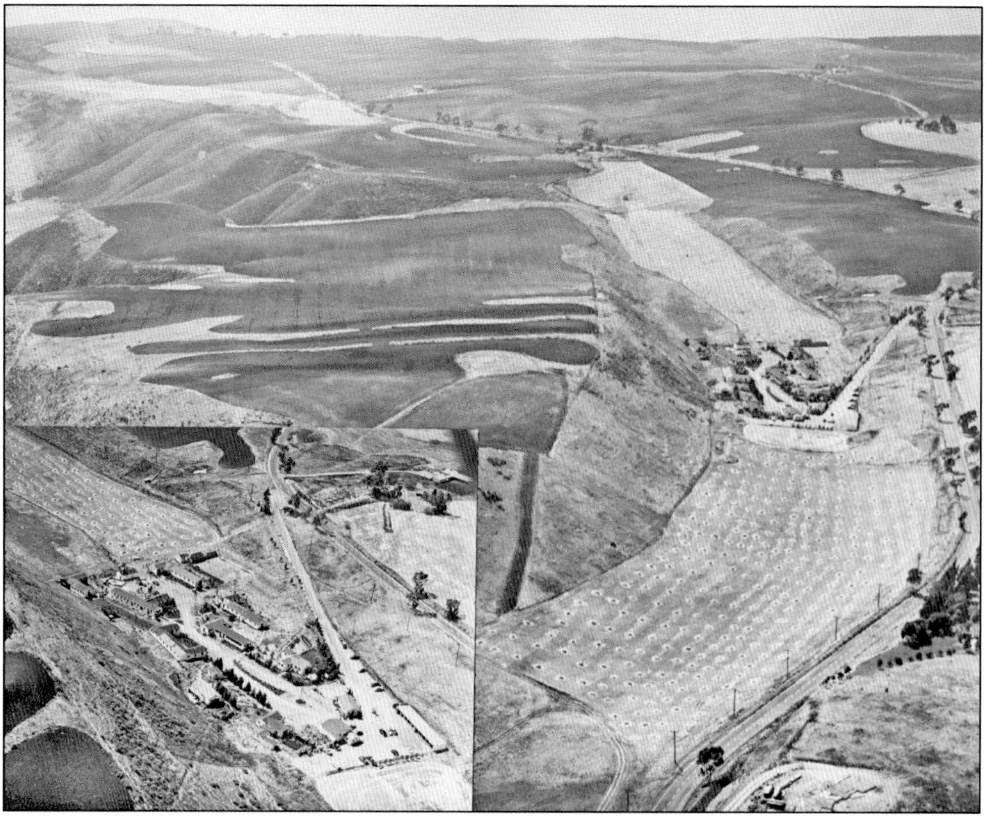

This photograph with the odd inset of the college is a good view across the hills of the McCarrell farmland surrounding the campus. Wallace McCarrell began sharecropping hundreds of acres in 1909. His twin sons, Roy and Raymond, farmed, married, and raised families alongside him. Wallace McCarrell continued farming until an auto accident took his life in 1944. (Courtesy Local History Collection, Palos Verdes Library.)

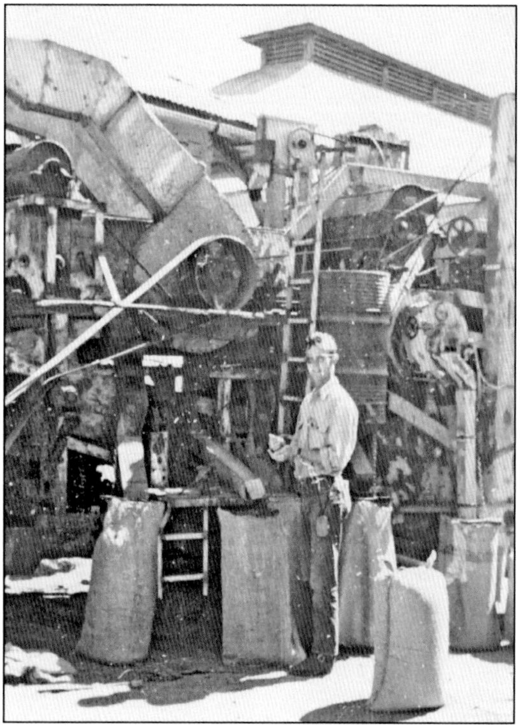

The 1940s brought the third generation of McCarrells. Wallace had three sons; the eldest, Herbert, died of polio, and one other son, Roy Sr., offered his own eldest son, one-year-old Roy McCarrell Jr., born in 1929, for his father, Wallace, to raise. Roy Jr. worked beside his grandfather's farmhands, and by the time he was 18, here in 1947, he knew enough to run the farm. (Courtesy Rosalee McCarrell Orr.)

“Fifty years ago, my granddad was farming with horses and mules,” said Roy Jr. When he was seven years old, he drove his first tractor, a 1936 John Deere that he would start by jumping on the flywheel to get it to turn to create a spark. “One of my biggest thrills was to drive that tractor,” he added. “Mule power or hydrocarbons, it all came from the land.” (Courtesy Rosalee McCarrell Orr.)

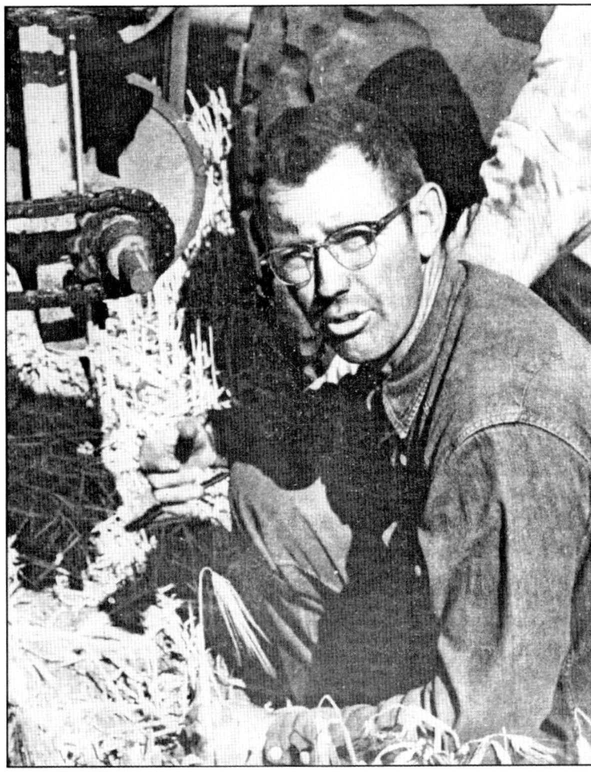

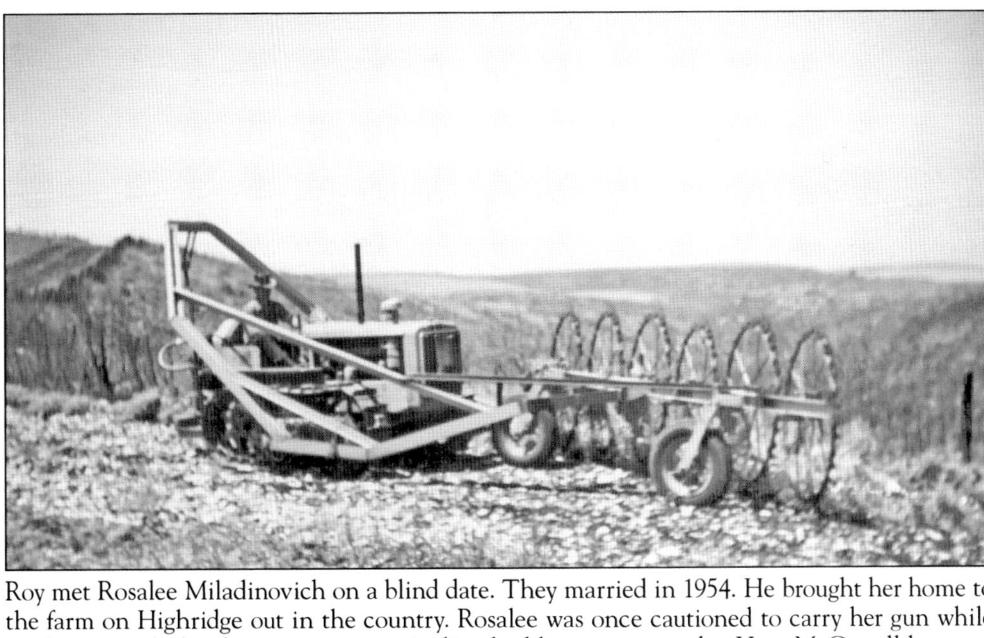

Roy met Rosalee Miladinovich on a blind date. They married in 1954. He brought her home to the farm on Highridge out in the country. Rosalee was once cautioned to carry her gun while out hanging clothes because a mountain lion had been seen nearby. Here McCarrell harvests garbanzo beans. Dry farming requires a lot of acreage because the yield per acre is lower without irrigation. (Courtesy Rosalee McCarrell Orr.)

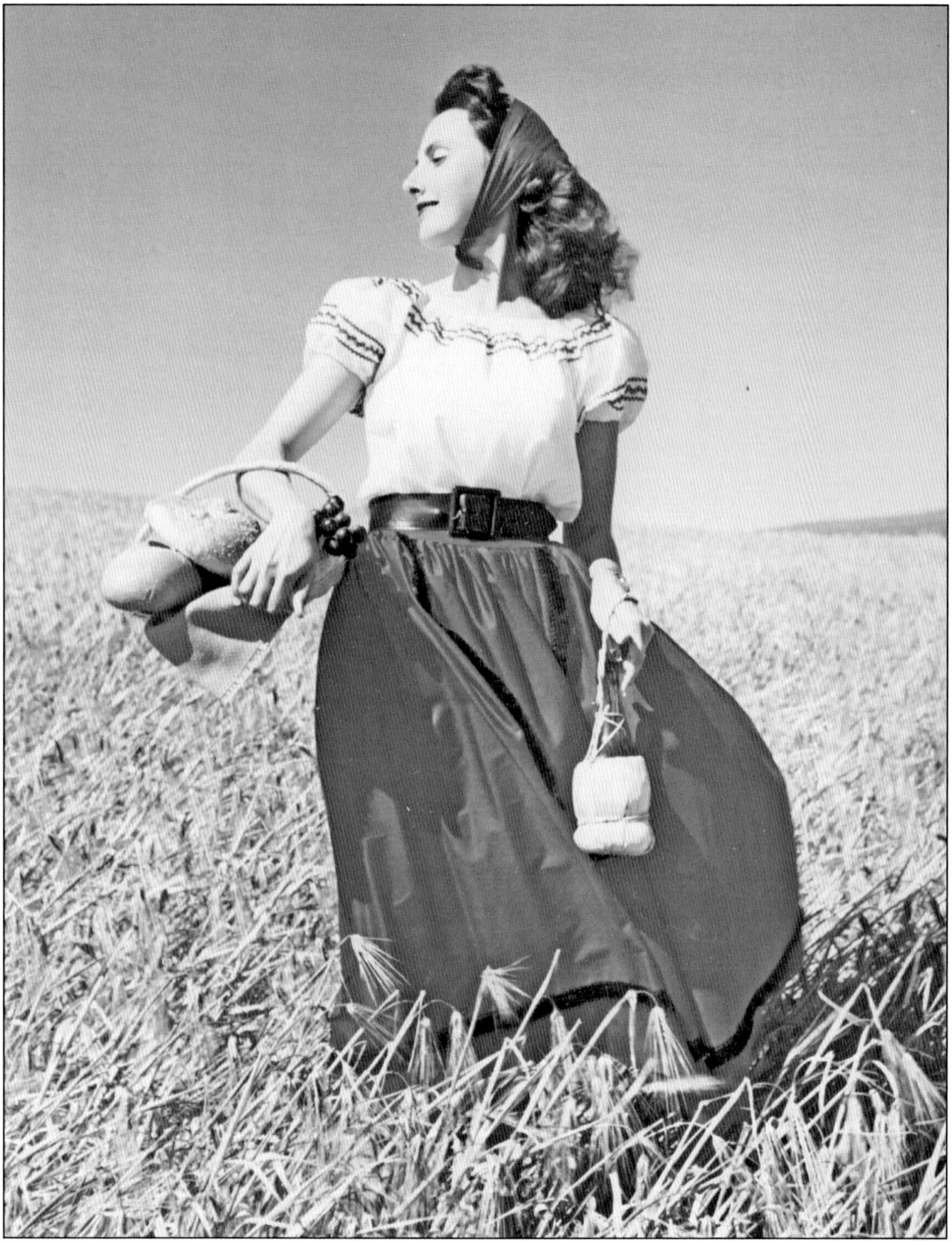

"It was a good life, a happy life," said Rosalee. "We didn't have a lot of money and some years we didn't make it. Farming is a gamble." Like the year they cut the garbanzo beans and a windstorm dumped all the beans into the ocean. "We didn't get paid that year," she said. Here Rosalee poses for an artist friend who wanted to paint a peasant girl. (Courtesy Rosalee McCarrell Orr.)

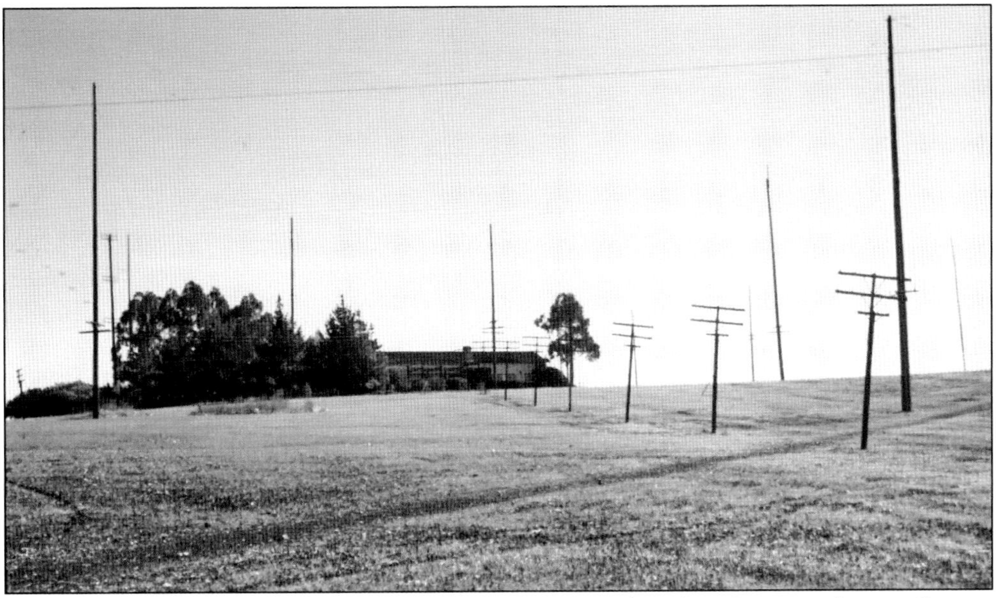

In the 1930s, Press-Wireless, owned by a group of newspapers, bought 105 acres at Armoga Springs and Highridge Roads and erected antennas to receive news dispatches from around the world. The Vanderlips had agreed to allow antennas on Palos Verdes only after a discussion with their friend Norman Chandler of the *Los Angeles Times*, a discussion arranged by Long Beach ham Don Wallace, W6AM. (Courtesy Dennis Yonker, NE6I.)

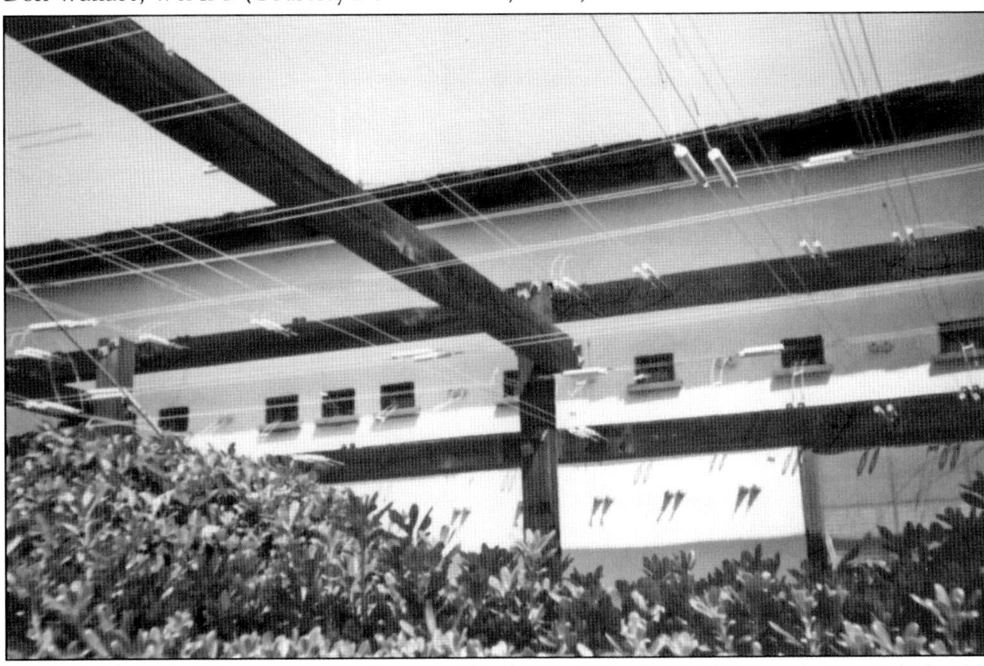

Press-Wireless played an unexpected part in World War II. In 1942, William Arthur Schuler, 23, who lived in Palos Verdes Estates and worked for Press-Wireless, was arrested by the FBI for spying. He had offered to transmit messages to foreign agents using the Press-Wireless transmitters in Playa del Rey. He got six years in the federal penitentiary. Pictured are the wires feeding into the receiving station. (Courtesy Dennis Yonker, NE6I.)

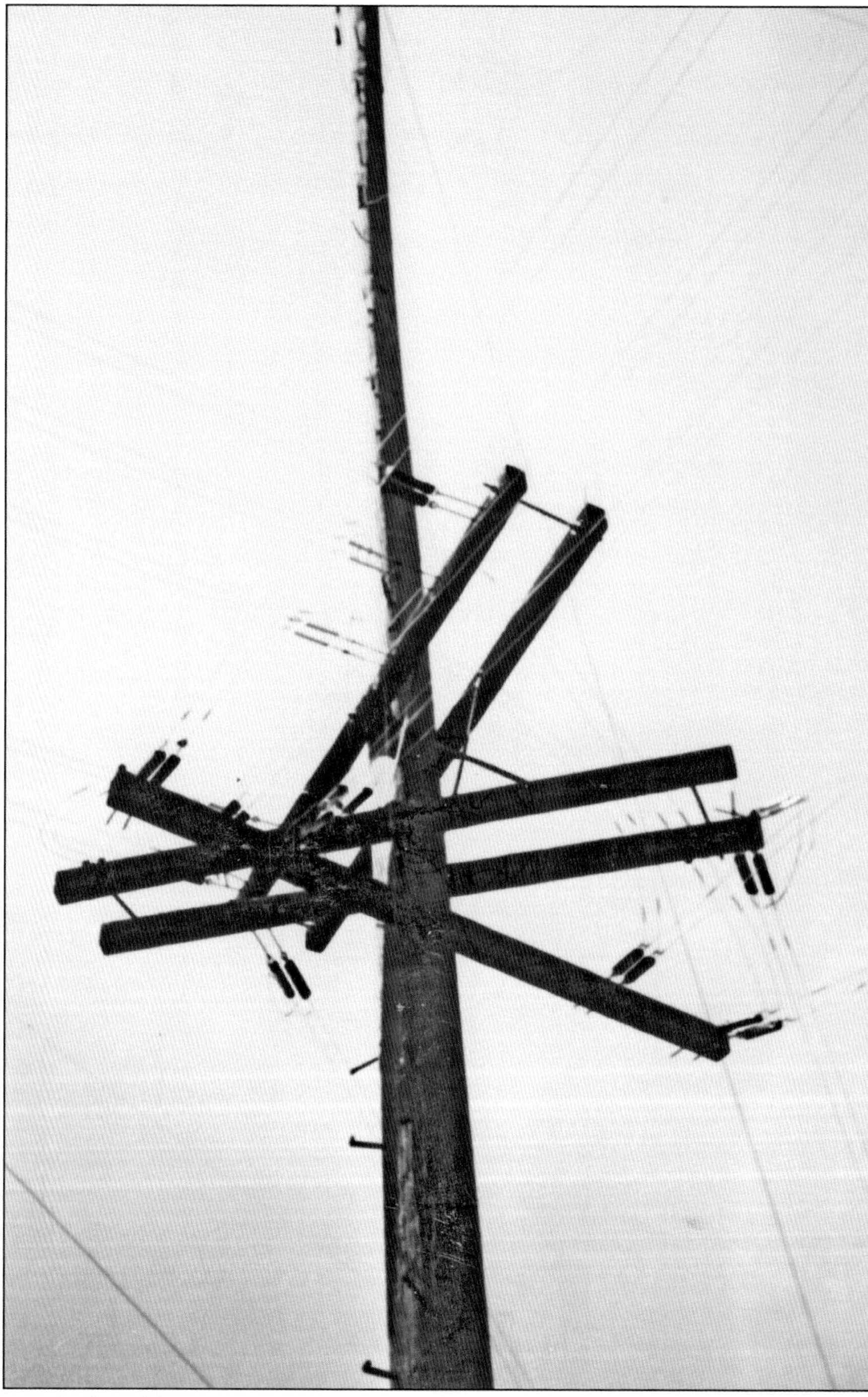

By the end of World War II, Press-Wireless had eight rhombic antennas—15 miles of wire in the air. A rhombic antenna is wire strung between four poles in a diamond shape and then run back to the radio. A radio station is only as good as its antennas, and rhombics are superior for receiving and sending signals. Each of these poles supported at least one end of a rhombic wire and sometimes even two or three. (Courtesy Brian Tilley, KA6UHM.)

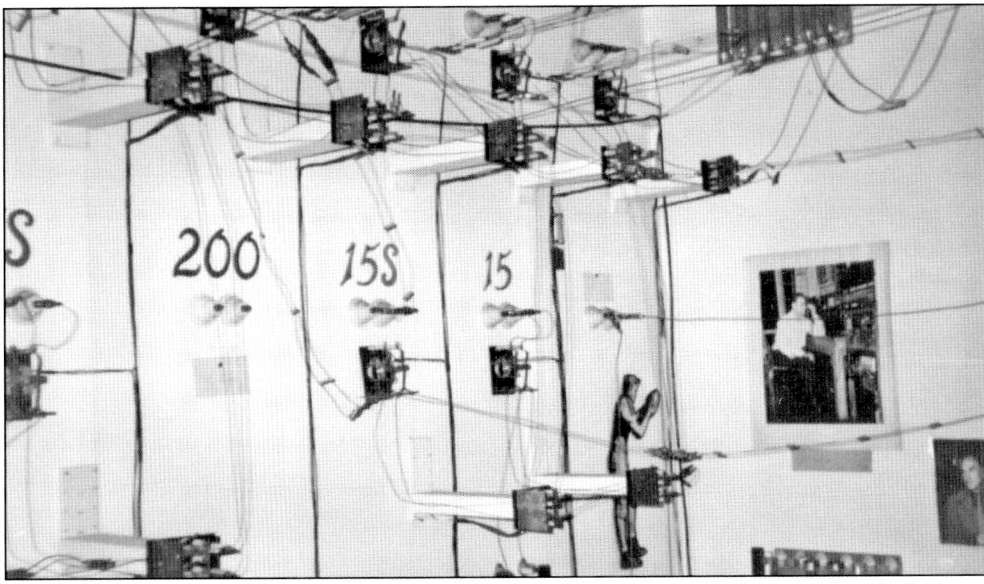

Two pairs of transmission lines ran from each rhombic to its own panel (shown here). One pair was connected to a transmitter and the other to a load resistor. The antenna would transmit and receive toward the load resistor. When the wires were reversed, the relays would go "kathunk, kathunk" and the antenna would receive and transmit signals in the opposite direction. (Courtesy Dennis Younker, NE6I.)

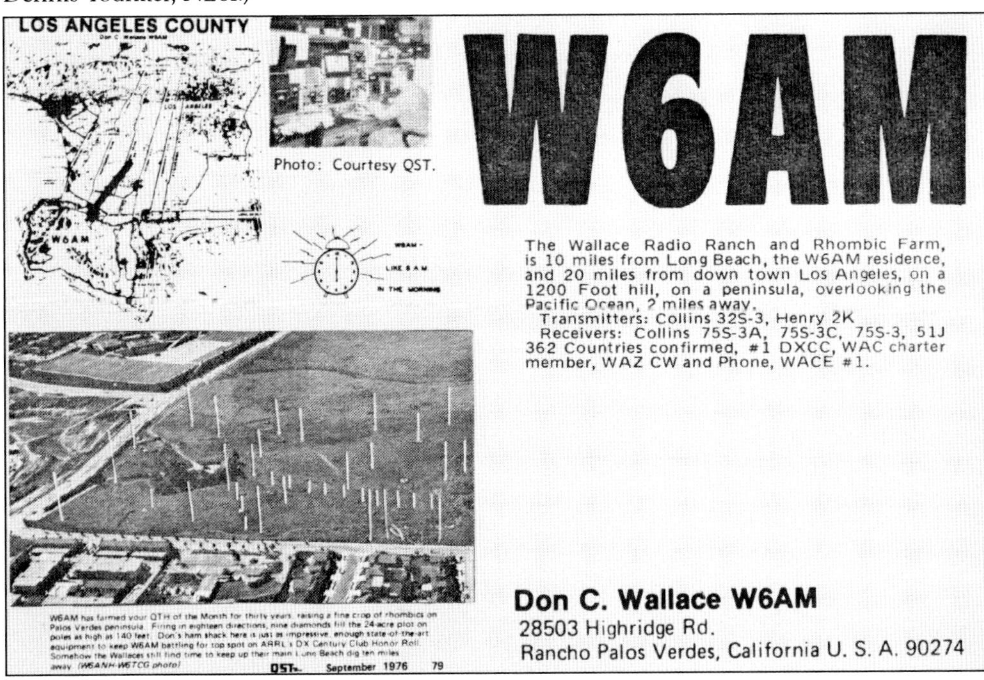

In 1945, Don Wallace bought the land from Kelvin Vanderlip who, in order to control deed restrictions, had bought the land from Press-Wireless. Wallace built one more diamond-shaped rhombic, and W6AM became a legend among hams around the world. In thanks, Wallace kept Rolling Hills in the news with press releases, which boosted Vanderlip's land sales. Wallace mailed this card to each radio contact. (Courtesy Dan Colburn, W6DC.)

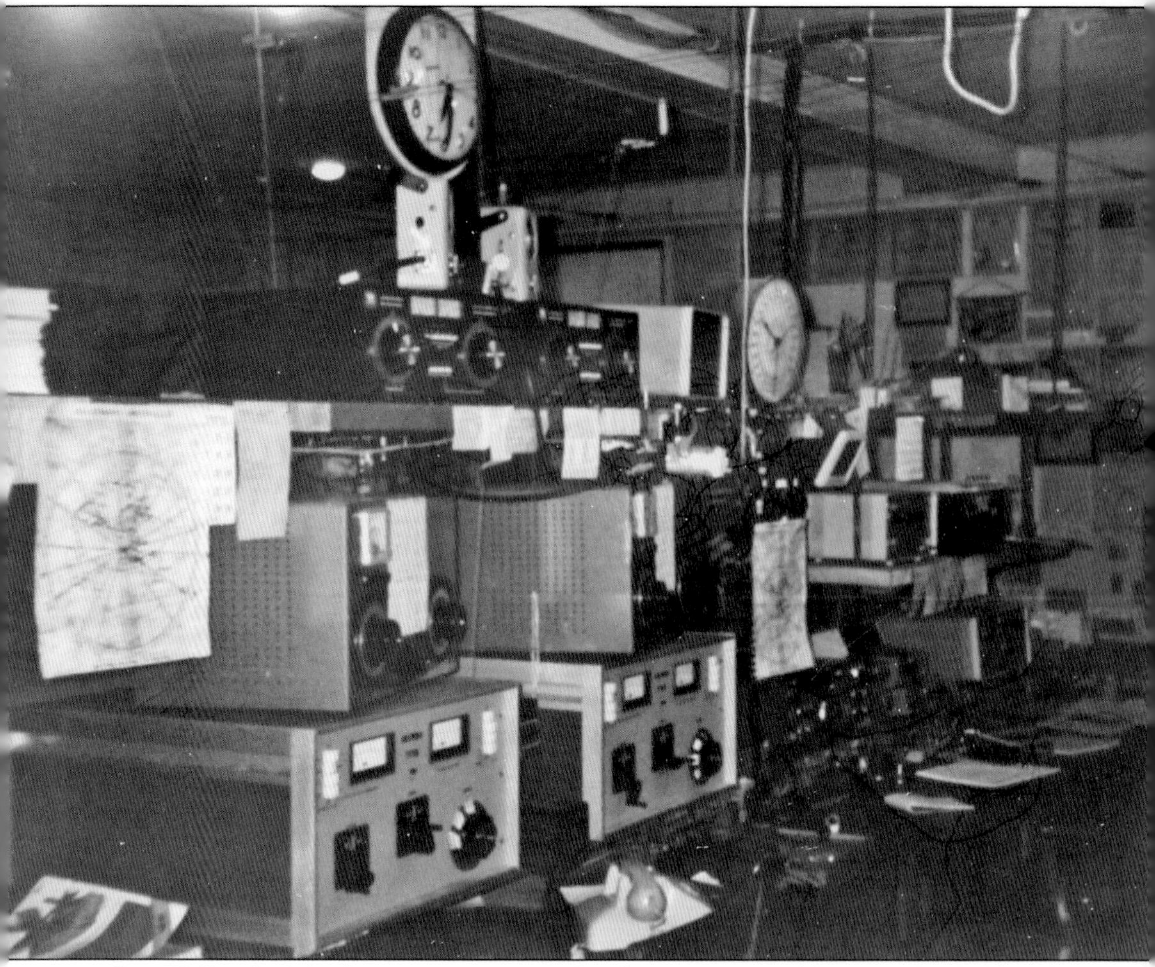

Don Wallace built his first receiver in 1909 when he was 11 years old. His timing could not have been better. Thomas Edison and Nikola Tesla were fighting over electricity, Lee de Forest had just improved the Fleming vacuum valve, and more inventions were to come. Here is the W6AM ham shack. The hanging chart on the left told the operator which rhombics covered which parts of the world. (Courtesy Dennis Younker, NE6I.)

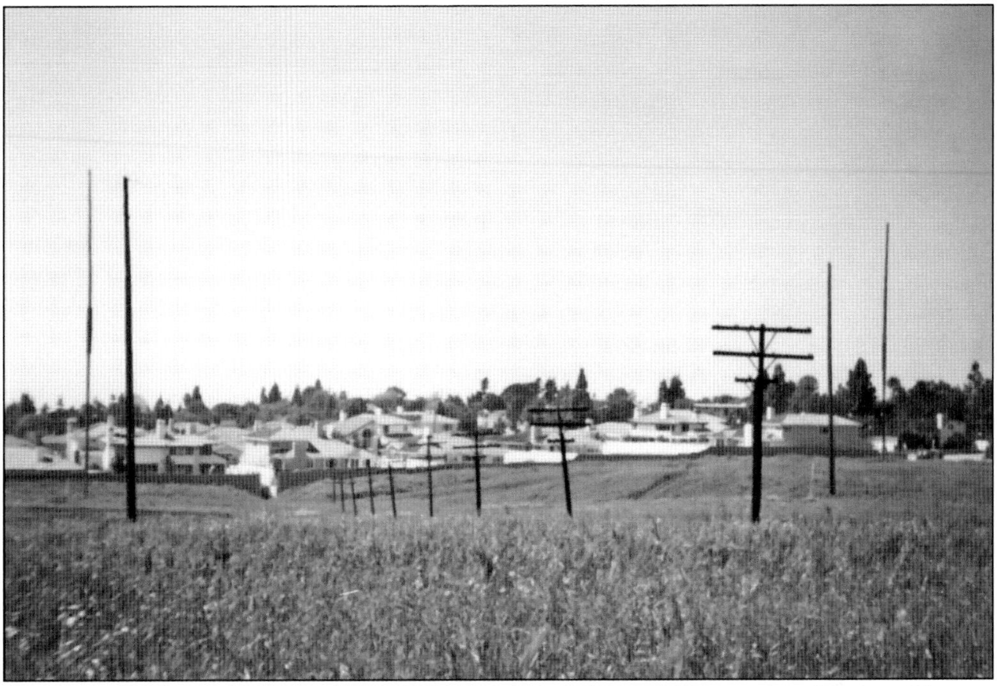

Over time, Wallace sold much of his valuable land, consolidating his nine rhombics into 24 acres. He stacked telephone poles (far left, far right) to make tall rhombics. The shorter telephone poles held the wires that transmitted the information between the rhombics and the "ham shack" where his radios were. Wallace climbed all of these poles well into his 80s to tension and repair the wires. (Courtesy Dennis Younker, NE6I.)

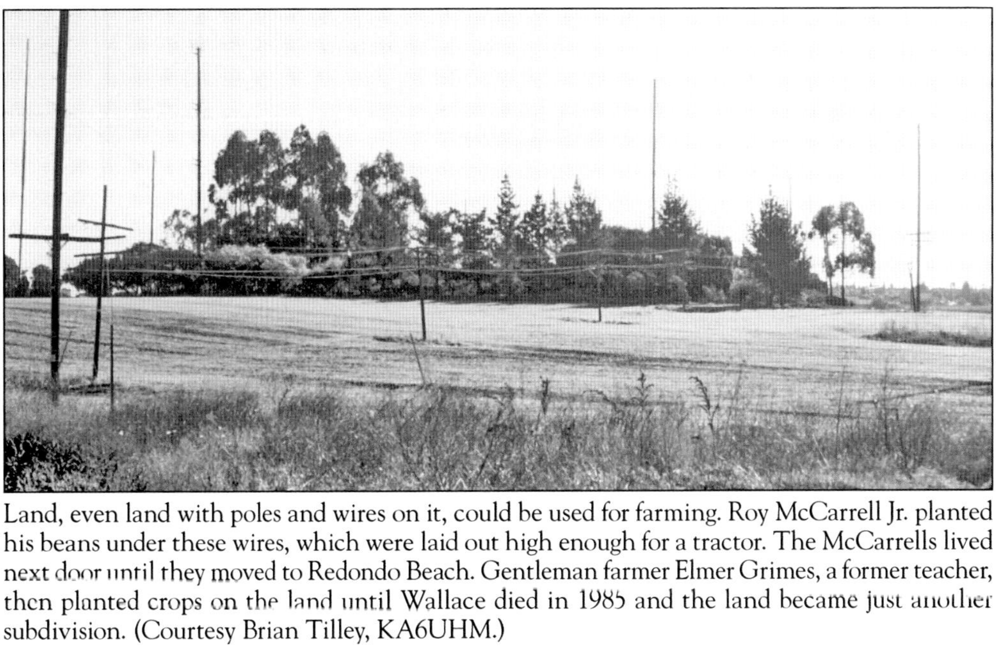

Land, even land with poles and wires on it, could be used for farming. Roy McCarrell Jr. planted his beans under these wires, which were laid out high enough for a tractor. The McCarrells lived next door until they moved to Redondo Beach. Gentleman farmer Elmer Grimes, a former teacher, then planted crops on the land until Wallace died in 1985 and the land became just another subdivision. (Courtesy Brian Tilley, KA6UHM.)

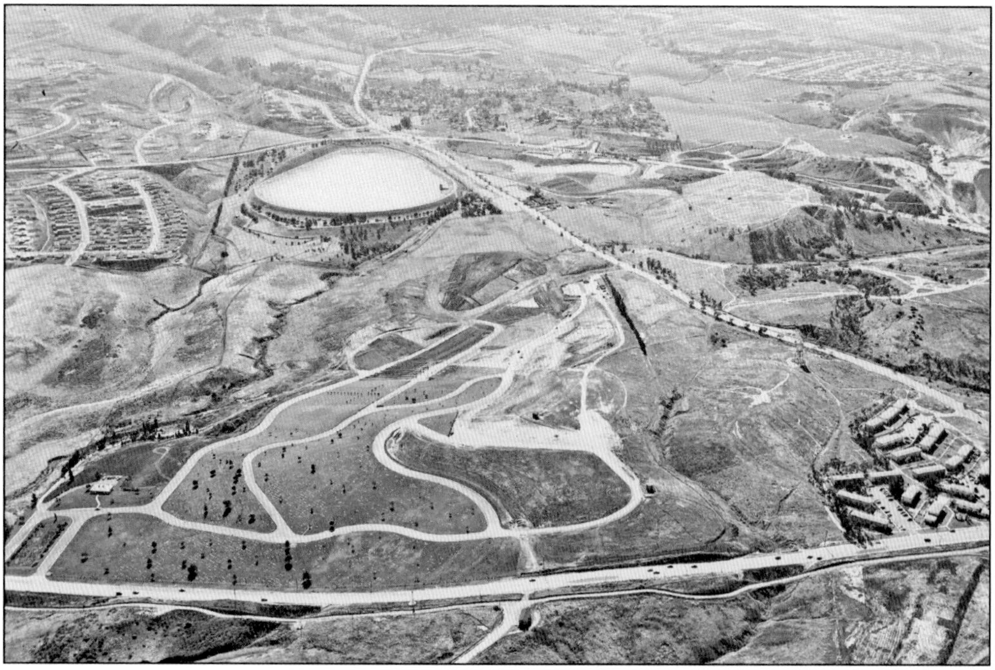

Green Hills Memorial Park was built in 1948 on property bought for $100,000 from the Vanderlips by Robert McNerney and a partnership of local businessmen. According to Frank Vanderlip Jr., it included an unenforceable deed restriction banning funeral processions on Palos Verdes Drive North. Green Hills is between Western Avenue (bottom) and the reservoir. The road along the side is Palos Verdes Drive North. (Courtesy San Pedro Historical Society.)

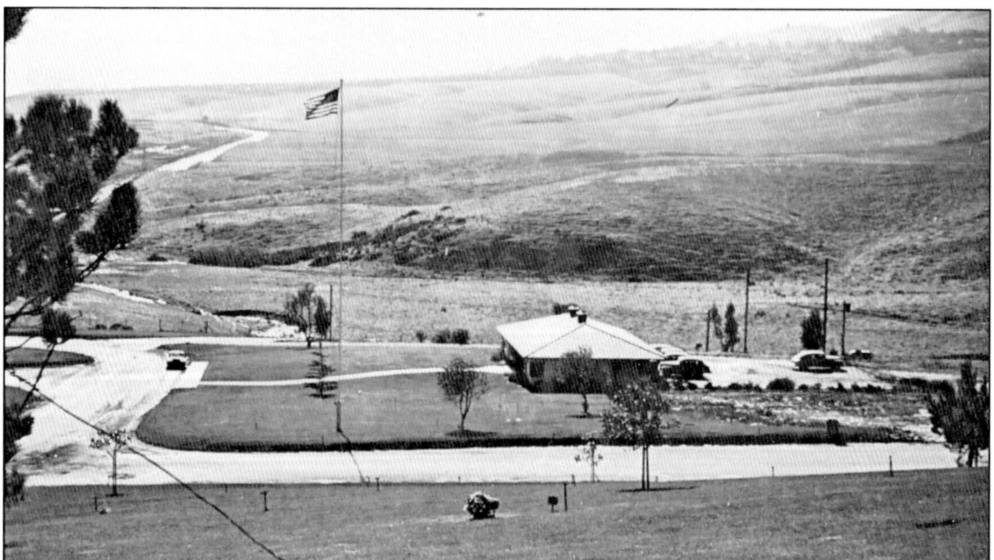

The 12th burial at Green Hills, six months after it opened, was Virginia Wilderman, an eight-year-old girl who had contracted a virulent form of polio. Her mother, Maxine, came to visit her daily in the Harbor View section. "There were no roads, no trees, nothing. I would take flowers in a fruit jar. The guys would drive me up on a Caterpillar tractor to her grave," she said. (Courtesy Green Hills Memorial Park.)

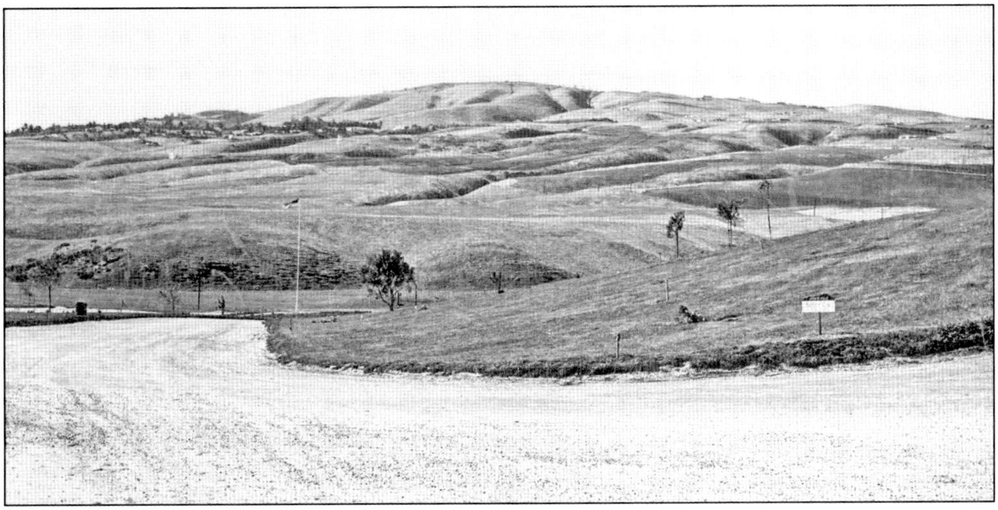

Maxine (Wilderman) Patalano became the top pre-need salesperson at Green Hills. "I wanted the place to grow, to be beautiful—make it a memorial for my daughter," she said. At first the land was bare and secluded. One day, when Patalano was working alone, a man came in with a shotgun. She was terrified, but he just wanted permission to shoot jackrabbits up the hill. (Courtesy Green Hills Memorial Park.)

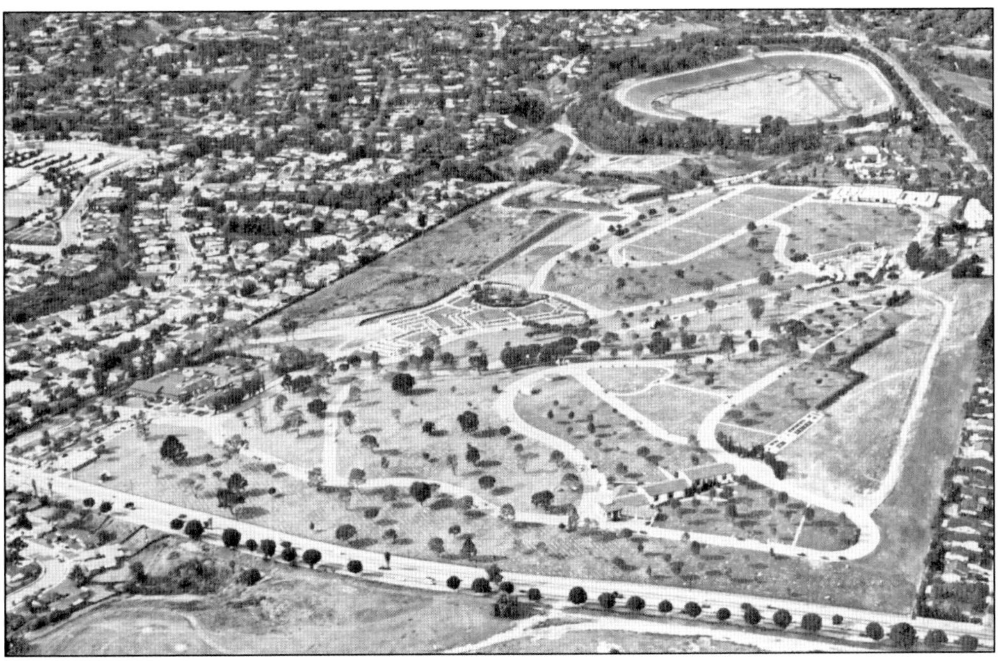

The entrance is on the lower left of this 1995 photograph of Green Hills Memorial Park. Many people from Palos Verdes are buried here, the Ishibashis and the McCarrell twins for example. Catholics were not buried here until the priests offered to visit, and the black community was not allowed until the Civil Rights Act made its inclusion mandatory, but now Green Hills is part of the Palos Verdes community. (Courtesy Green Hills Memorial Park.)

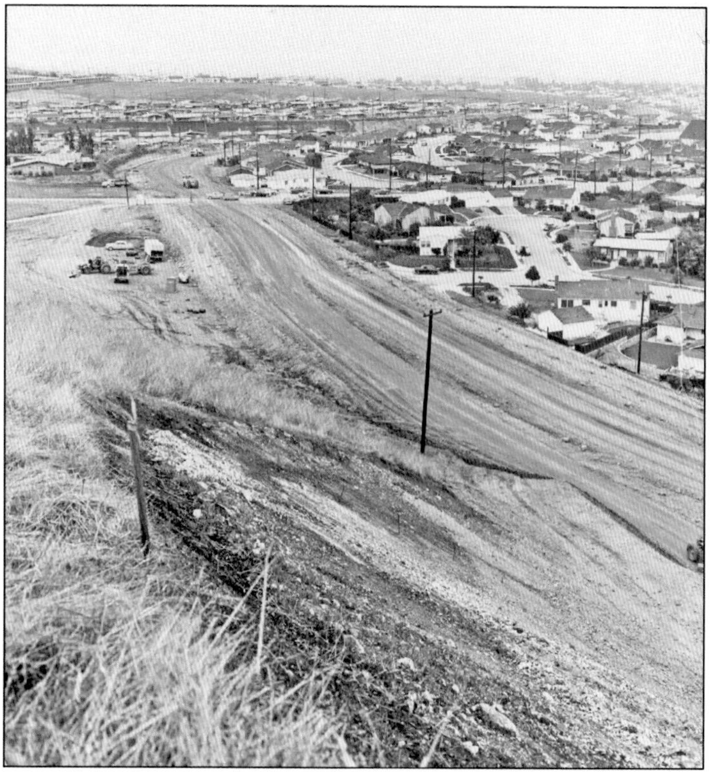

By 1959, Western Avenue was completed. Running along the east side of the Palos Verdes hills along the edge of San Pedro, the new road provided an easier access to coastal Palos Verdes. Twenty years later, a few years after the city of Rancho Palos Verdes was formed, a strip along Western Avenue would vote to leave Los Angeles County and join the city. (Courtesy San Pedro Historical Society.)

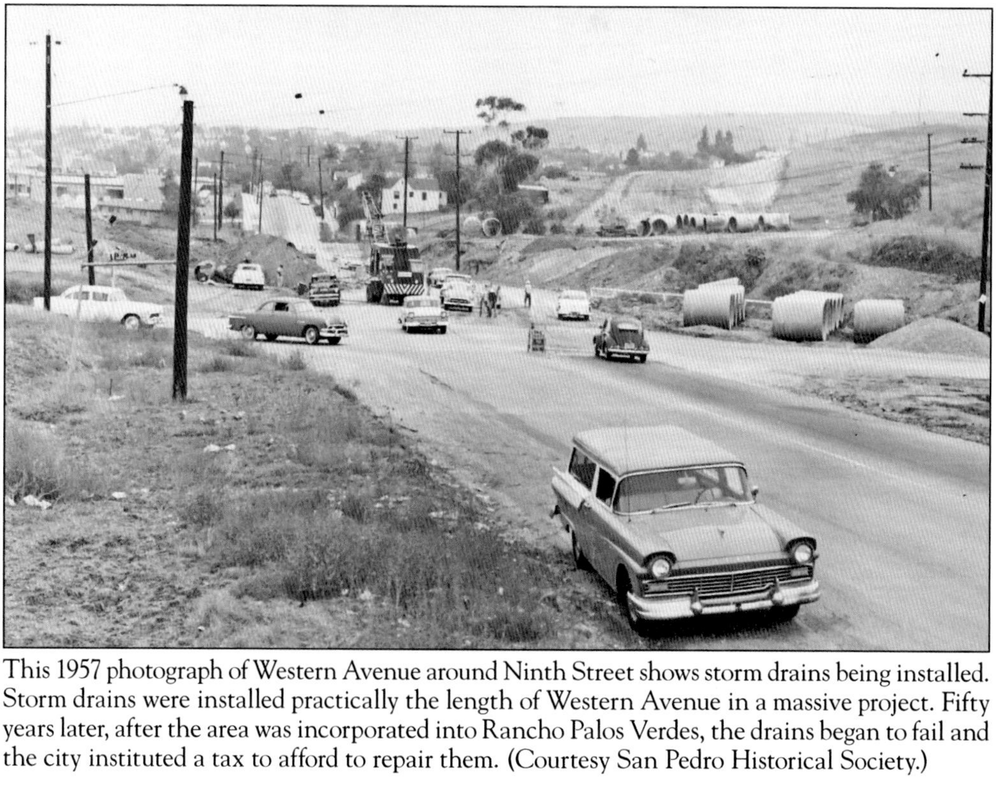

This 1957 photograph of Western Avenue around Ninth Street shows storm drains being installed. Storm drains were installed practically the length of Western Avenue in a massive project. Fifty years later, after the area was incorporated into Rancho Palos Verdes, the drains began to fail and the city instituted a tax to afford to repair them. (Courtesy San Pedro Historical Society.)

Four

Landslide of the Elbow

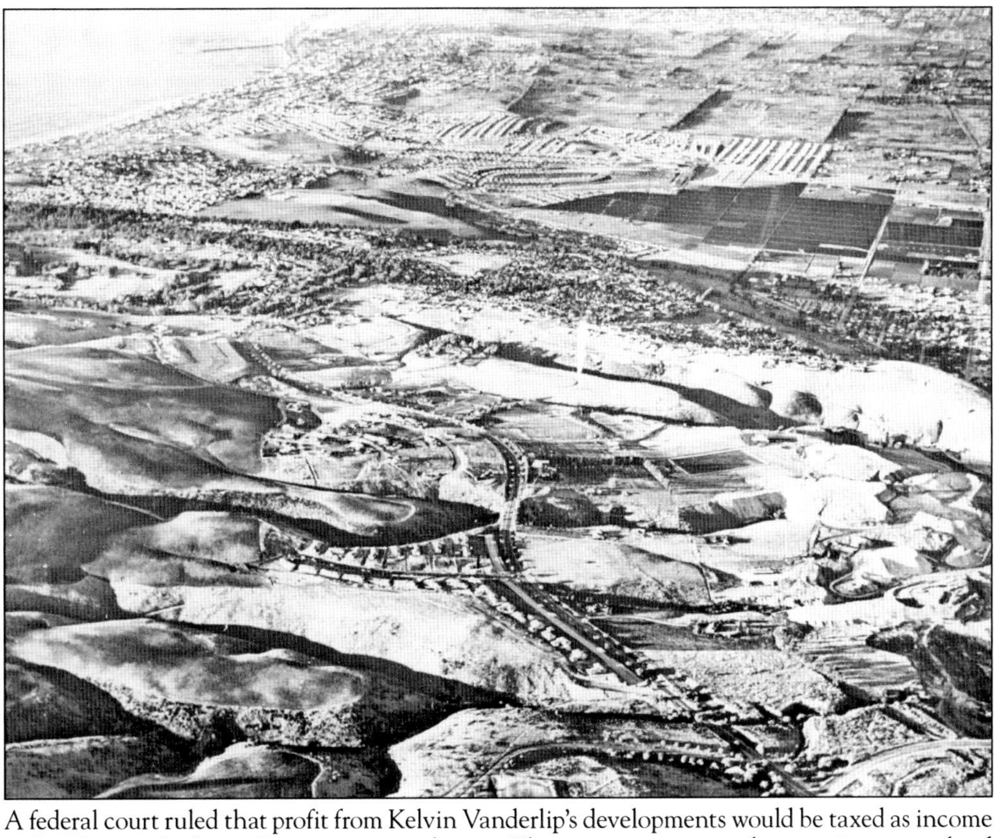

A federal court ruled that profit from Kelvin Vanderlip's developments would be taxed as income rather than at the lesser 25 percent capital gains. The consequence was the most important land transaction on Palos Verdes since 1913. In 1953, Frank Vanderlip Jr. sold the remainder of Palos Verdes to Great Lakes Carbon Corporation, which had been mining diatomite from area quarries (right) since 1930. (Courtesy Local History Collection, Palos Verdes Library.)

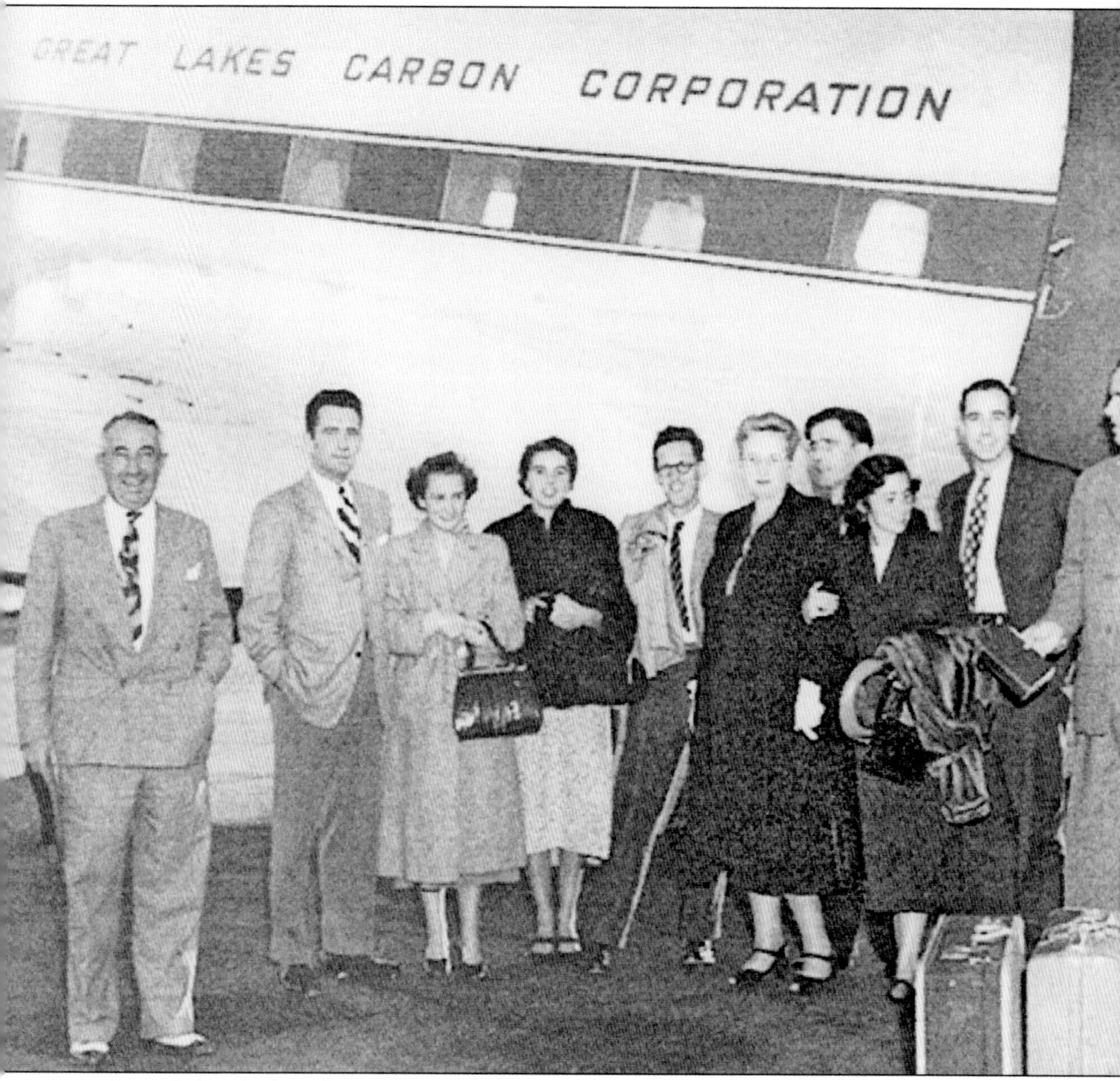

Great Lakes Carbon Corporation was owned by George and Ann Skakel along with their family and extended family. They had six children, one of whom, Ethel, married Robert Kennedy. George Skakel learned that the diatomite mine he had planned to work on Crest Road was unusable but realized that Palos Verdes would be profitable for development. What his exact plans for the peninsula were will never be known. In 1955, this company plane crashed with George and Ann on board. George Skakel Jr. became president of the corporation and ran it for 10 years until he, too, died in a plane crash. (Courtesy Kennedy Family Forum.)

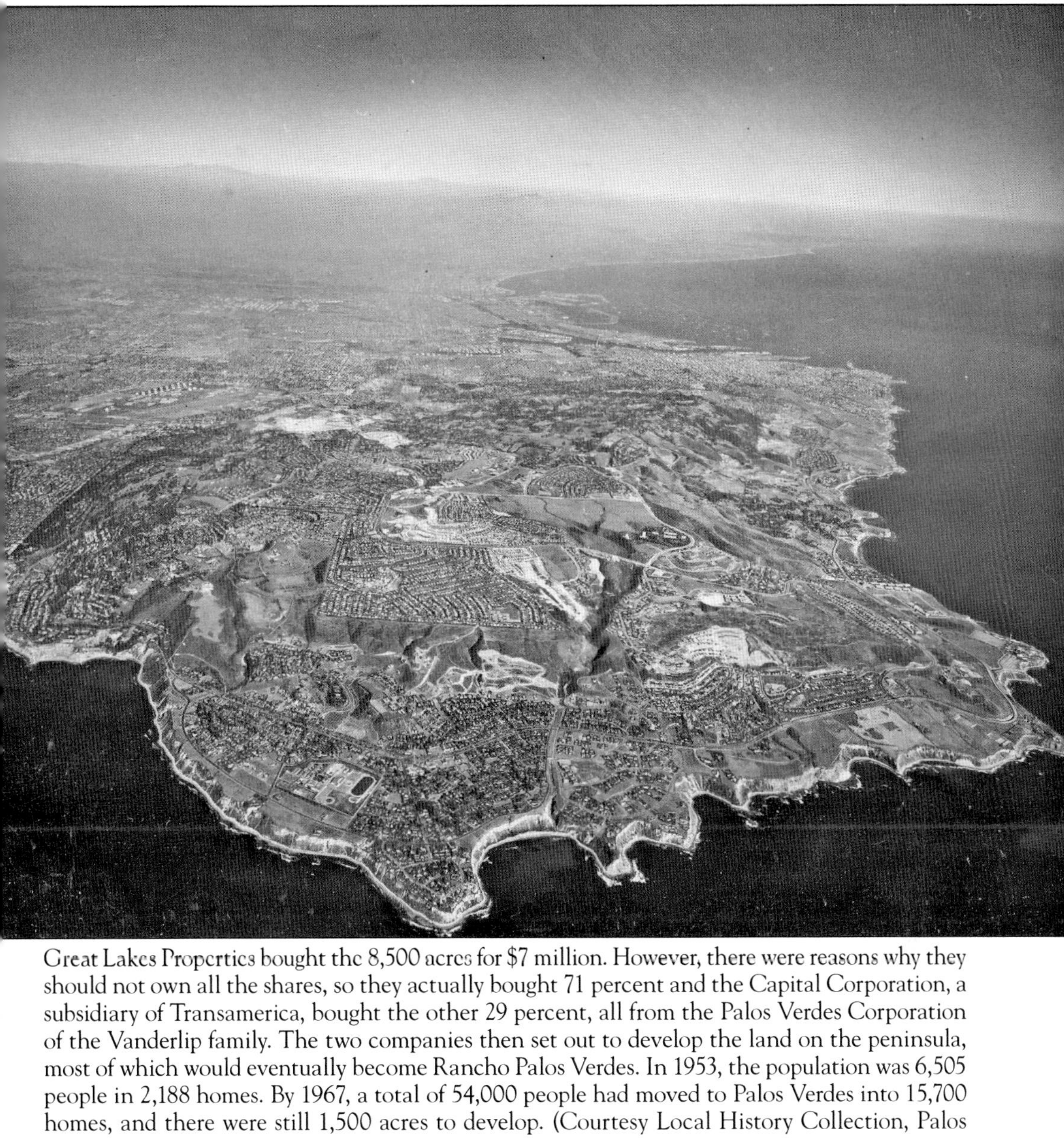

Great Lakes Properties bought the 8,500 acres for $7 million. However, there were reasons why they should not own all the shares, so they actually bought 71 percent and the Capital Corporation, a subsidiary of Transamerica, bought the other 29 percent, all from the Palos Verdes Corporation of the Vanderlip family. The two companies then set out to develop the land on the peninsula, most of which would eventually become Rancho Palos Verdes. In 1953, the population was 6,505 people in 2,188 homes. By 1967, a total of 54,000 people had moved to Palos Verdes into 15,700 homes, and there were still 1,500 acres to develop. (Courtesy Local History Collection, Palos Verdes Library.)

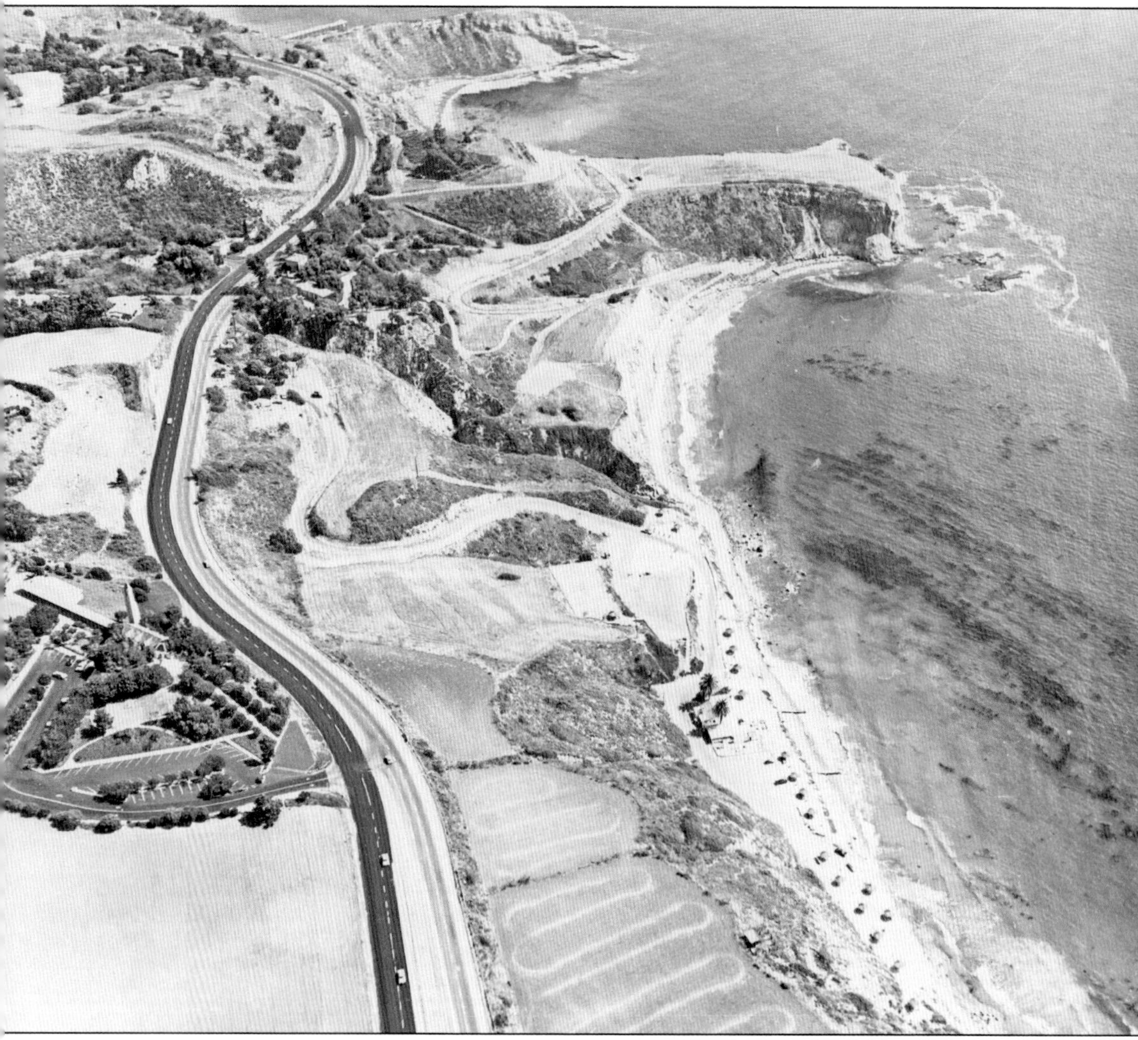

It is 1955. The bell tower at the Wayfarers' Chapel is completed. The Abalone Cove Club, flanked by its distinctive Canary Island date palms, has become a nursery school, which was created in 1953 by Elin Vanderlip for her four little children and their Portuguese Bend neighbors. Just visible at the top of the photograph, beyond Portuguese Point and Inspiration Point, is the Portuguese Bend Club pier. Life is simple, but that will change soon. (Courtesy Point Vicente Interpretive Center.)

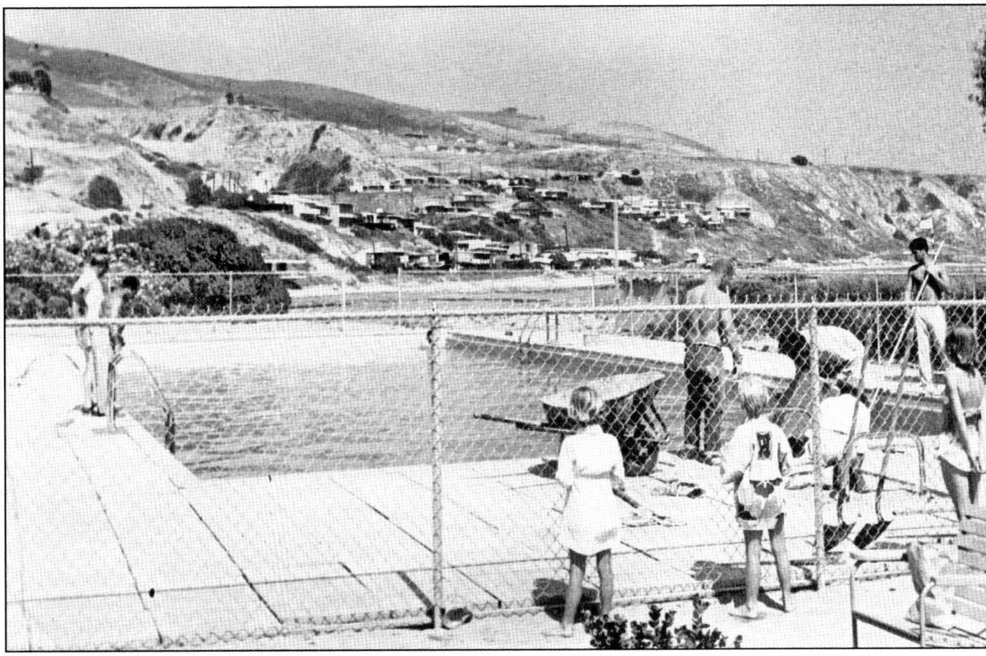

In 1955, the pool at the Portuguese Bend Club started cracking and leaking. Everyone got mad at the pool builder. They constructed another pool with a plastic lining and concrete block paving to correct any problems. It worked for a while, then it did not work. The problem may not have been the pool builder; the problem may have been the land on which the pool was built. (Courtesy Dennis Jaconi.)

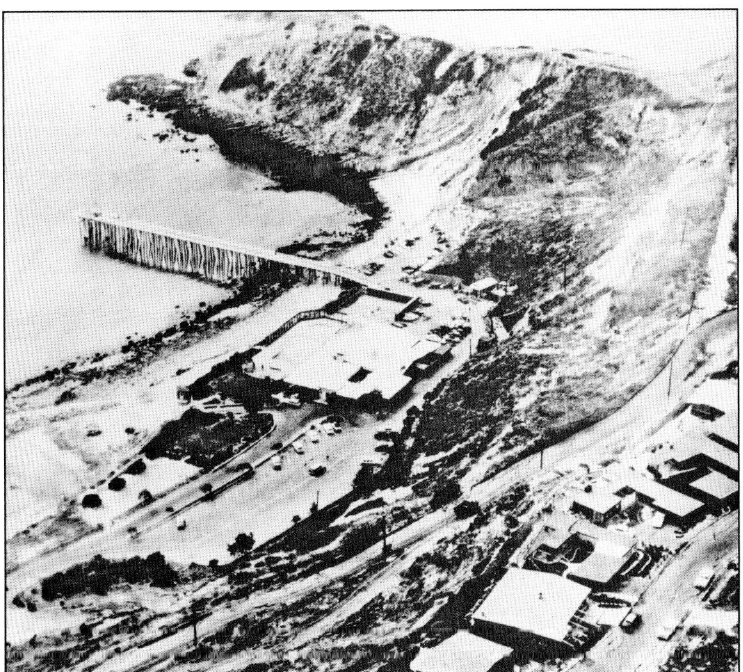

Back in 1947, before the Portuguese Bend Club was created, George Fisher took Fritz Ripley to the site and said, "This is where we're going to build the club." Ripley replied, "George, this whole damn thing is moving. I wouldn't be caught dead in it." This was something Ripley knew from years of observation. He was right. Here is the club and its pier, completed. (Courtesy Point Vicente Interpretive Center.)

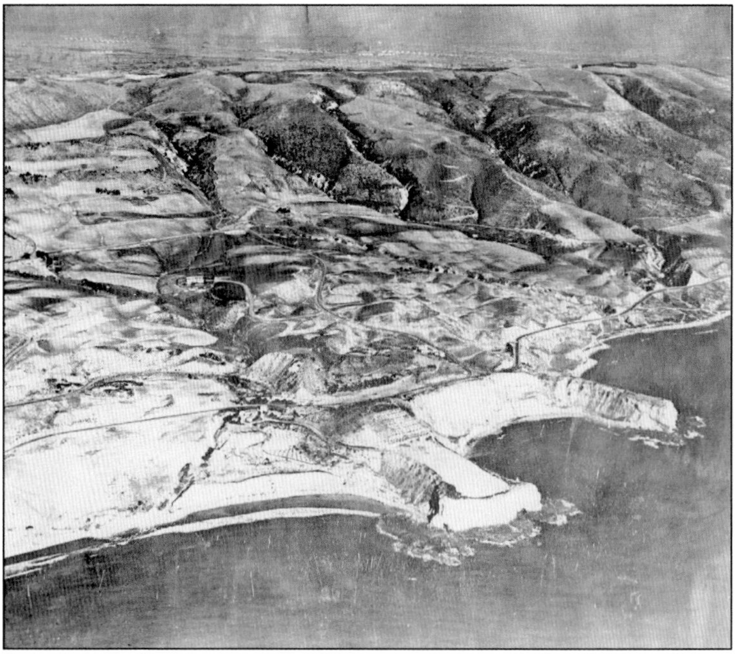

Fritz Ripley knew the ground was moving. He had driven this coast road for years and had seen a fence slowly work its way over the cliffs. James Ishibashi knew the ground was moving because his straight furrows were crooked by the end of the year. And the Spaniards in the 1800s called the coastline "Landslide of the Elbow." The elbow was Point Vicente. (Courtesy Local History Collection, Palos Verdes Library.)

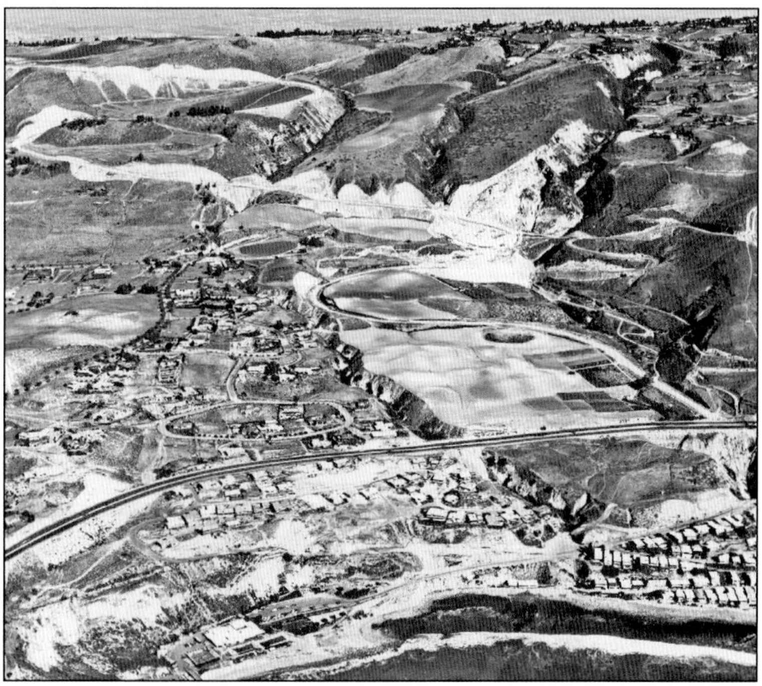

In the foreground along the coast is the Portuguese Bend Club. Above Palos Verdes Drive South is the community of Portuguese Bend going up into the hills. That circle drive is Cherry Hill Lane. The Ishibashi farm is on the right. The white line is the cut made for Crenshaw Road. In 1955, the county began work to make a highway of it. (Courtesy Local History Collection, Palos Verdes Library.)

Plans to extend Crenshaw Boulevard to the coast had been in the works for years. As the Los Angeles County Road Department cut across Portuguese Canyon going down the hill, they moved about 500 tons of dirt and placed it just below what turned out to be the escarpment of an ancient landslide. The weight of the dirt reactivated the landslide—seen as a white gash. (Courtesy Point Vicente Interpretive Center.)

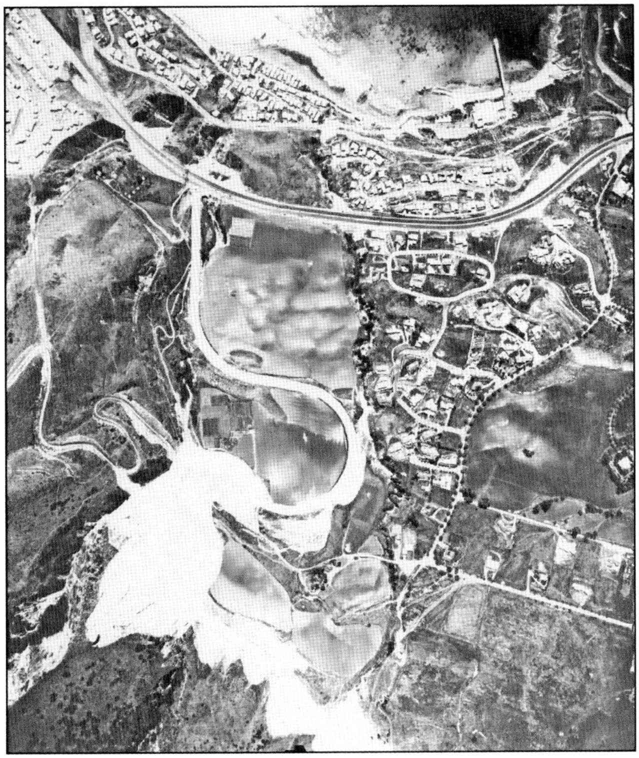

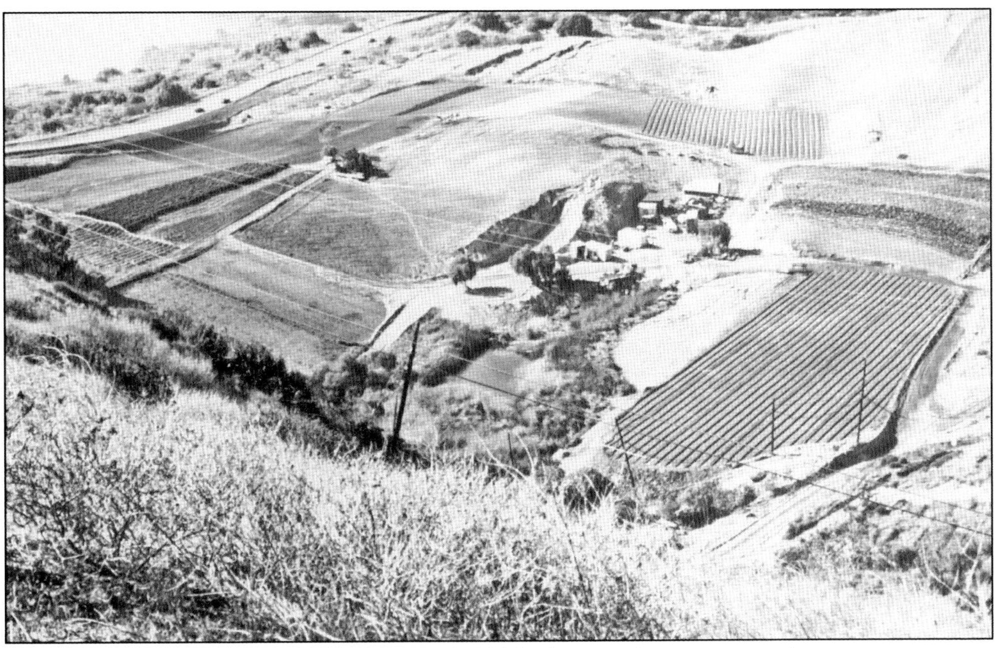

The first indication was on Friday, August 29, 1956, when cracks were noticed in a masonry storm culvert. In the next month, houses in Portuguese Bend began to shift and crack. Roy McCarrell Jr. reported that the swale where Palos Verdes College had been had become a lake. A low point on the farm (center) along Palos Verdes Drive South became Lake Ishibashi. (Courtesy Point Vicente Interpretive Center.)

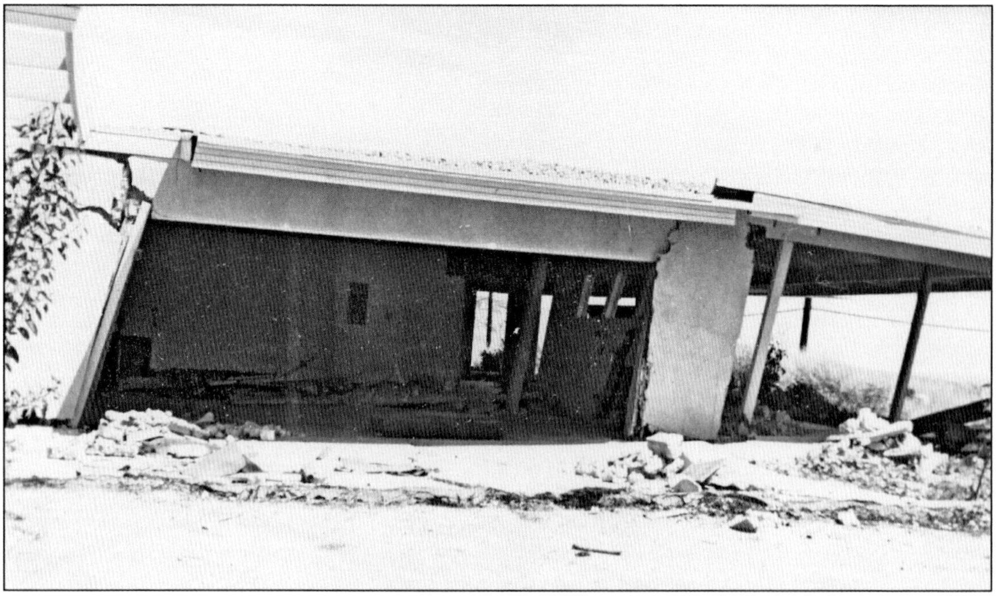

Much of the rock that Palos Verdes sits on is Altamera Shale. While the oldest shale was forming, an underwater volcano was active. This old shale, at least on the south side of the peninsula, is shot-through with a volcanic material called tuff that turns into Bentonite. Bentonite is incredibly slippery when wet. The weight of the dumped dirt began the slide, but water has kept it going. (Courtesy Point Vicente Interpretive Center.)

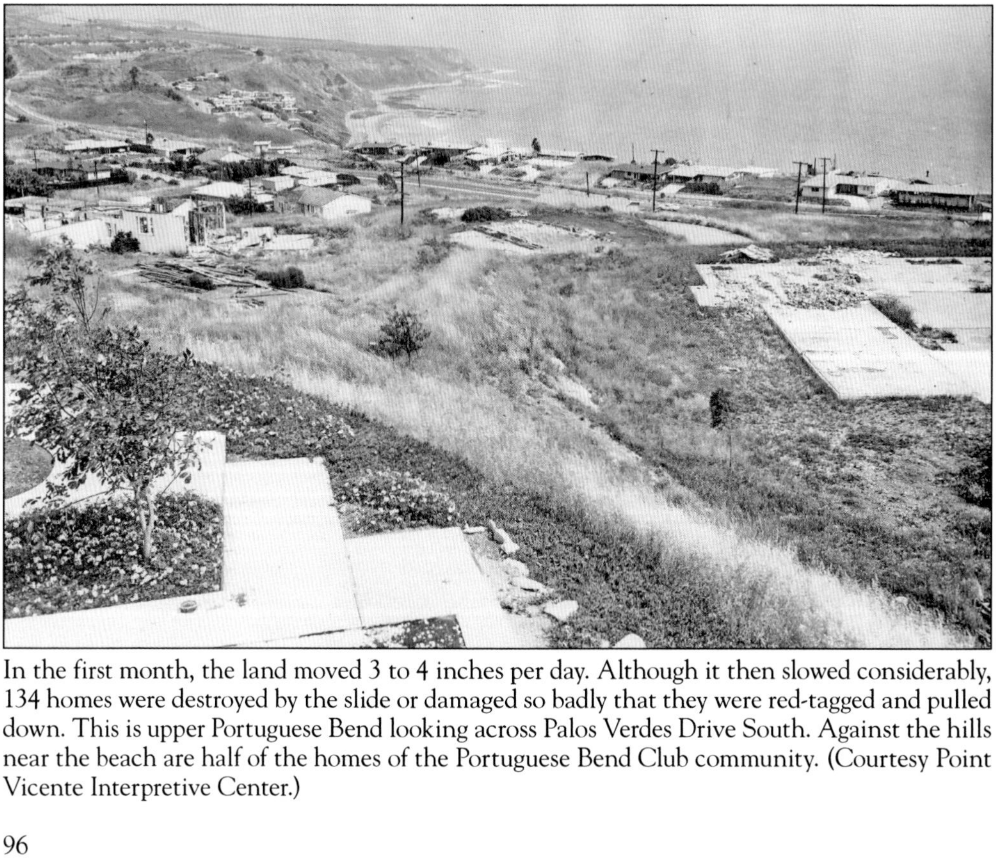

In the first month, the land moved 3 to 4 inches per day. Although it then slowed considerably, 134 homes were destroyed by the slide or damaged so badly that they were red-tagged and pulled down. This is upper Portuguese Bend looking across Palos Verdes Drive South. Against the hills near the beach are half of the homes of the Portuguese Bend Club community. (Courtesy Point Vicente Interpretive Center.)

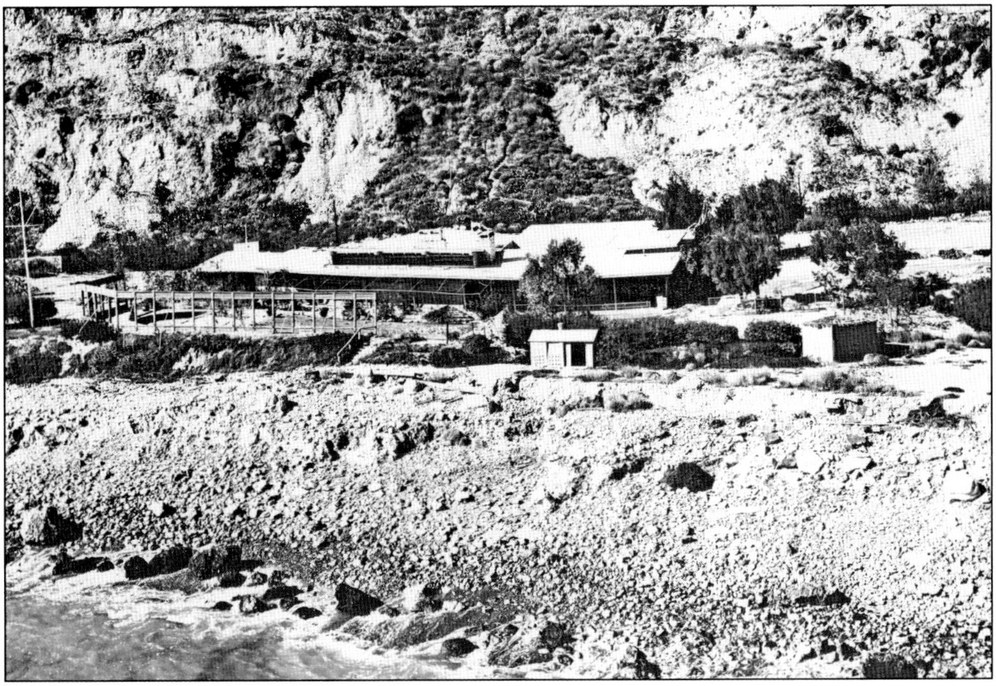

The slide headed straight for the Portuguese Bend Club, pier, and homes. By September 1956, Palos Verdes Drive South had a 4-inch offset, and the cliff began moving into the Portuguese Bend Club parking lot. Nineteen months later, in April 1958, Los Angeles County engineers declared the building unsafe and closed it. Ivar O. Hanson, club president, mailed the bad news to the residents. (Courtesy Point Vicente Interpretive Center.)

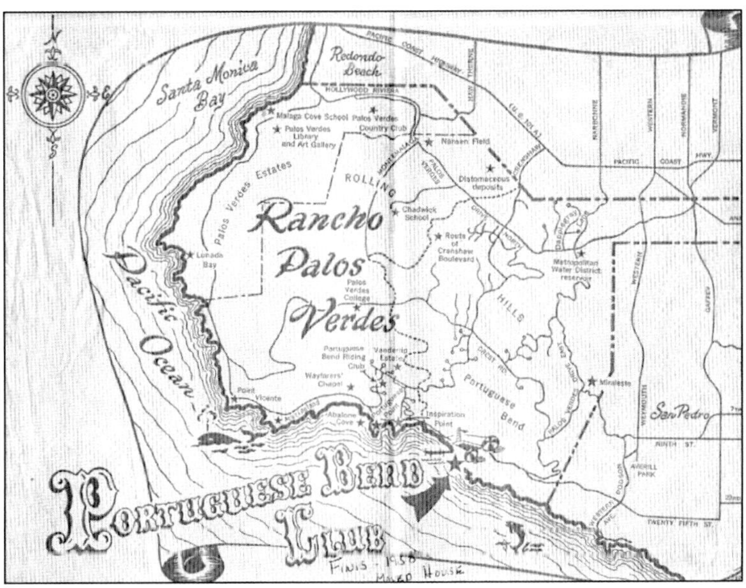

The slide cut a swath through half of the Portuguese Bend Club community. The homes were owned, but the land was leased from Palos Verdes Properties, who offered to move endangered homes to stable land along the east hillside. Here, on the bottom of a Club place mat, Ed Fabian has written "Finis—1958 moved house." (Courtesy Mike Fabian.)

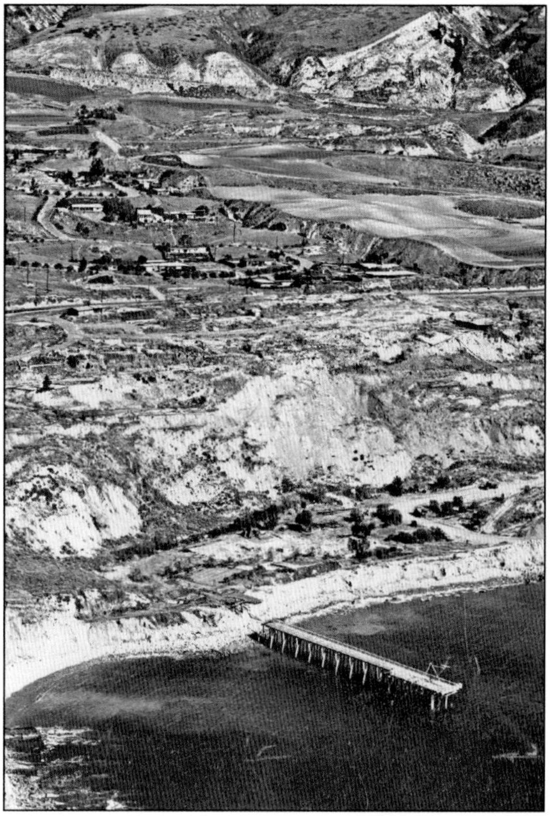

The pier stayed the same—the pilings did not budge—but the slide brought down so much earth that it raised the ground underneath the land end and the pier broke off. It was not until many years later that what was left of it was razed as an "attractive nuisance." (Courtesy San Pedro Historical Society.)

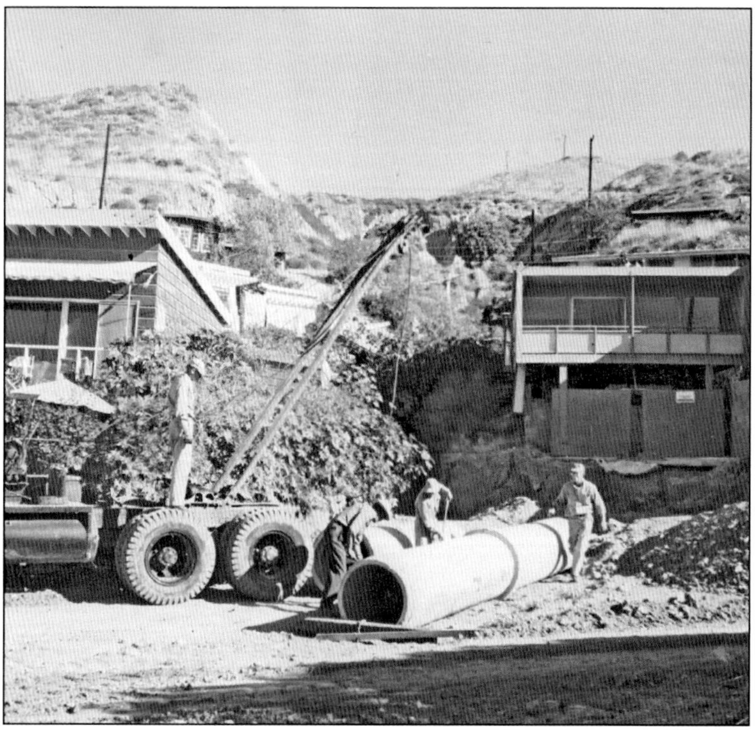

In March 1957, two 20-foot concrete cylinders like these were driven 10 feet into the ground with strain gauges attached to calculate the force of the slide. Unexpectedly, the slide slowed. Assuming the cylinders had caused the slowing, the county and Palos Verdes Properties installed 23 more cylinders seaward of Palos Verdes Drive South. The slide slowed for six months, then sped up again. (Courtesy Dennis Jaconi.)

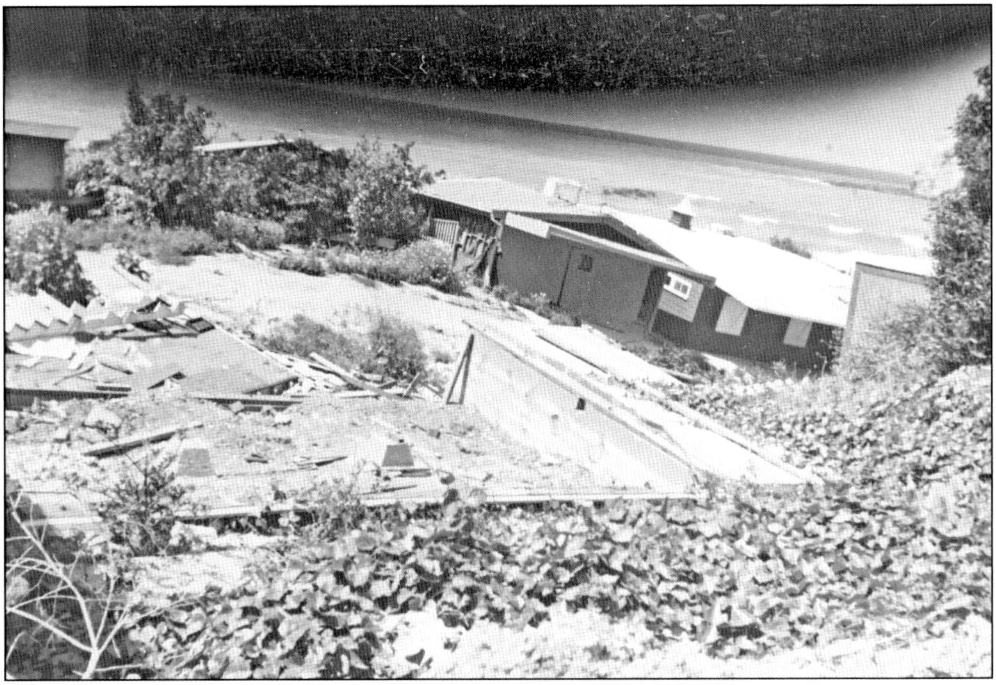

Amid rumors in 1959 that Palos Verdes Drive South would be abandoned, a worried William Monahan, Marineland president, wrote to Los Angeles County supervisor Burton Chase encouraging the county to maintain access to Palos Verdes. It did, and 1966 was the first of three times the road was returned to its legal right of way. This house was on the bluff side of the road and went from home to rubble. (Courtesy Point Vicente Interpretive Center.)

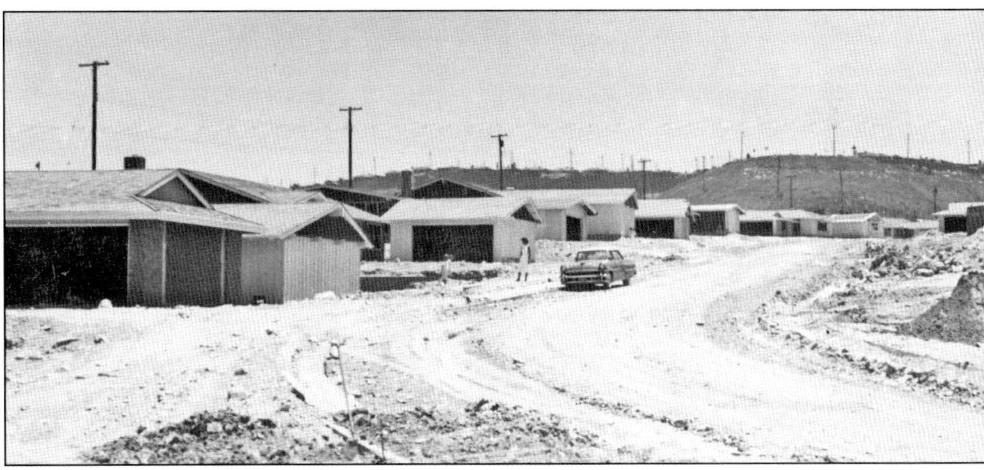

Elsewhere buildings were going from rubble to home. The change in ownership to Great Lakes Carbon brought a change in land-use philosophy. Building and real estate companies bought large pieces of land and created hundreds of homesites. The Grandview Building Company, an Edward Zuckerman and Bernie Morris partnership, was first. They built single-family homes with Grandview in the name. The view is from lower Grayslake toward another Grandview tract in early 1961. (Courtesy Rose Jensen.)

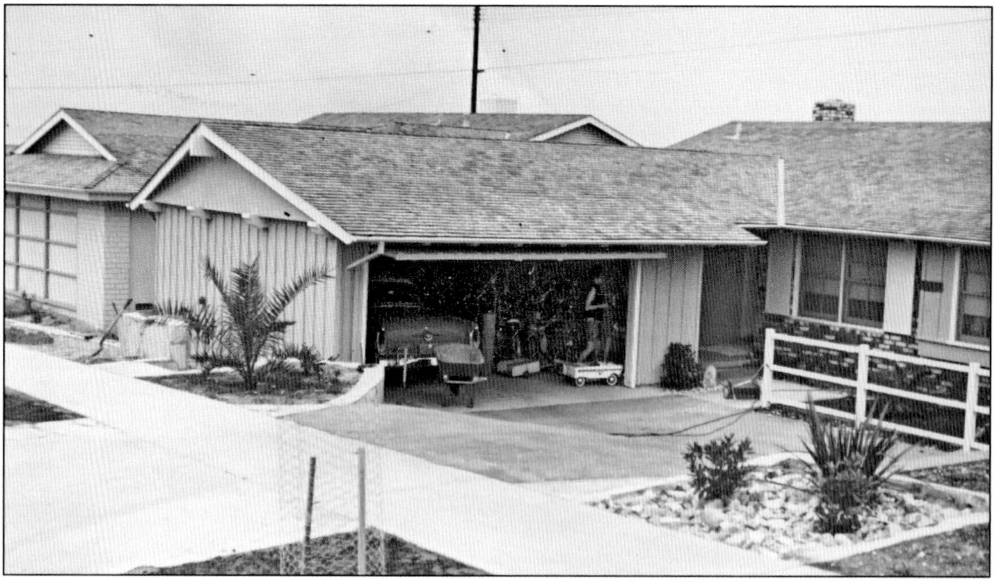

Young families, many of them engineers working in the booming aerospace industry, drove to Palos Verdes on weekends, drawn by real estate advertisements and word-of-mouth from their colleagues. They found new, affordable homes built by Palos Verdes Properties, Filliorum, Great Lakes Properties, and others, with views and good schools nearby. Palos Verdes became a wonderful place to raise a family. (Courtesy Rose Jensen.)

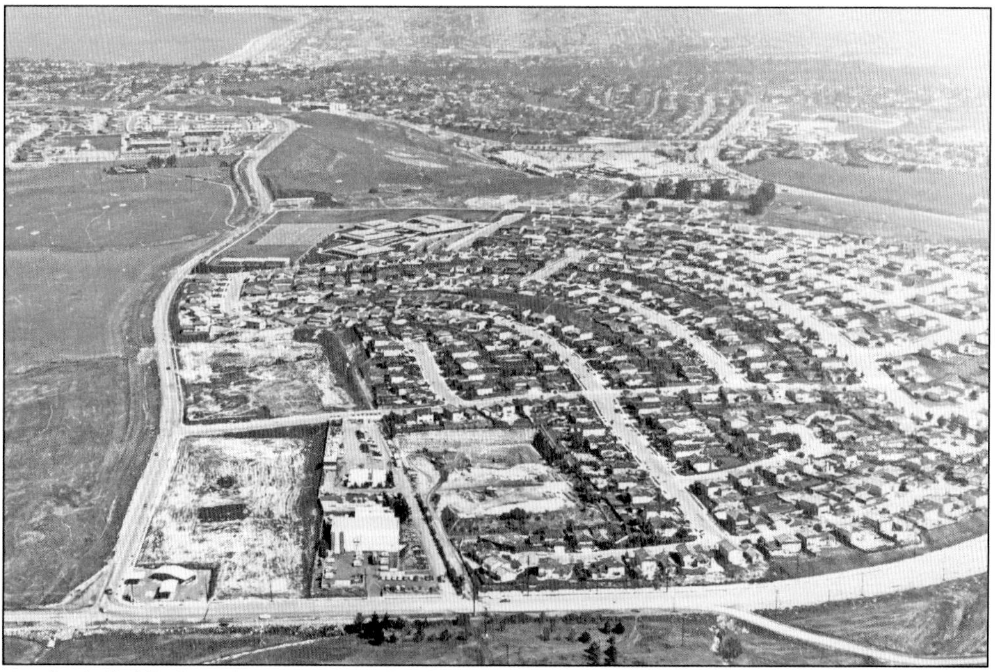

As the hill filled in, farming was edged out. One of the final areas farmed was under Don Wallace's,W6AM, rhombic antennas along the left side of this photograph. The new subdivision on the right was built in the early 1960s. Crest Road runs along the bottom of the photograph. The Palos Verdes Water Company is next to the empty lot on Crest Road. (Courtesy California Water Company.)

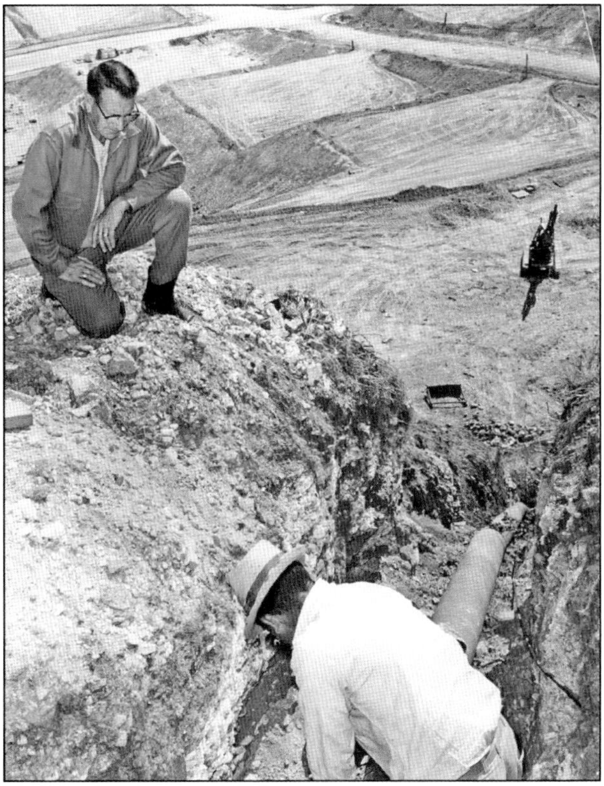

Trimble and Pierce Doty kept the water company ahead of the building boom. They laid new pipe, often in difficult places using ingenious methods. Over the years, the Doty Brothers have laid over two million feet of pipe in Palos Verdes. Above is a view of the company employees running pipe down the face of a cliff to the building sites below. Seen below is the view of the steep cliff with the pipe running down it and the building pads along the side of the cliff. (Both photographs courtesy California Water Service.)

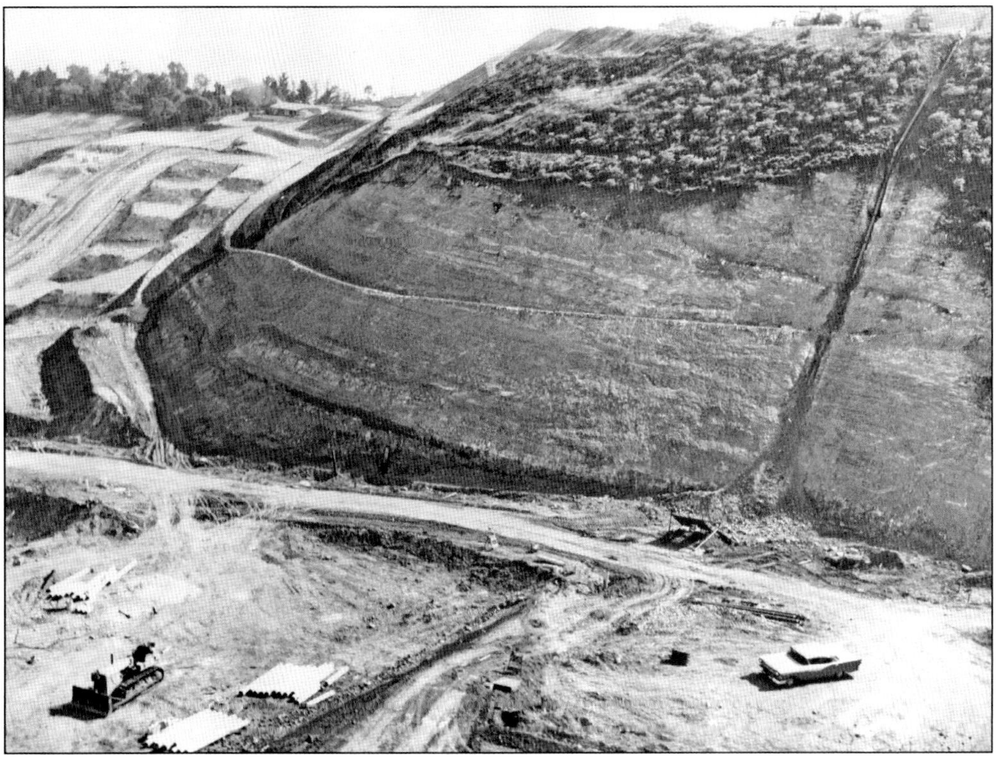

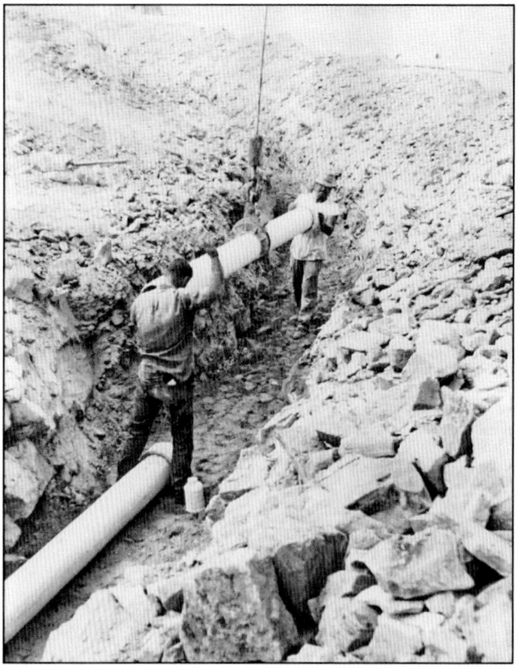

The Palos Verdes Water Company raced to keep up with the pace of the building. Back in the 1940s, water was leaking out of their lines, dirt was seeping in, and money was tight. The Doty Brothers, of Bellflower, thriftily replaced the redwood stave line with reclaimed, sterilized oil pipe. Said Trimble Doty, "We found the old mains easily. We just followed the trail of cattails." The photograph is of later pipelines. (Courtesy Point Vicente Interpretive Center.)

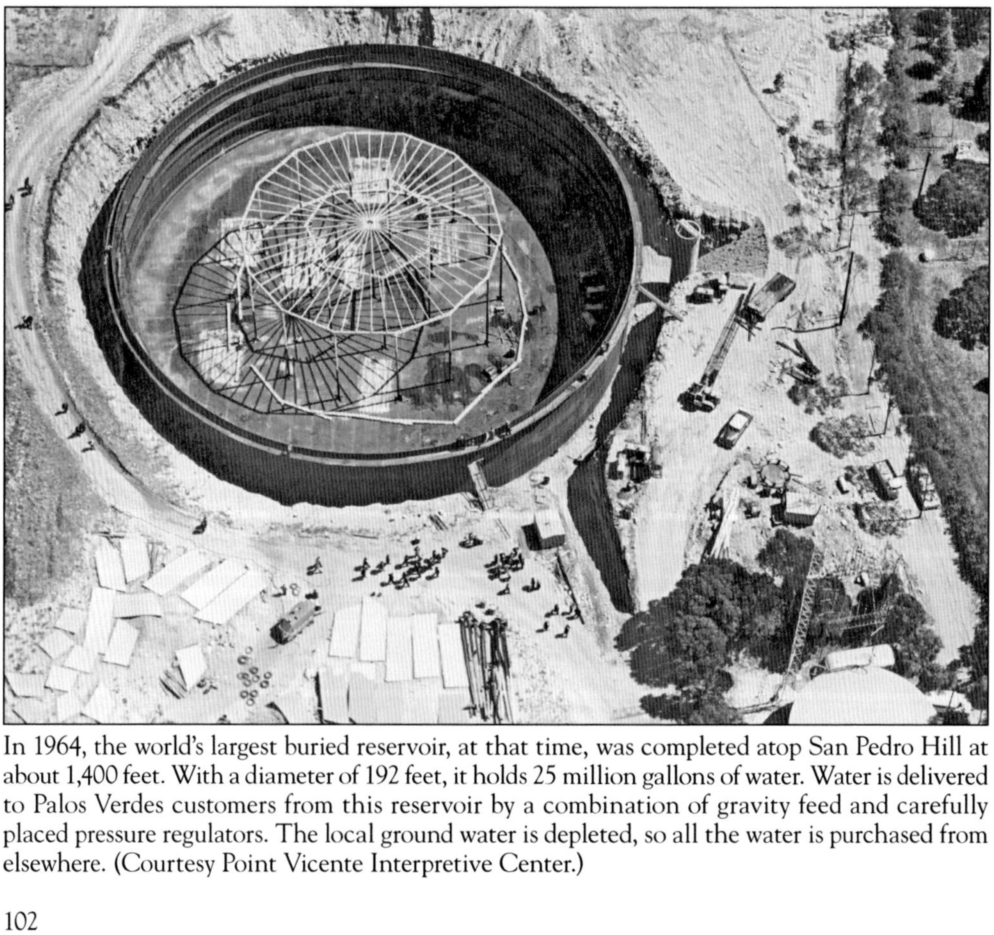

In 1964, the world's largest buried reservoir, at that time, was completed atop San Pedro Hill at about 1,400 feet. With a diameter of 192 feet, it holds 25 million gallons of water. Water is delivered to Palos Verdes customers from this reservoir by a combination of gravity feed and carefully placed pressure regulators. The local ground water is depleted, so all the water is purchased from elsewhere. (Courtesy Point Vicente Interpretive Center.)

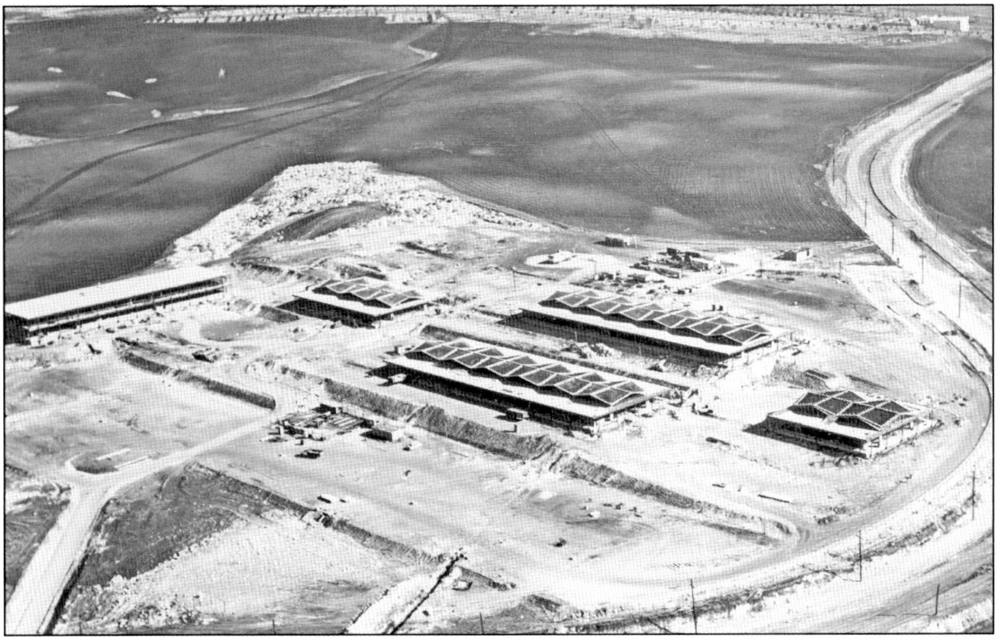

In 1960, Northrup began what was to be a scientific research park, a multi-company think tank where scientists could live and work in peace and seclusion. On the corner of Crest Road and Hawthorne Boulevard, it was zoned for "light manufacturing" so scientific prototypes could be built. Various city agencies and groups objected, and by 1962, much of the land became tract homes. Nortronics left in 1991. (Courtesy Homer Meek, K6HKT.)

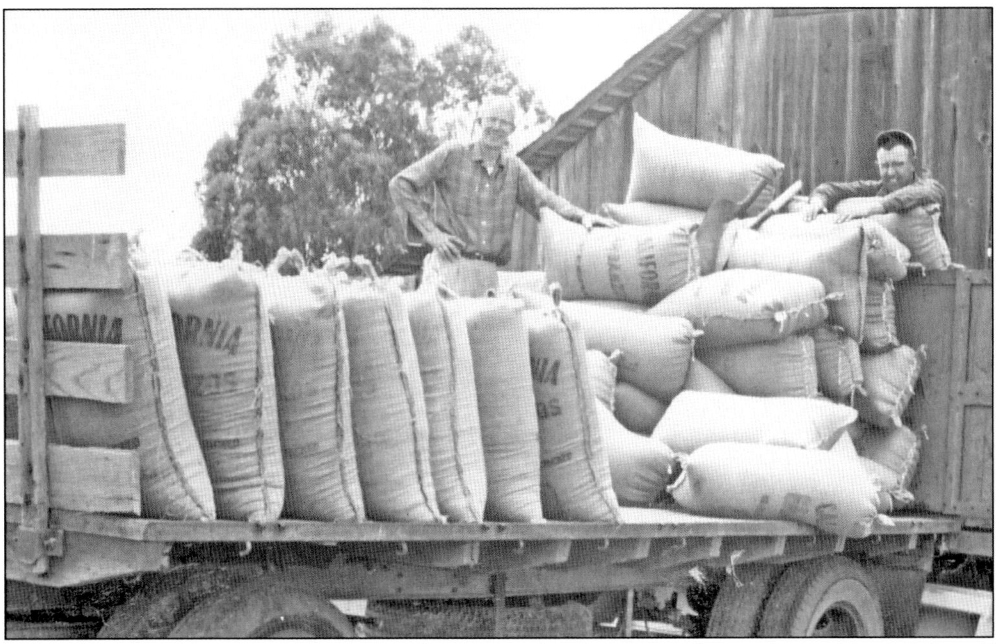

Roy McCarrell Sr. introduced the profitable garbanzo bean crop to Palos Verdes, and Roy McCarrell Jr. invented a garbanzo bean resistant to toxic mold. Their best customer was Cuba, until the borders closed. Here stands the younger McCarrell (on right) with some of his garbanzo bean crop. On alternate years, they raised barley. (Courtesy Rosalee McCarrell Orr.)

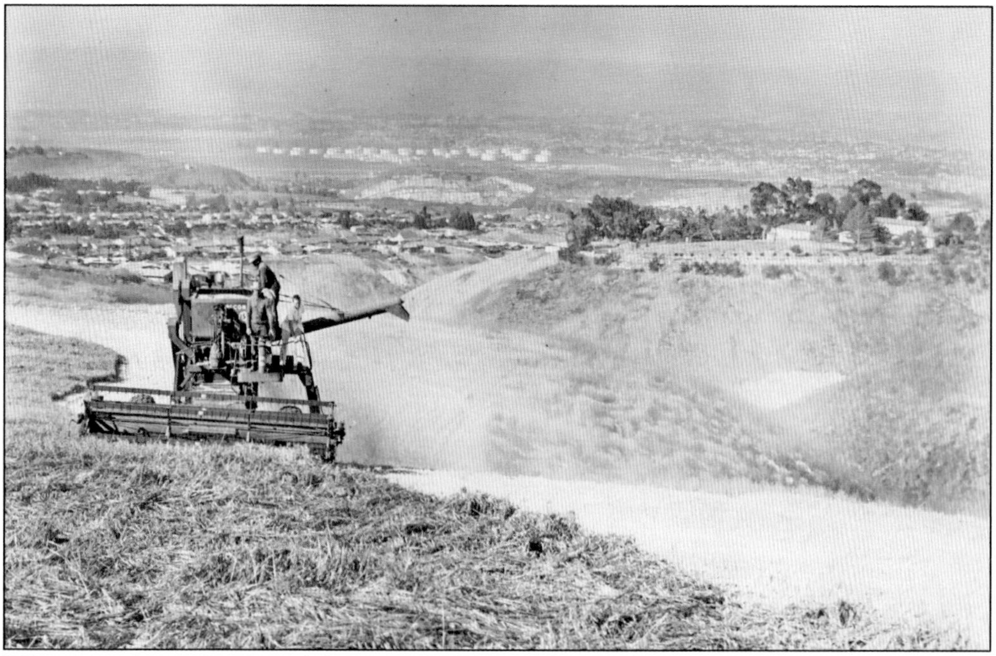

When Hawthorne Boulevard was extended from Palos Verdes Drive North and connected to Crest Road at the top of the hill, it was the beginning of the end for making a living with farming. With roads came people and homes, shrinking the land available for farming. "Highridge went right through the barn," said Rosalee McCarrell. This photograph was taken near Hesse Park. (Courtesy Rosalee McCarrell Orr.)

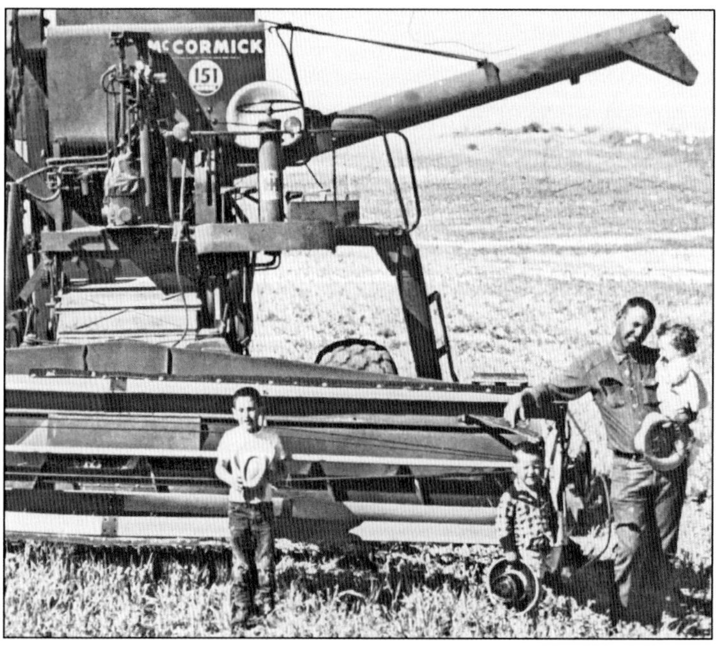

By 1973, there was not enough contiguous land to farm. The McCarrells moved to Redondo Beach, and Roy Jr., grandson of Wallace McCarrell, went into construction and weed abatement just as the grandsons of Harry Phillips did. Roy Jr., who had a farmer's love and understanding of the land as his father and grandfather had, said, "I'm suggesting to my sons that they prepare for occupations other than farming." (Courtesy Rosalee McCarrell Orr.)

Five

They Didn't Let Us Say Goodbye

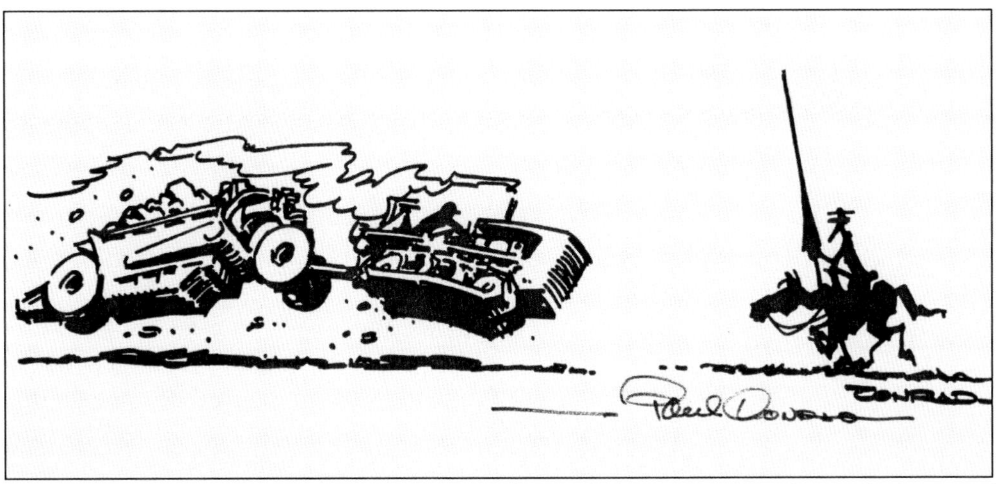

The pace of development was startling and created a backlash. In 1967, the Palos Verdes League of Woman Voters issued a spiral-bound book: *The Time is Now*, a summary of peninsula land use and development. It was "the Bible for incorporation," said Barbara Cleghorn later. A campaign called Save Our Coastline began. Their viewpoint was adroitly depicted in this drawing by *Los Angeles Times* political cartoonist Paul Conrad. (Courtesy Barbara Gleghorn and Paul Conrad.)

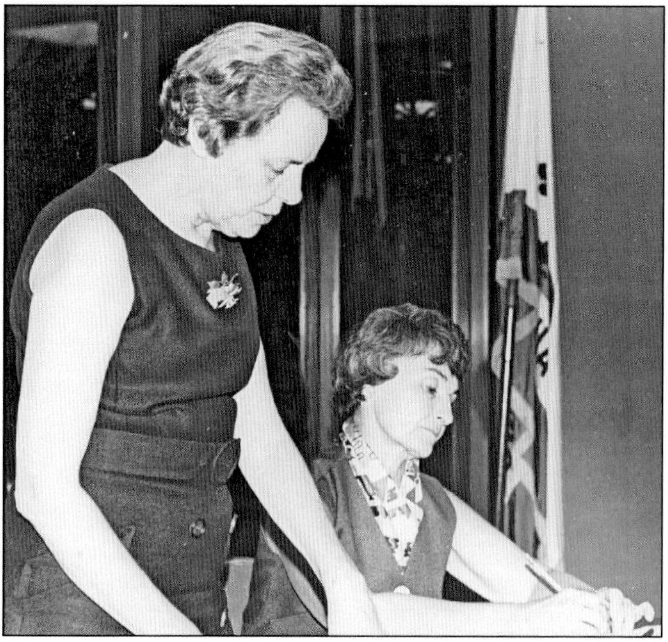

In 1969, Save Our Coastline (SOC) was formed. Co-chair Dorothy LeConte (left) from Rolling Hills spearheaded the effort with a well-run campaign using the Peninsula Advisory Council of Homeowners' Associations. SOC's goals were to stop coastal development and to create a fourth city. The Local Agency Formation Commission (LAFCO) refused their initial petition to explore incorporation when 55 percent of the landowners, led by Bill Monahan at Marineland, filed an objection. (Courtesy Ken Dyda.)

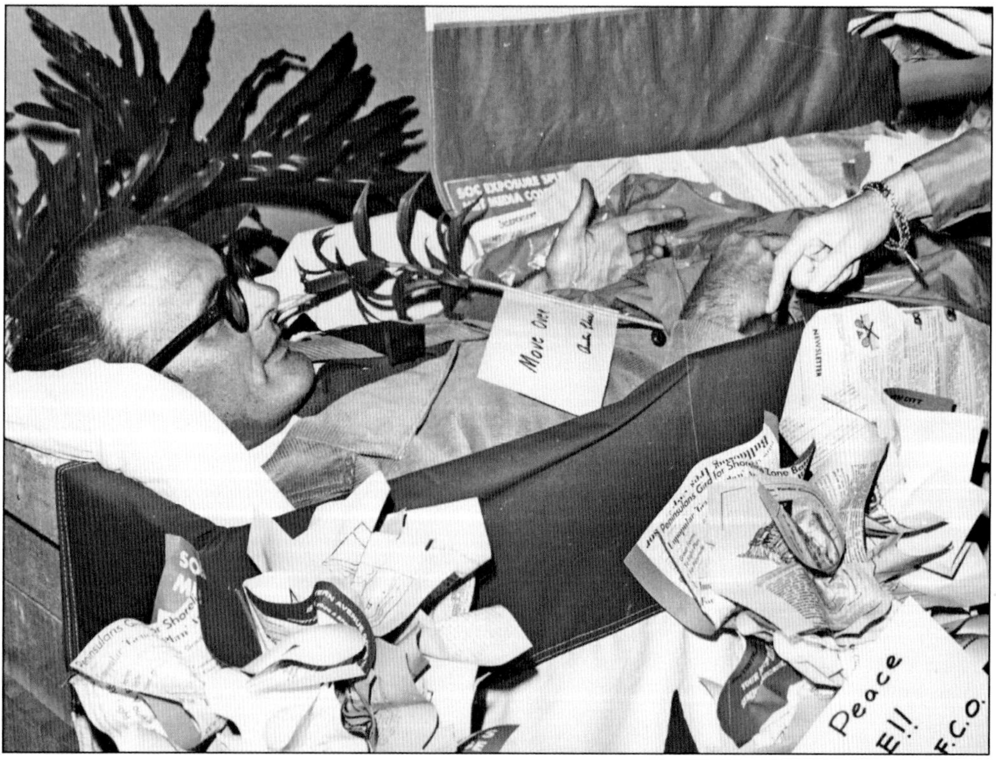

SOC lost in the Federal District Court and was sent back to state courts. Then they lost at the California State Appellate Court. People were saying that SOC was dead, so they held a *Finnegan's Wake* party in which *Los Angeles Times* political cartoonist Paul Conrad, who lives in the county area in Palos Verdes, played the down (but not out) Finnegan. (Courtesy Ken Dyda.)

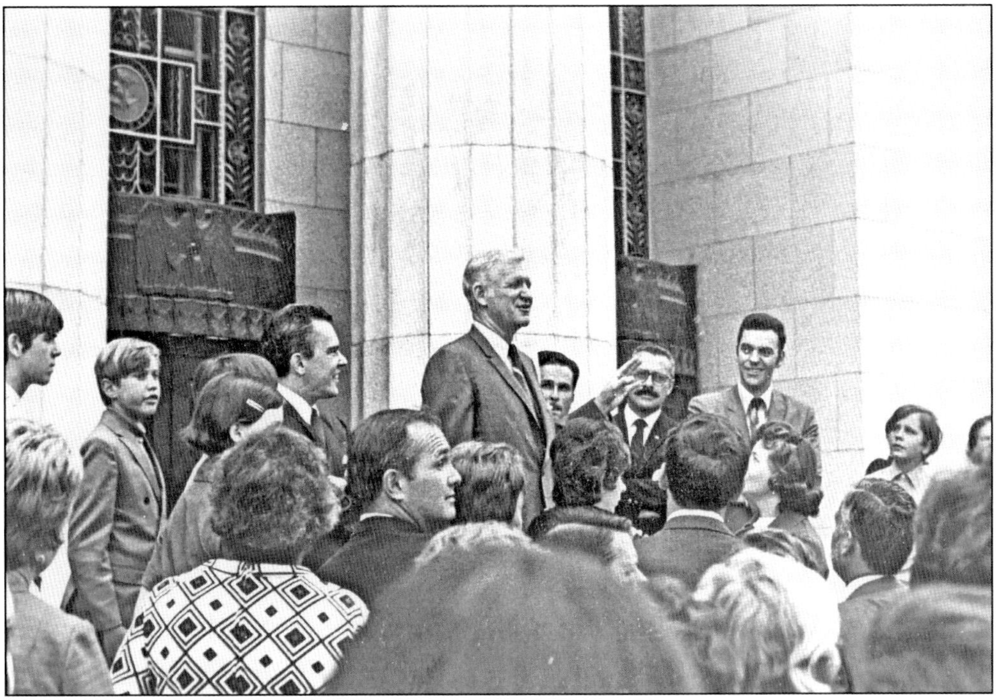

No city could be incorporated if 51 percent of the landowners objected. Save Our Coastline needed to have that law changed to create Rancho Palos Verdes, and they finally did it in the California Supreme Court. Henceforth, cities could be incorporated by a majority of voters regardless of land ownership. Gordon Curtis, from Portuguese Bend, represented the unincorporated area in these lawsuits. He stands here on court steps. (Courtesy Jean Curtis Wells.)

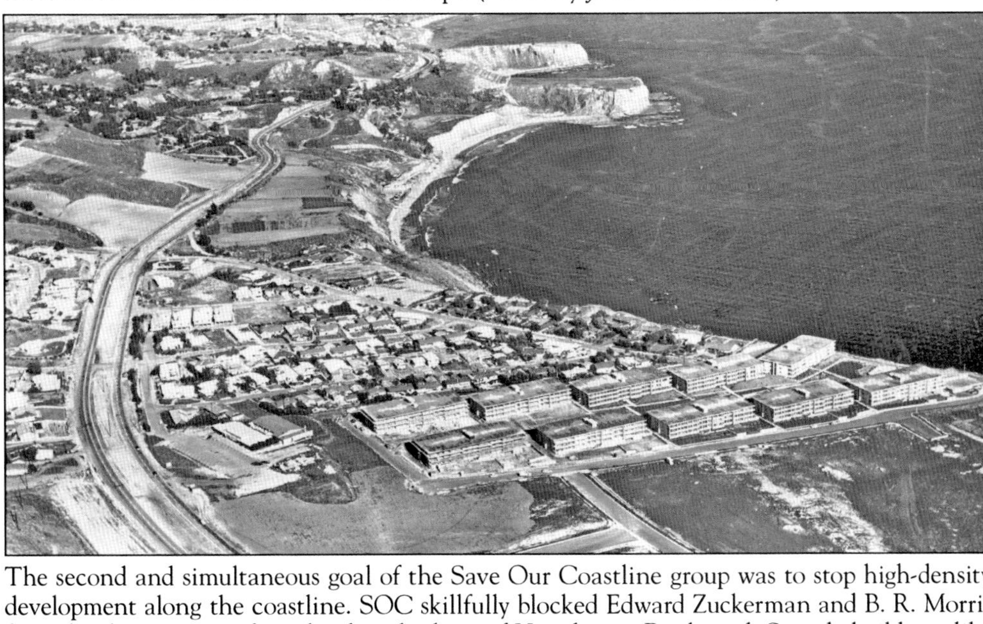

The second and simultaneous goal of the Save Our Coastline group was to stop high-density development along the coastline. SOC skillfully blocked Edward Zuckerman and B. R. Morris from developing oceanfront land at the base of Hawthorne Boulevard. Seaside buildings like the Bay Club condominiums near Long Point, built in the 1960s (shown here), were almost all successfully halted before the city was formed. (Courtesy Point Vicente Interpretive Center.)

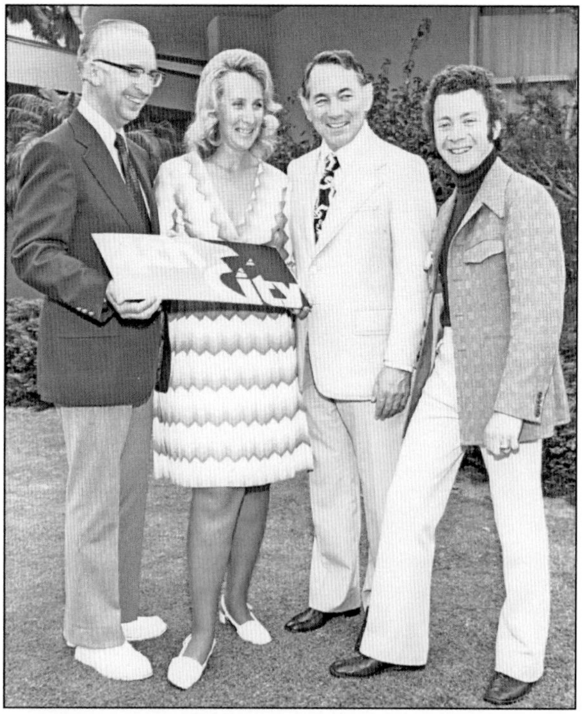

The Fourth City campaign began with fund-raisers. The mayors of the surrounding three cities had all been strong campaigners for a fourth city to limit the development and population increase that burdened the peninsula's infrastructure. Here standing with Los Angeles County supervisor Jim Hayes (center) are mayors Joseph Barnett, Palos Verdes Estates (left); Nell Mirels, Rolling Hills Estates; and Tom Heinsheimer, Rolling Hills. (Courtesy Ken Dyda.)

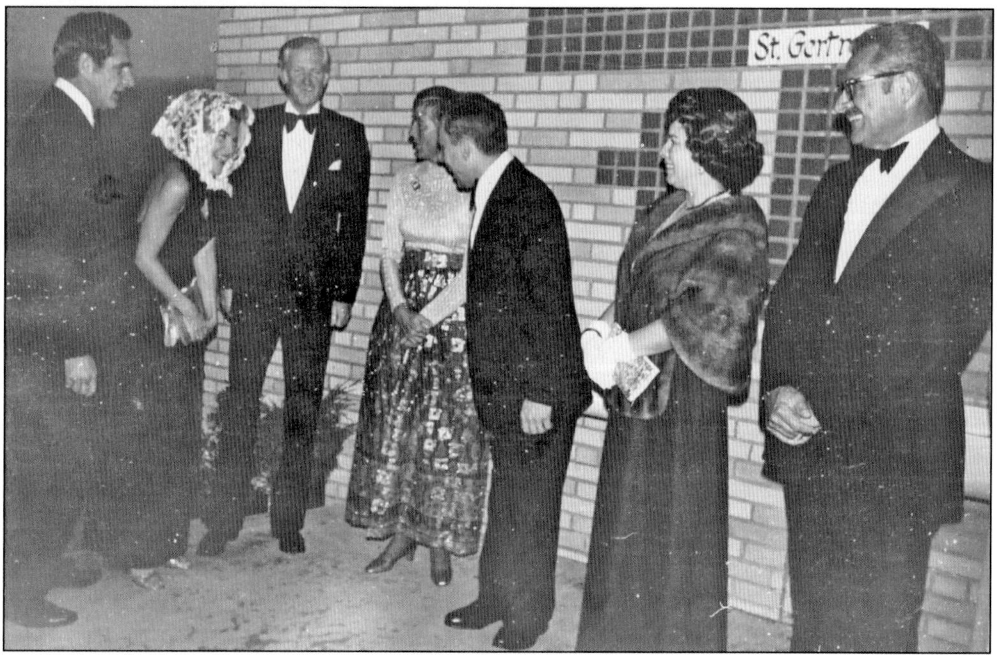

Twenty-four candidates ran for office. An impressive 68 percent turnout voted 83 percent for city incorporation—a tribute to Dorothy LeConte's organizational skills and political savvy. The inaugural ball was held at Marymount College on Hawthorne Boulevard on October 14, 1973. From left to right are an unidentified couple; Gordon Curtis; Nel Curtis; Mayor Pro Tem Ken Dyda, who had the second-highest number of votes; Lorraine Dyda; and councilman Cisco Ruth. (Courtesy Jean Curtis Wells.)

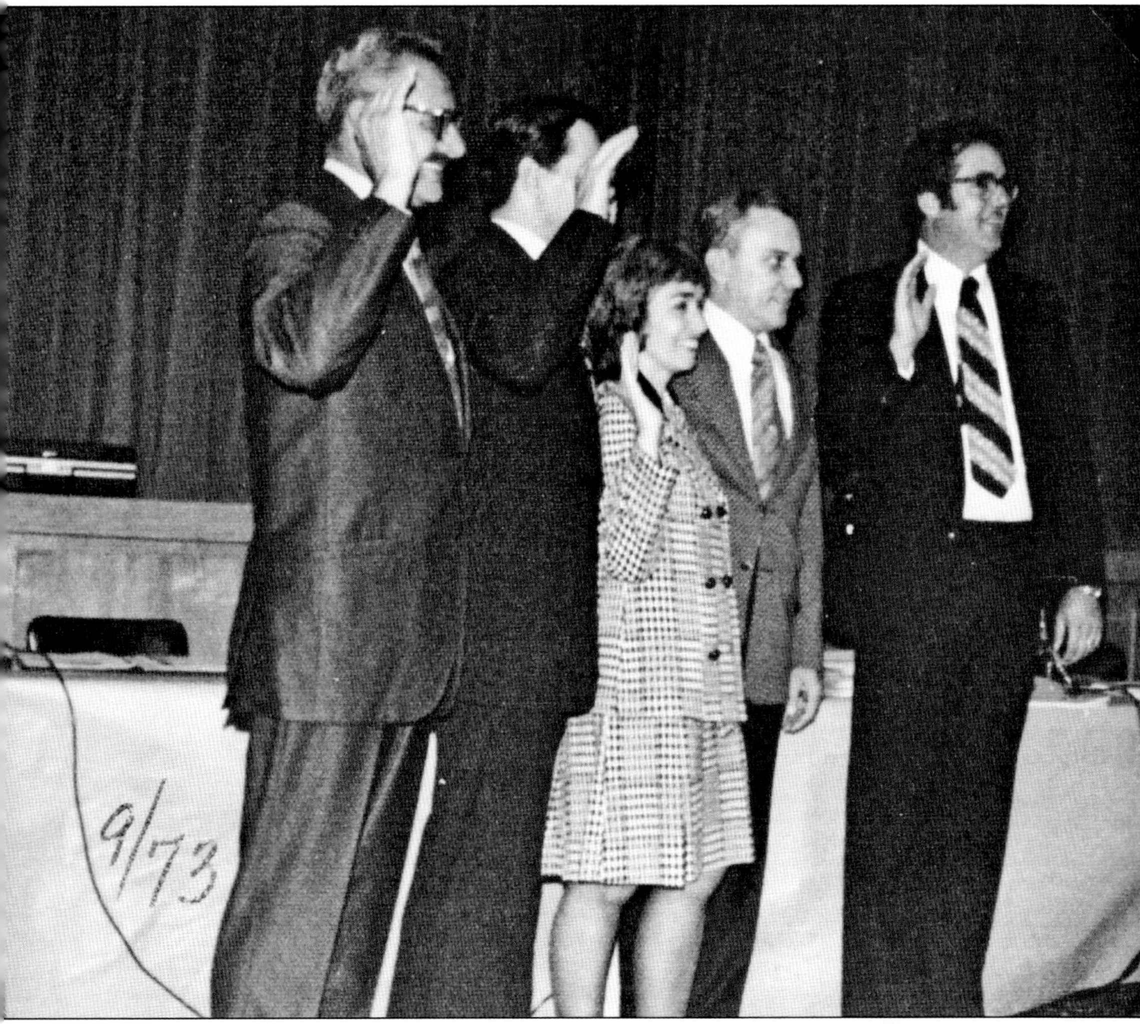

In September 1973, the first city council was sworn in. From left to right are Francis D. "Cisco" Ruth, Gunther Burke, Mayor Marilyn Ryan, Mayor Pro Tem Ken Dyda, and Robert Ryan. They put a moratorium on development and then changed the zoning on those properties. The fight to form the city and stop coastline development had been skillfully run and, had been at times, acrimonious. It was all over now except for some hard feelings. Marilyn Ryan, who had been president of the League of Women Voters when *The Time Is Now* was published, went on to successfully run as a state representative. (Courtesy Ken Dyda.)

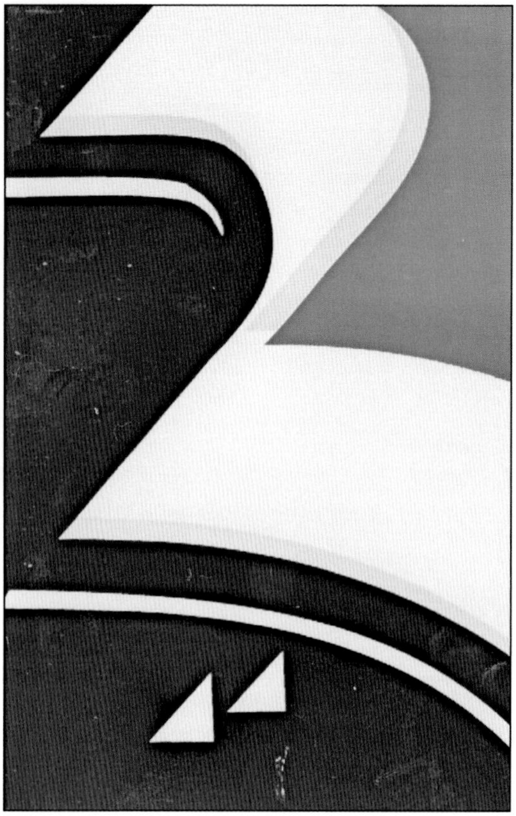

The city ran a logo contest, which was won by professional graphic artist Tom Hollingsworth. Hollingsworth had also designed the Fourth City logo for the fund-raising parties. The Rancho Palos Verdes logo shows the coastline with blue water, green land, and a white boundary between. He says both logos are similar to the view from his backyard. (Courtesy City of Rancho Palos Verdes and Carolyn Petru.)

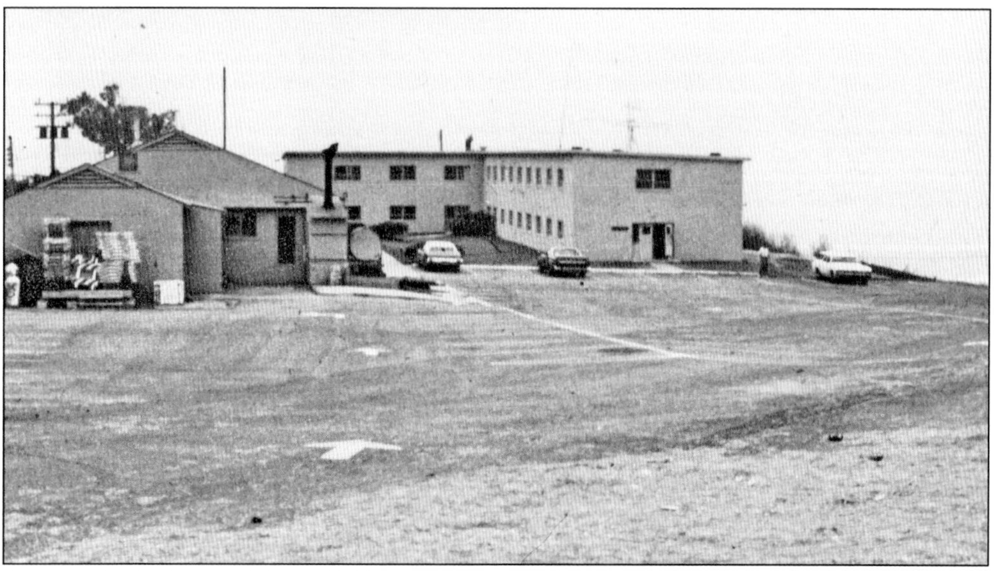

Seven and a half acres of the old Nike missile site overlooking Point Vicente and the ocean were deeded to the new city by the federal government through the efforts of retired colonel Francis D. "Cisco" Ruth, who was then a city councilman. The barracks, with its beautiful view, became the Rancho Palos Verdes city hall, reaffirming the newly elected council's campaign promises to always be frugal. (Courtesy Mel Hughes.)

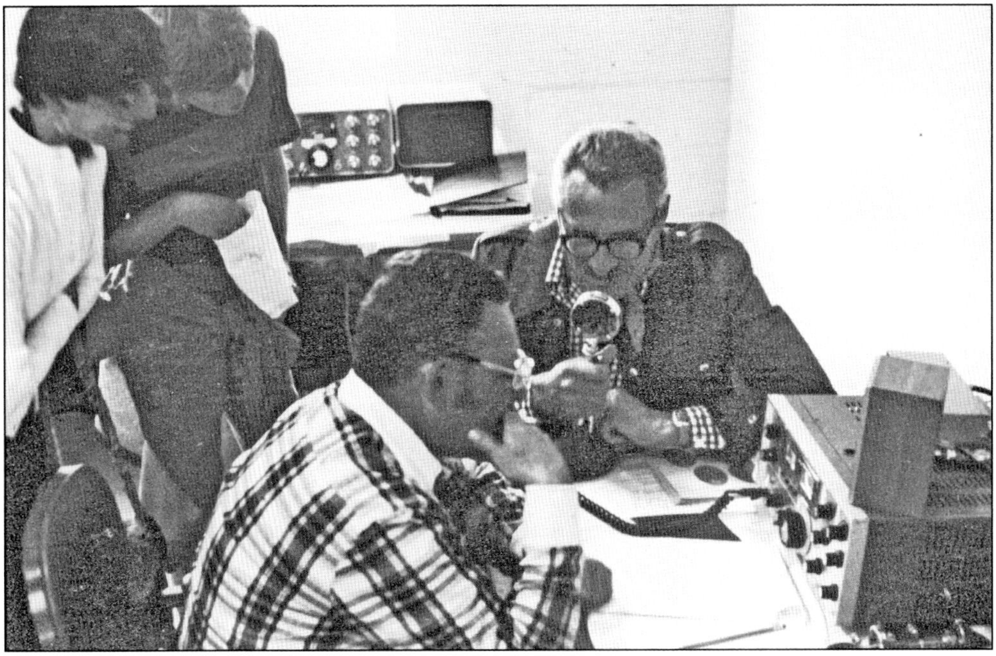

Adopted in the new city's general plan was a surprisingly restrictive amateur radio antenna ordinance. Alarmed hams formed the peninsula-wide Rancho Palos Verdes Amateur Radio Association and began a campaign to educate the public. During the city's celebration of the bicentennial, the club set up a ham station for visitors. Here councilman Cisco Ruth tries out the microphone with Paul Weiss, W6YQ. (Courtesy Mel Hughes, K6SY.)

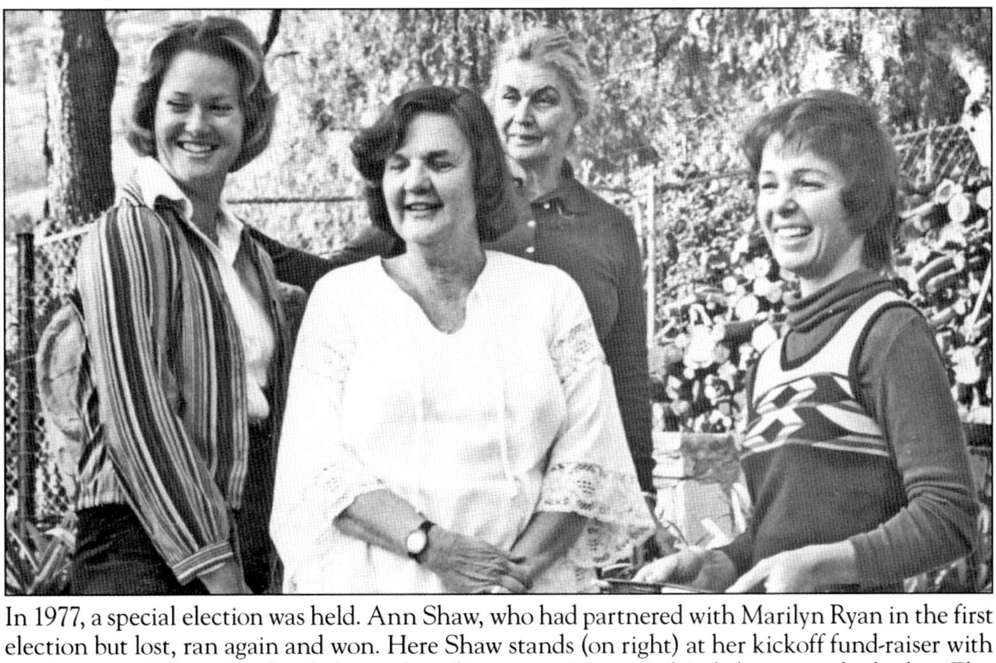

In 1977, a special election was held. Ann Shaw, who had partnered with Marilyn Ryan in the first election but lost, ran again and won. Here Shaw stands (on right) at her kickoff fund-raiser with co-chairmen Donna Lanferiek (center) and Maurine Potter. Behind them stands the late Elin Vanderlip, at whose home the event was held. The Vanderlips, Elin, and Elin's neighbors John and Suzanne often hosted political fund-raising parties. (Courtesy Ann Shaw.)

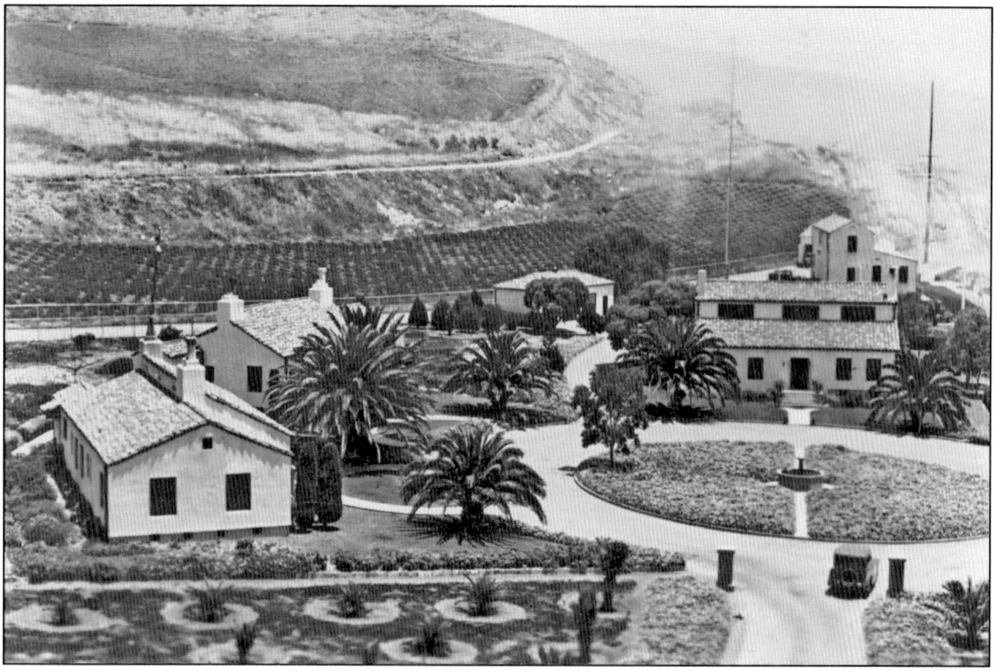

By 1951, the lighthouse radio station (antennas on right) had 34 coast guard personnel. Working around the clock, the radio operators listened for distress signals from mariners on the Pacific Ocean. They relayed emergencies to coast guard search and rescue using either voice transmission or international Morse code. The radio station acted as a lifeline to thousands of vessels in southland waters. (Courtesy Linda Cherney.)

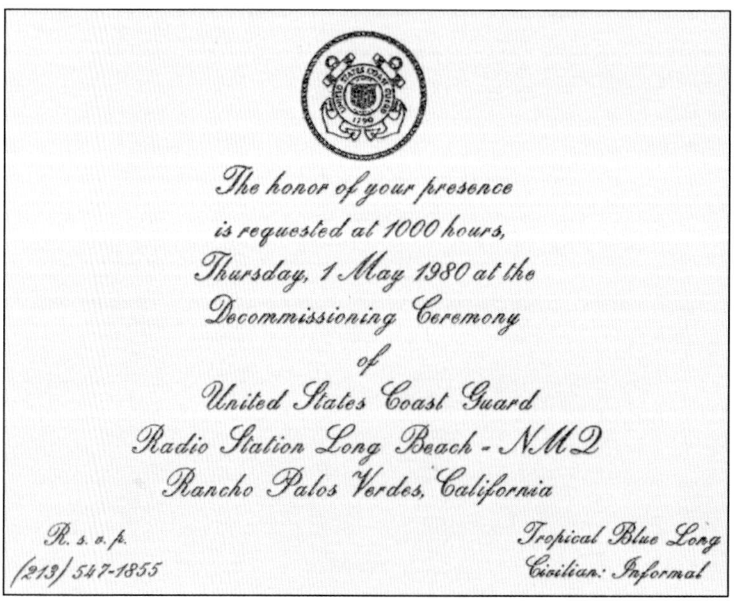

The honor of your presence
is requested at 1000 hours,
Thursday, 1 May 1980 at the
Decommissioning Ceremony
of
United States Coast Guard
Radio Station Long Beach - NMQ
Rancho Palos Verdes, California

R. s. v. p.
(213) 547-1855

Tropical Blue Long
Civilian: Informal

In 1971, the Point Vicente lighthouse was automated, and in 1979, some frequencies were transferred to the communication station in San Francisco. The lighthouse station was decommissioned as a manned operating facility in 1980 and became a fully remote communications facility. Since then, it has been run by the Coast Guard Auxiliary. (Courtesy Ken Dyda.)

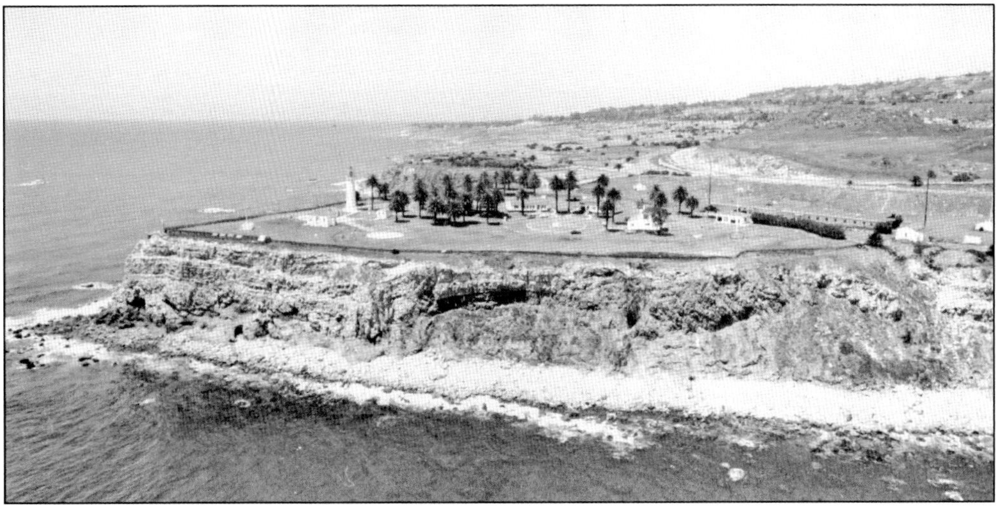

The radio room building—which had been visible behind the clothesline in the backyard of the main house—has been taken down, and the lighthouse has become a home for coast guard personnel and their families. The land on the rest of Point Vicente also belonged to the federal government, as did the land up the hill that had been a Nike missile-launching site. (Courtesy Point Vicente Interpretive Center.)

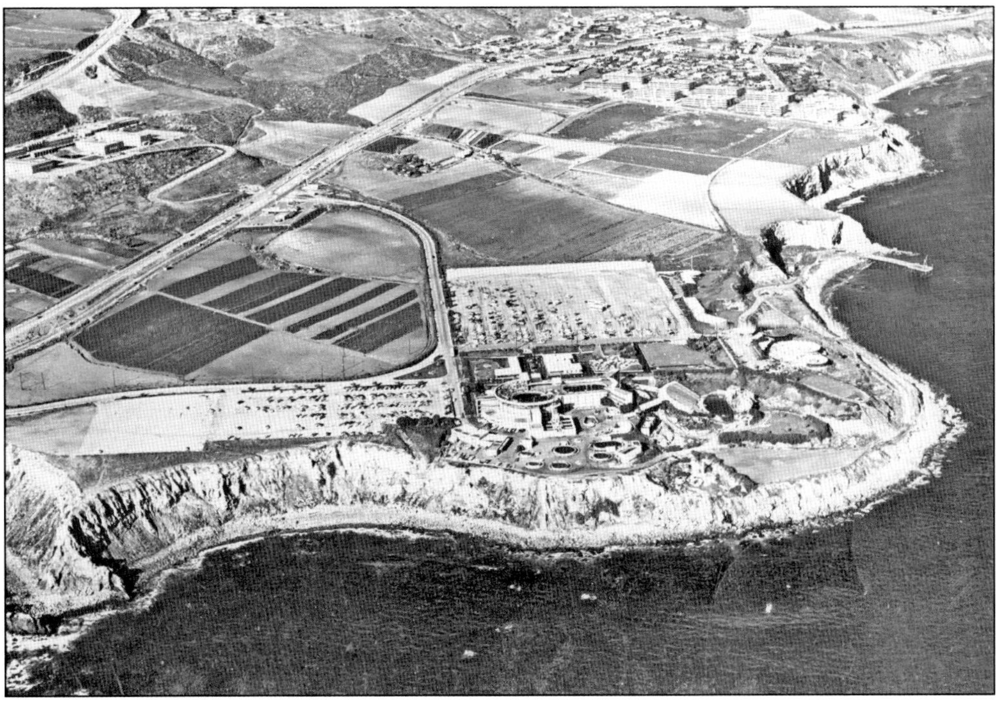

Marineland's heyday was 1965, but in 1971, it was sold. After Bill Monahan left, maintenance suffered and attendance slipped. Finally, in December 1986, Harcourt Brace Javanovich bought Marineland vowing to change nothing and improve the park as the company had done for Sea World. Midnight, January 19, 1987, trucks left for Sea World carrying Orky and Corky. Sea World had needed a breeding pair of killer whales. (Courtesy Point Vicente Interpretive Center.)

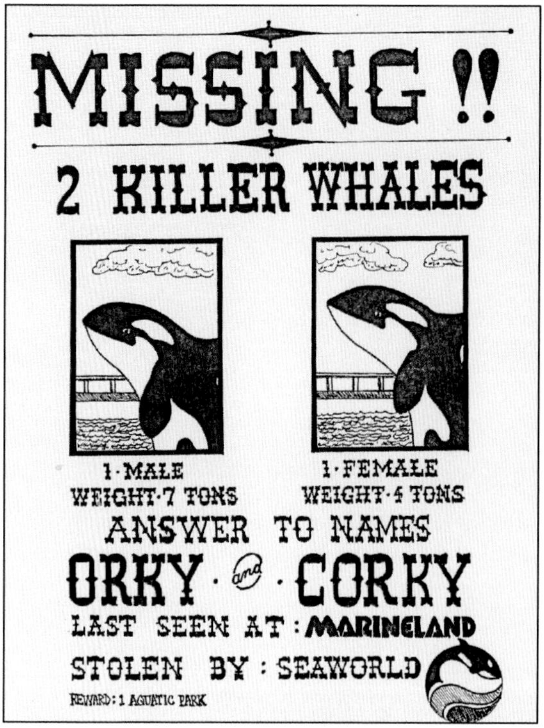

The community that had cherished Orky and Corky was devastated and enraged but not speechless. Residents and employees filed into the Palos Verdes Estates home of Bryant and Helen Winchell and formed Citizens to Save Marineland. They organized pickets and publicity like this broadside. One member raged, "They didn't give us a chance to say goodbye!" (Courtesy Point Vicente Interpretive Center.)

To The Citizens of San Diego

Bubbles is now with you — for 23 years she has been with us; for 15 years her likeness has stood at the entrance to Marineland to greet visitors from many lands. Although Marineland has had different owners over the years, no one here considered that one day someone could take Bubbles away.

When you go to Seaworld, would you tell her we love her — she's used to hearing that — and that we miss her very much, and we're sorry.

From The Citizens of Greater Los Angeles

Paid for by the Citizens to Save Marineland
(Our group will be picketing outside Seaworld this Saturday, Feb. 28 at noon.)

Within weeks of taking the killer whales, the new owners, after claiming vandalism to a tank, fired Marineland's employees and closed the park, taking the rest of the animals, including the beloved pilot whale, Bubbles. Within a few months, seven of the animals had died. Fury at Harcourt Brace Javanovich was so intense that they were boycotted and sales suffered. William Javanovich was blamed for the fiasco and ultimately edged out. (Courtesy Point Vicente Interpretive Center.)

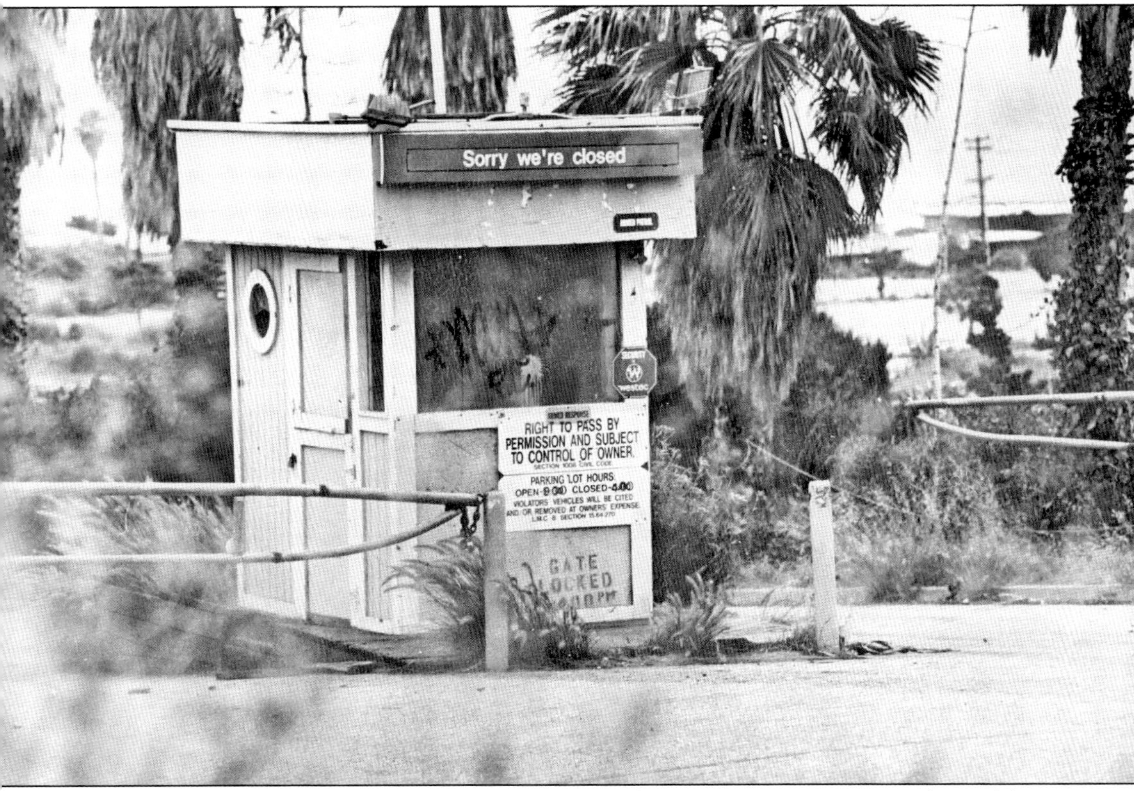

For Rancho Palos Verdes mayor Mel Hughes, dealing with Harcourt Brace Javanovich was like dealing with shadows. They would talk with him about the future of the Marineland property and then they would disappear. His constituents were asking him to take action. They wrote and phoned, beseeching him to do something, but he was powerless and frustrated. Eventually the property was sold and all dreams of a replacement park were over. It was the end. (Courtesy Point Vicente Interpretive Center).

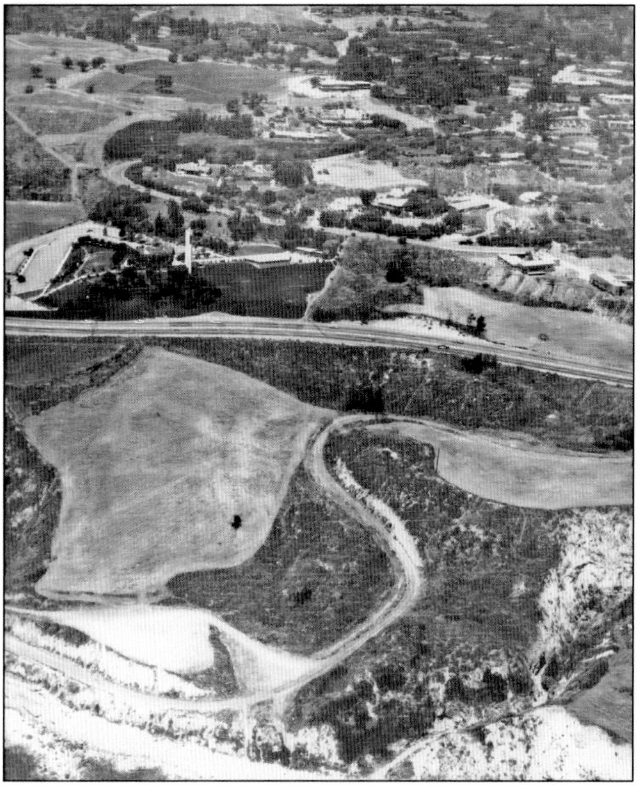

The slippery bentonite deep in the Altamira Shale was not limited to Portuguese Bend. It caused the less spectacular Abalone Cove landslide in 1974 that damaged the Wayfarers' Chapel Visitor's Center (far right of the bell tower) ultimately causing its removal. A new one was built on the west side of the property under the direction of Eric Lloyd Wright, son of the architect Lloyd Wright. (Courtesy Point Vicente Interpretive Center.)

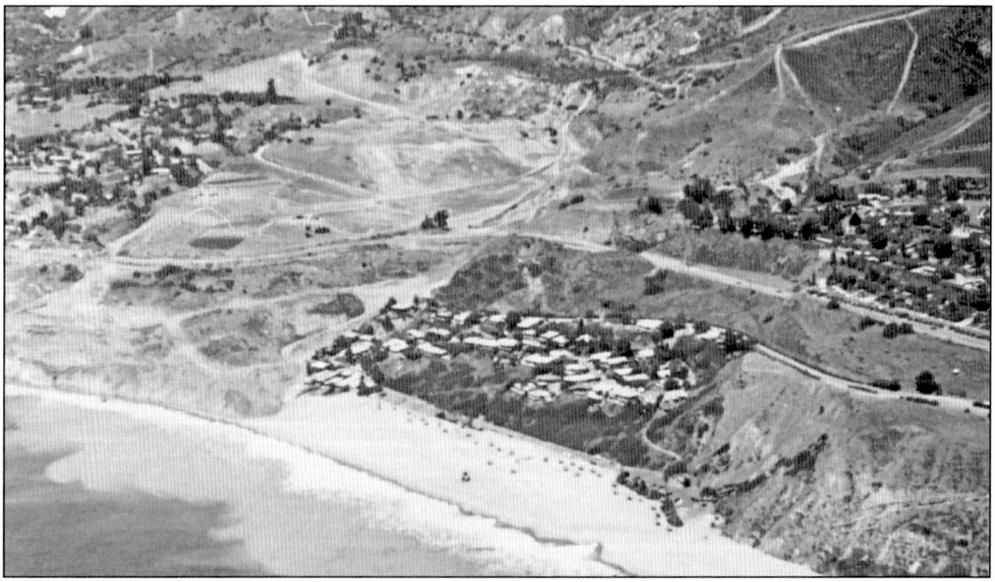

By 1980, the Portuguese Bend slide had settled to about .25 inches per day. On the left is the mass of land that has moved to the shore. On the right are the Portuguese Bend Club homes huddled off the path of the slide. The homes remaining in the upper community are on moving ground. Because the east side of the slide moves faster than the west side, the houses are slowly rotating clockwise. (Courtesy Point Vicente Interpretive Center.)

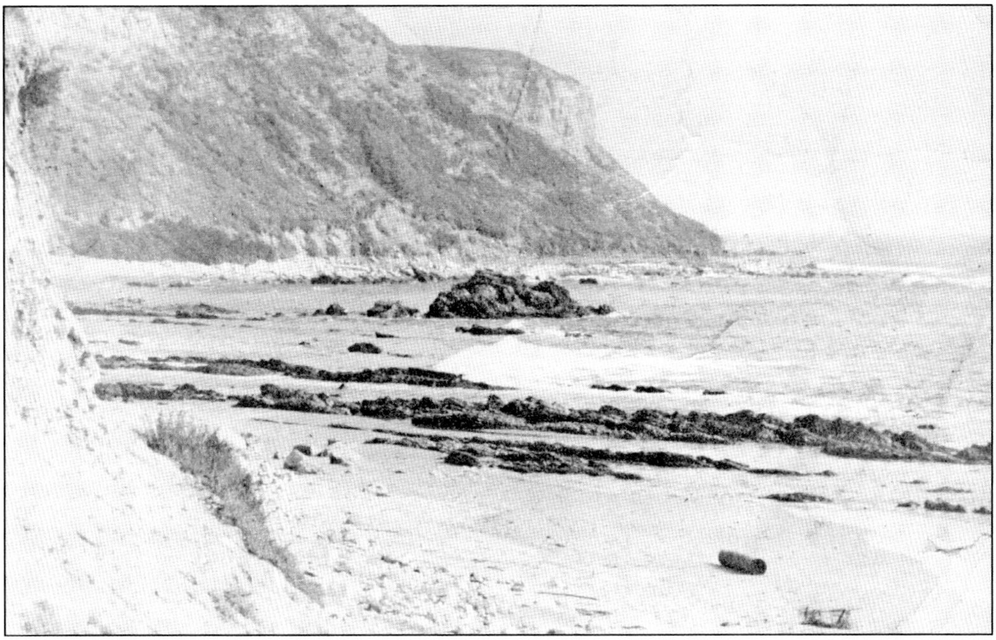

The slide caused an interesting and unexpected thing to happen to the beach at Portuguese Bend: sand began to accumulate, and the beach began to grow. Portuguese Bend is bound by Inspiration Point on the west end and Halfway Point on the east. The rock in the middle of the cove, looking toward Halfway Point, is Crab Rock. In the photograph below, although the angle is slightly different, you can see that Crab Rock has been covered by sand, and Lulu Jaconi—half boxer, half dalmatian—is walking on sand where once there used to be water. It is not known whether the changed shape of the coastline slowed the wave action, keeping the sand from being swept out, or the slide itself was adding to the material, possibly both since the slide is still active and the material is washing into the sea and moving down the coast with the current. (Both photographs courtesy Dennis Jaconi.)

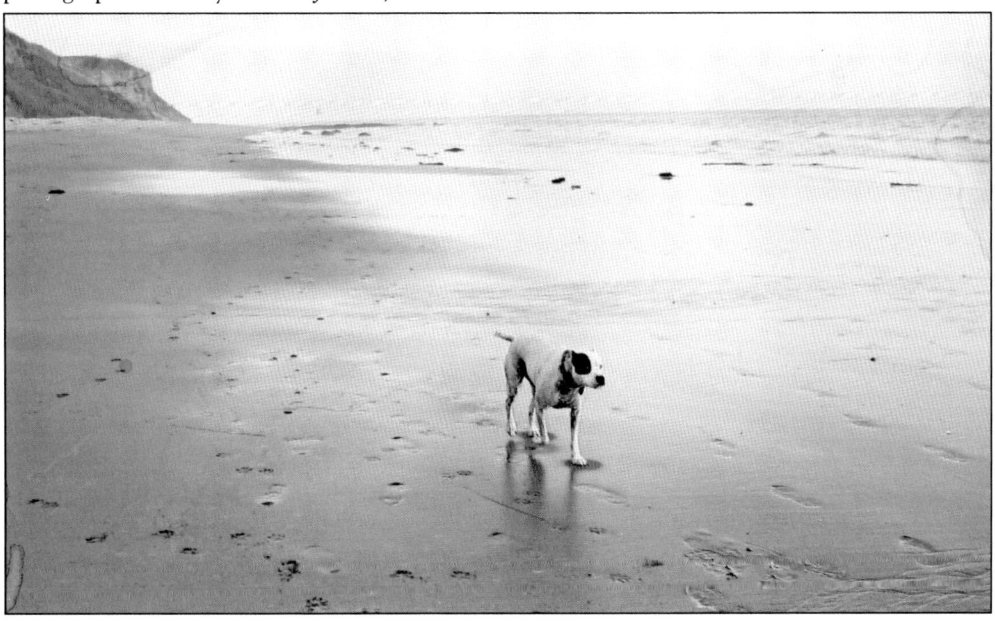

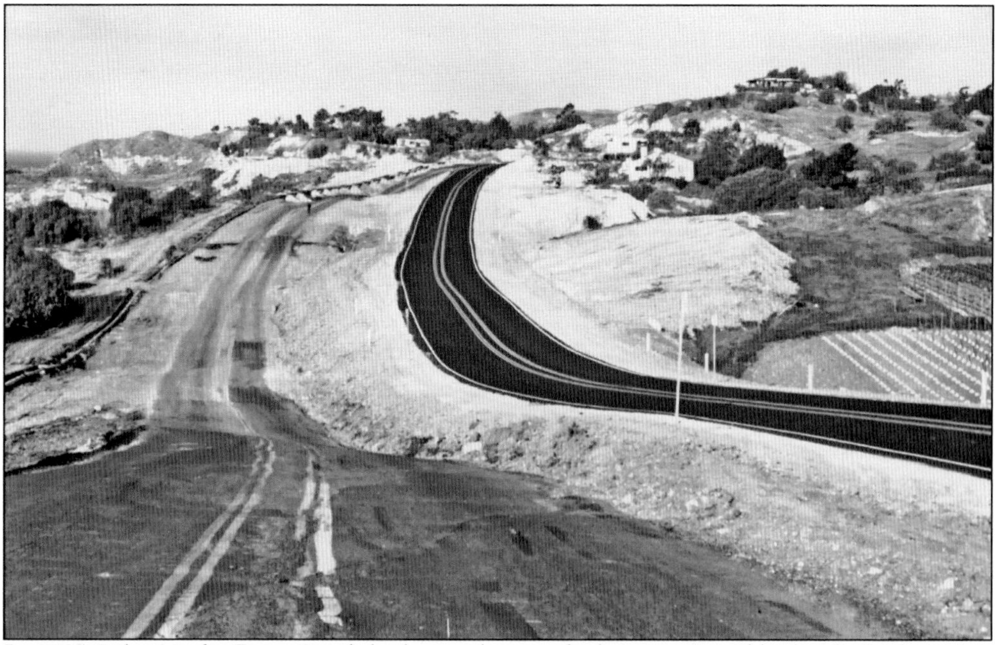

By 1985, Palos Verdes Drive South had moved so much that a new road had to be built farther inland to replace it. Homes that were on the north side of the highway were now on the south side of the road and headed for the cliff. The road was built right through Cherry Hill Circle. (Courtesy Mrs. Martin [Katherine] Reiter, Point Vicente Interpretive Center.)

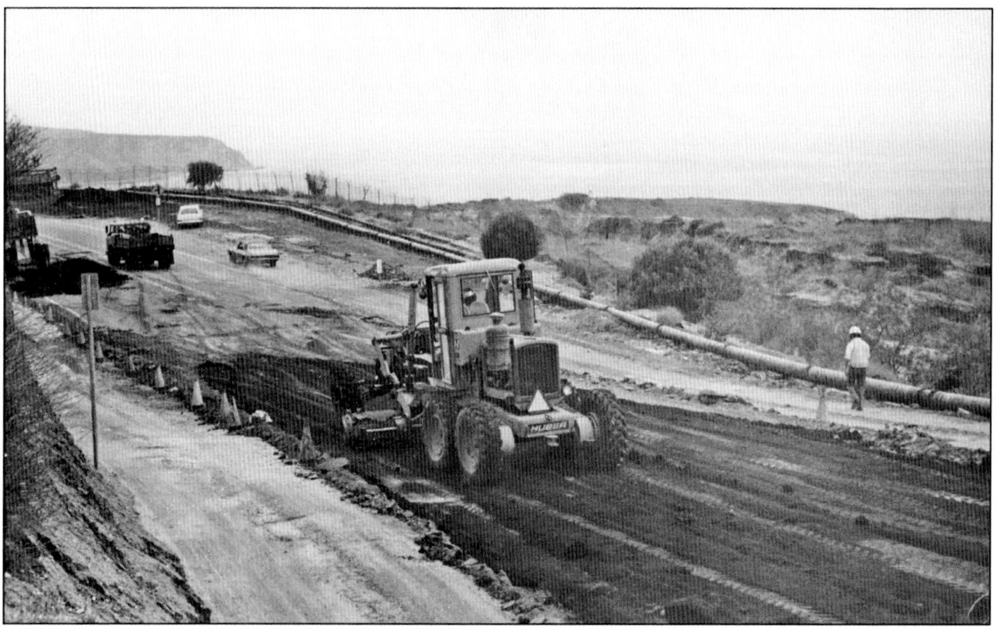

The slide and the cost to maintain the area's infrastructure belonged to the City of Rancho Palos Verdes. Although the county had told them it would cost about $45,000 per year to maintain the road, by 2008 the costs had escalated to $200,000 per year to the detriment of other roads under the city's care. (Courtesy Point Vicente Interpretive Center.)

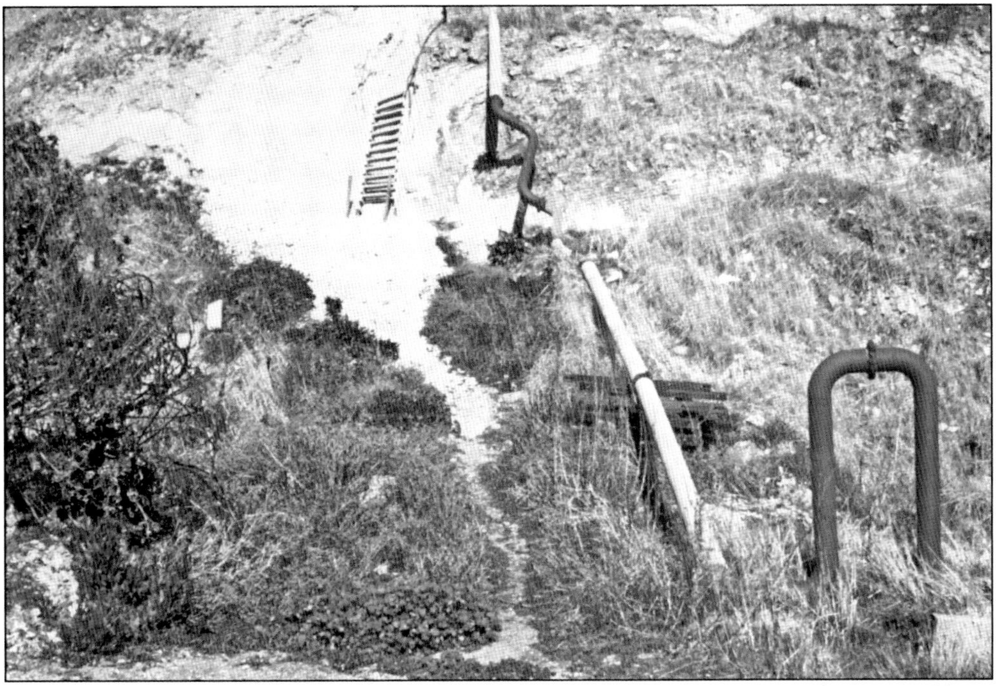

The utility companies had a different kind of problem. Obviously underground pipes would not work in moving ground. Water and gas pipes were relocated above ground with stress-relief kinks in them. (Courtesy Mrs. Martin [Katherine] Reiter, Point Vicente Interpretive Center.)

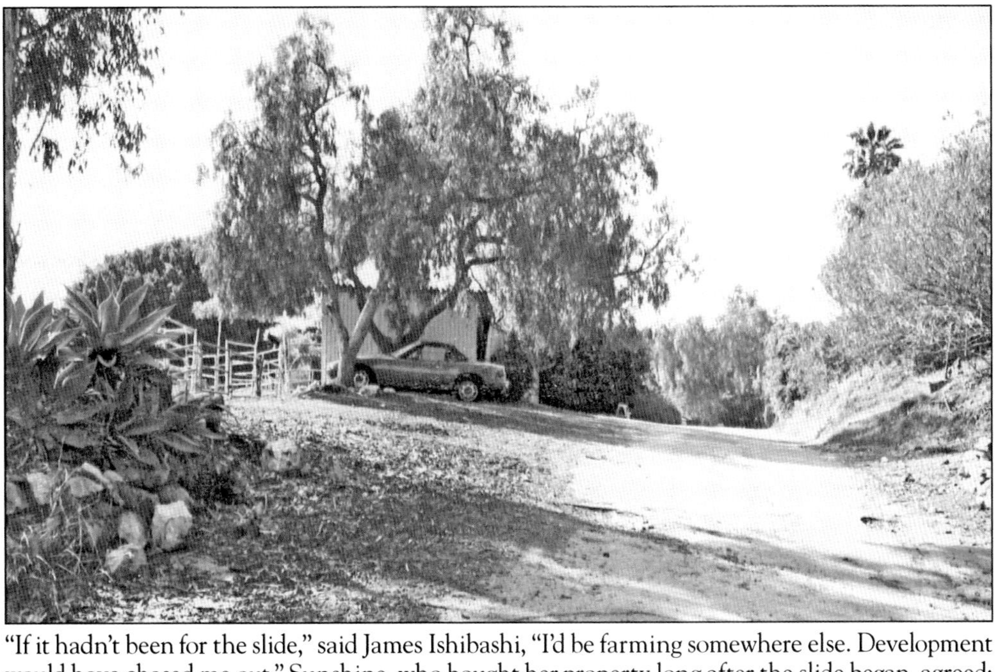

"If it hadn't been for the slide," said James Ishibashi, "I'd be farming somewhere else. Development would have chased me out." Sunshine, who bought her property long after the slide began, agreed: "That slide was the best thing that ever happened to Portuguese Bend." The peppertree-lined dirt roads, horses, the peacocks' call, and the sense of community—all are reminiscent of the older, simpler, undeveloped Palos Verdes. (Courtesy author.)

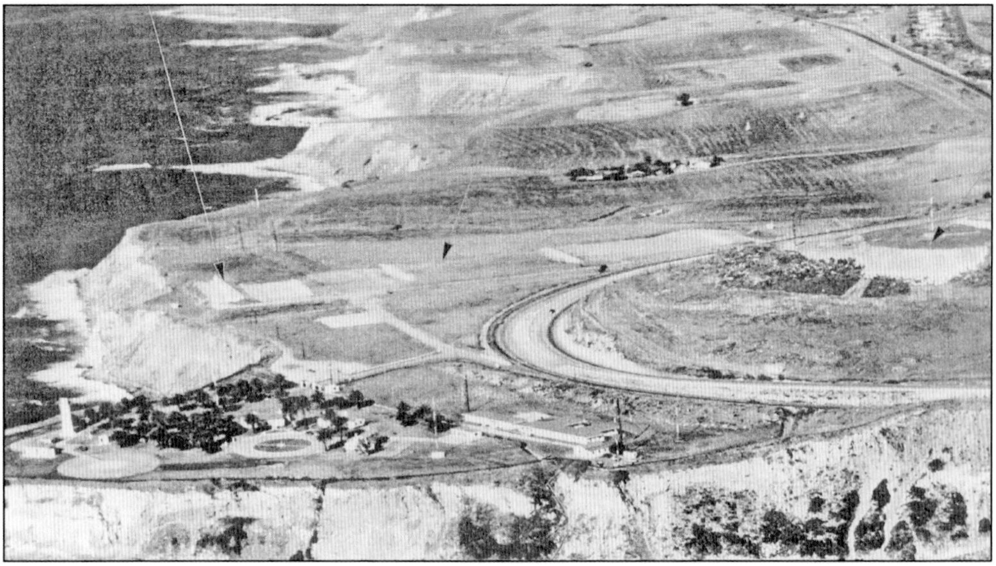

Point Vicente became federal property in 1923 when the lighthouse was built. Later, the property west of the lighthouse became an army rifle range and, across the road, a Nike missile-launching site. The land beyond, along the bluffs, was private and was bought in the 1960s by Zuckerman and Morris. Their bid to build condominiums on that site had been the flash point for the Save Our Coastline fight. (Courtesy Point Vicente Interpretive Center.)

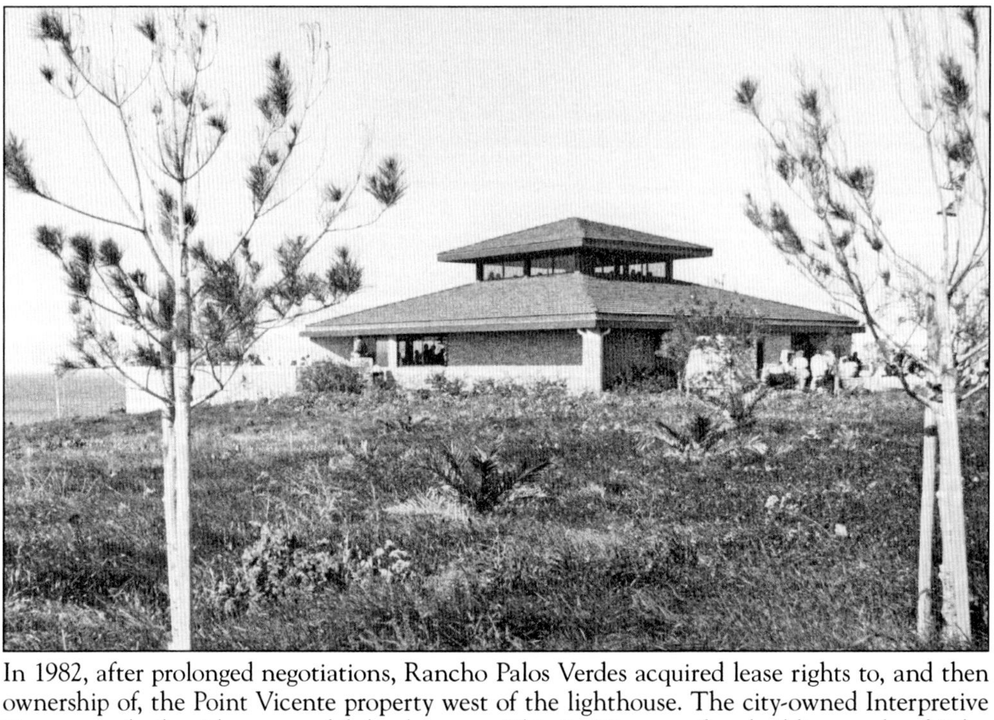

In 1982, after prolonged negotiations, Rancho Palos Verdes acquired lease rights to, and then ownership of, the Point Vicente property west of the lighthouse. The city-owned Interpretive Center was built with state and federal money. This 2,400-square-foot building made of Palos Verdes stone cost around $375,000. (Courtesy Point Vicente Interpretive Center.)

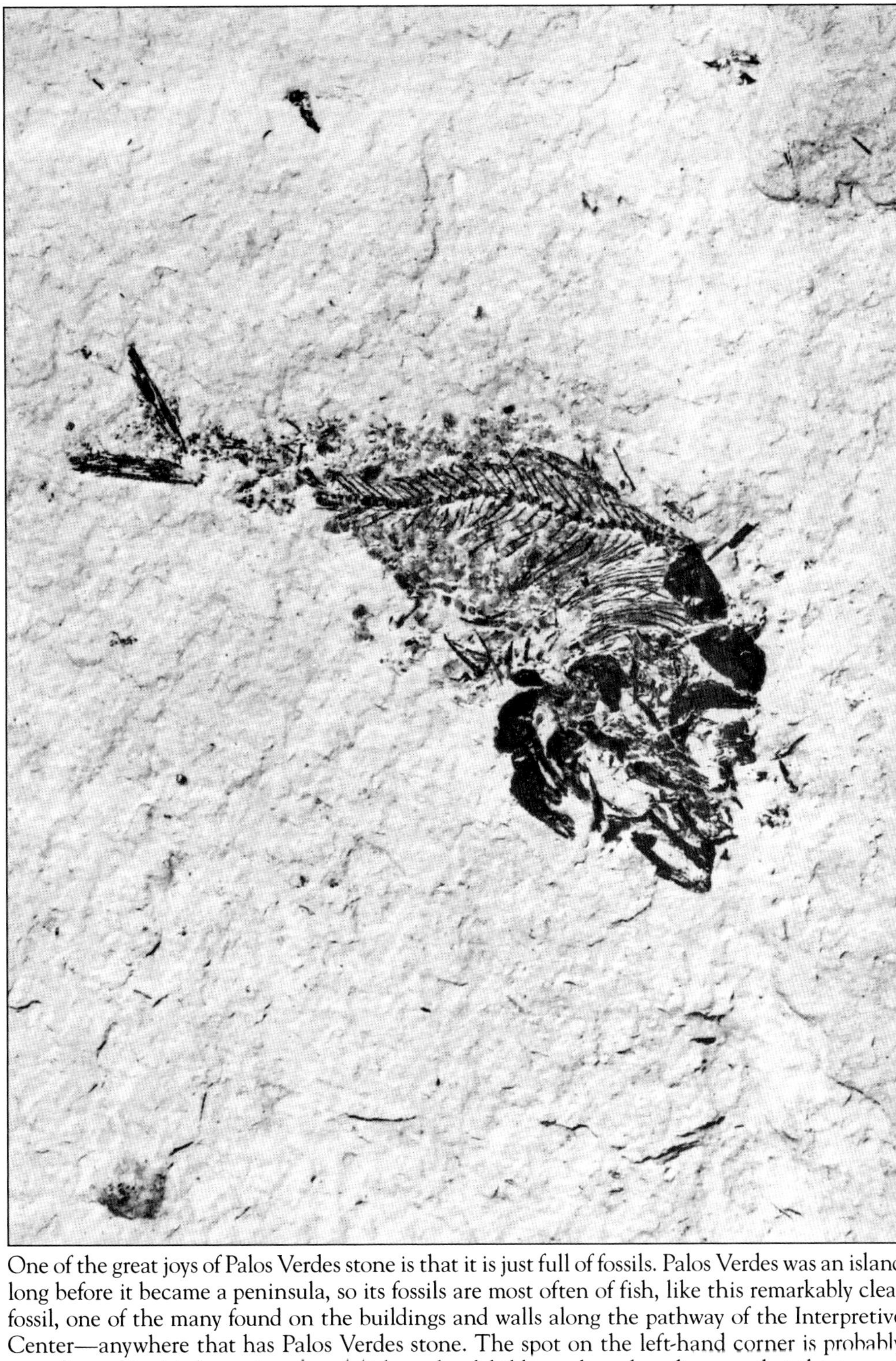

One of the great joys of Palos Verdes stone is that it is just full of fossils. Palos Verdes was an island long before it became a peninsula, so its fossils are most often of fish, like this remarkably clear fossil, one of the many found on the buildings and walls along the pathway of the Interpretive Center—anywhere that has Palos Verdes stone. The spot on the left-hand corner is probably coprolite, a bit of information that delights schoolchildren when they discover that this term is just another word for fossilized fish poop. (Courtesy Joe Cocke.)

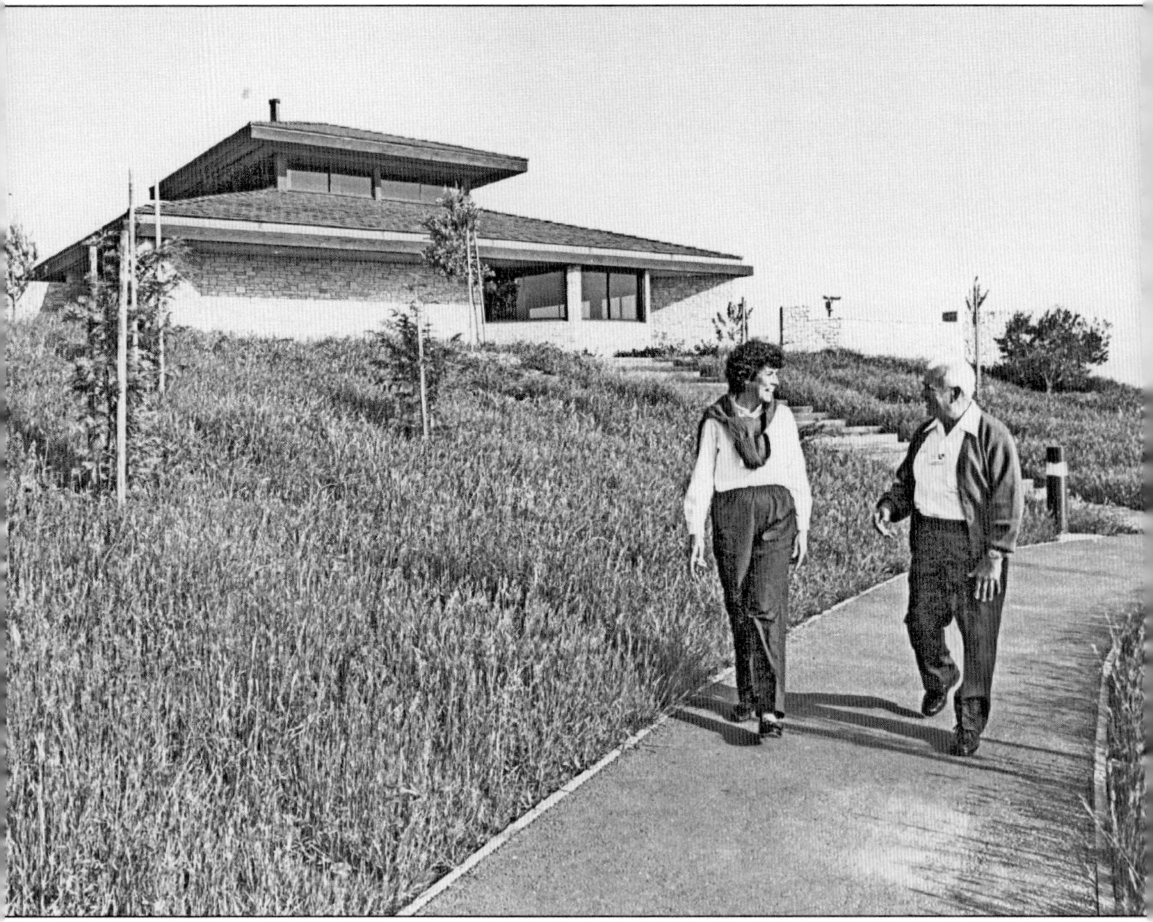

Diana McIntyre, assistant to the curator of mammals at the Natural History Museum of Los Angeles County and a Palos Verdes Estates resident, became docent coordinator for the new Interpretive Center. She tapped what she called "the pool of talent" on the peninsula and created Los Serenos de Point Vicente, her docent group. She created training classes where each prospective docent was required to write a paper on the history or natural history of some aspect of Palos Verdes. Over the years, these papers have provided a wealth of information about the peninsula and copies of them are available in the Palos Verdes Peninsula Local History Collection. Here are Donna Sanford and Carmen Marinella, graduates of the first docent class in 1984. (Courtesy Point Vicente Interpretive Center.)

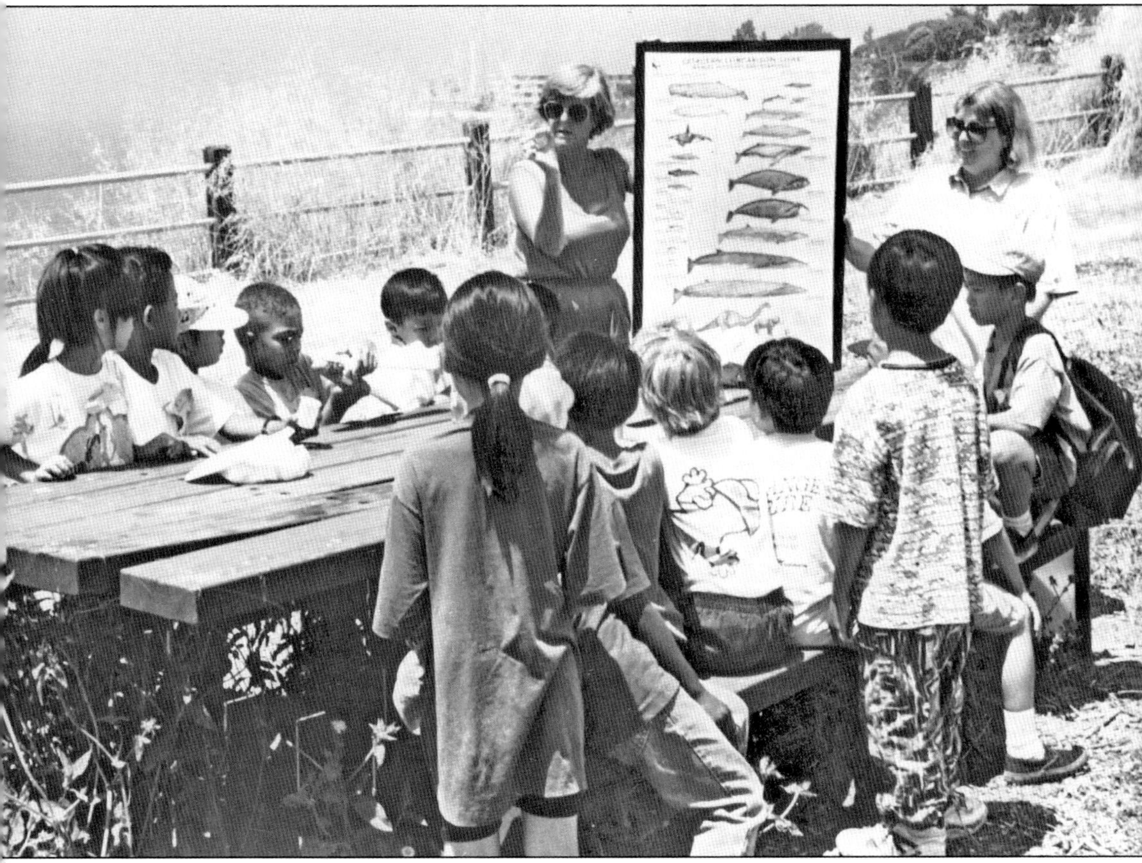

The Point Vicente Interpretive Center docents have a mission to teach the rich natural history of Palos Verdes. Diana McIntyre (left) holds a chart showing cetaceans, with the whales and dolphins organized by size, which she created in collaboration with the late John Heyning when he was curator of marine mammals at the Natural History Museum of Los Angeles County. Because Rancho Palos Verdes has the longest coastline of the four cities on the peninsula and because gray whales come close to Point Vicente on their migration, the Interpretive Center has adopted the gray whale as its own. (Courtesy Point Vicente Interpretive Center.)

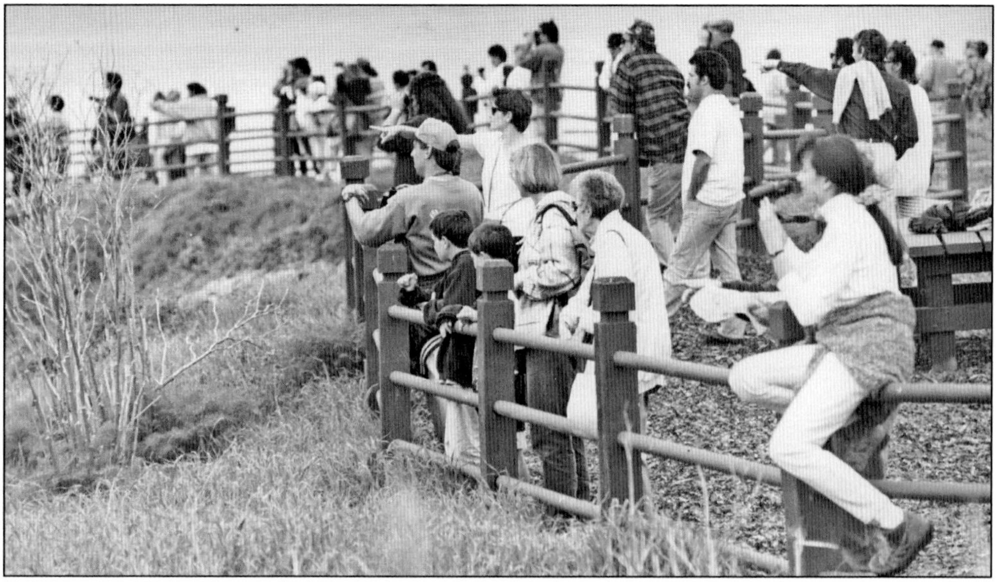

The Point Vicente Interpretive Center hosts gray whale census volunteers from the American Cetacean Society from December through May. On the terrace with their binoculars, they count gray whales passing close by the point on their annual migration between Alaska and Baja California. On the first Saturday in March, the docents host Whale of a Day (pictured), inviting the community to the center to celebrate the gray whale. (Courtesy Point Vicente Interpretive Center.)

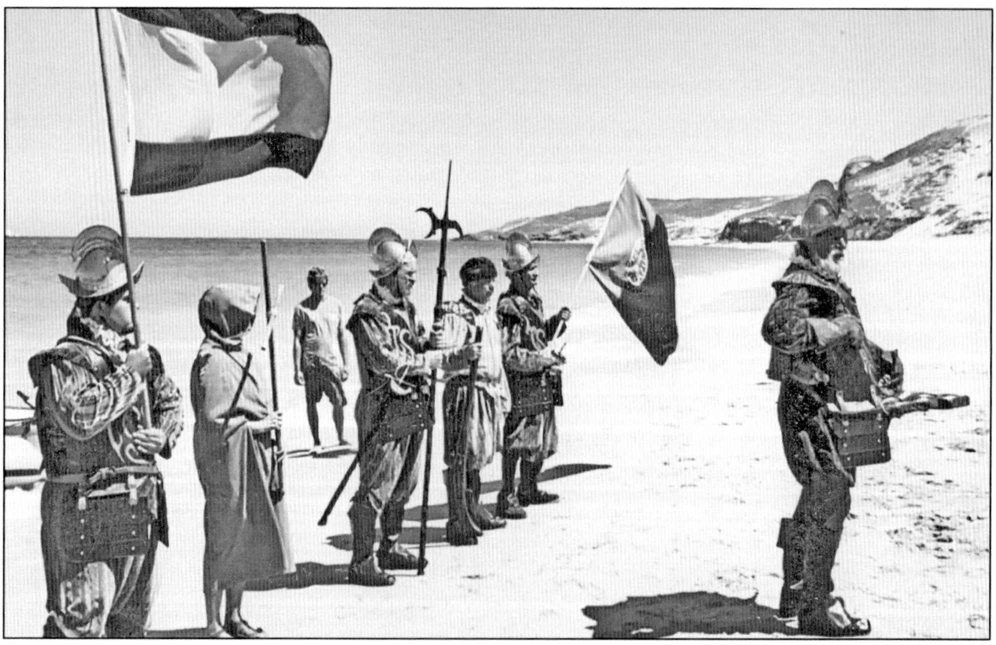

Every fall, well-known San Pedro resident John Olguin (right) leads a small crew dressed as Juan Cabrillo's expeditionary force to San Miguel Island, where a monument to Cabrillo stands on a hill. Onlookers pay to join them, and Island Packers motors them over to the island. There Olguin delivers a tribute to the man who discovered California. The priest this time is Point Vicente Interpretive Center curator Diana MacIntyre. (Courtesy Jo Woods.)

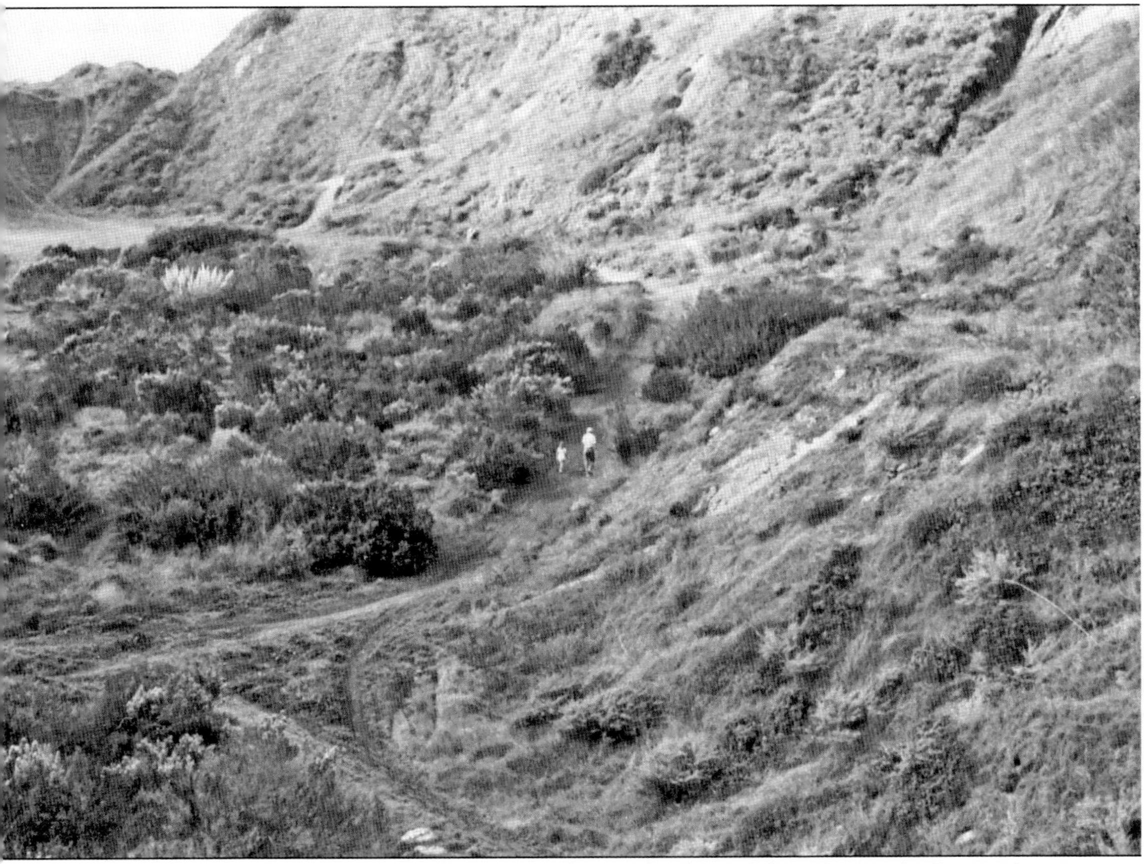

In 1988, Rolling Hills Estates residents Bill and Barbara Ailor formed the Palos Verdes Peninsula Land Conservancy. They wanted a nonconfrontational method to preserve the disappearing open space, so they worked with landowners, cities, and citizens, using government funds, grants, and donations to buy land. One of their first successes was negotiating the purchase of Forrestal by Rancho Palos Verdes from the Diamond Brothers. (Courtesy Point Vicente Interpretive Center.)

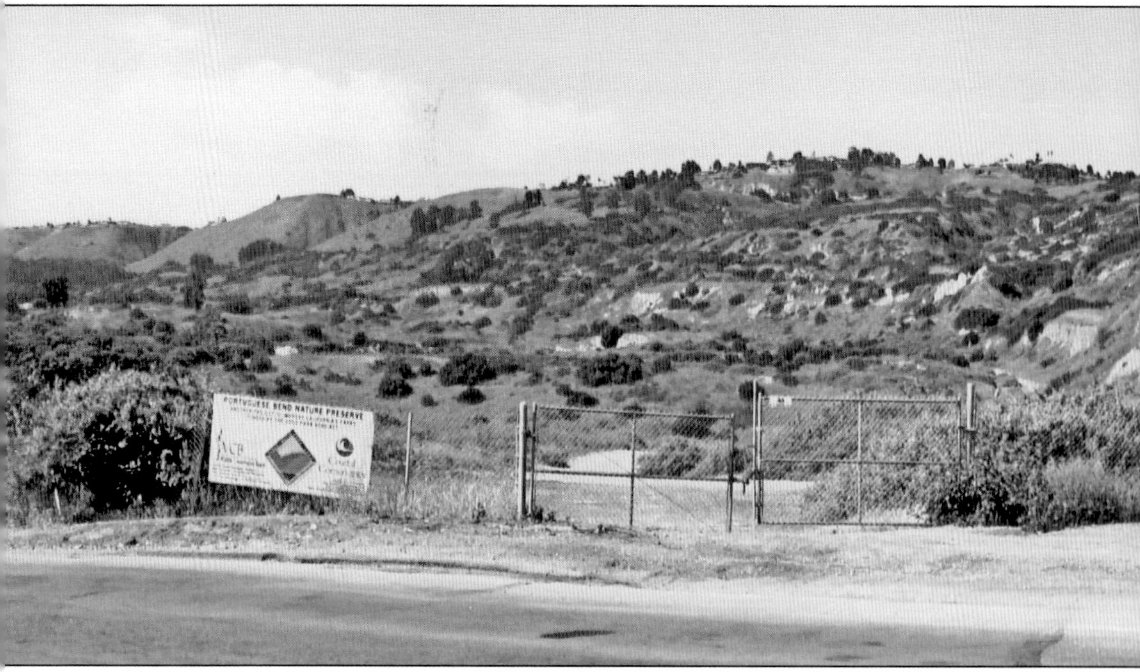

"We wanted to acquire the land in a way that preserves it," said Bill Ailor. "We had a better relationship with business than with environmental communities who felt that if we weren't with them, we were against them." The Land Conservancy's crowning achievement was the 2005 purchase of the Portuguese Bend slide area because it drew in the community, who donated $4 million. The balance of $13 million came from various government agencies and grants. (Courtesy Author.)

BIBLIOGRAPHY

David, Lester. *Ethel, The Story of Mrs. Robert F. Kennedy*. New York: The World Publishing Company, 1971.

Easton, Nina. "The Death of Marineland." *Los Angeles Times*. August 9, 1987.

Fink, Augusta. *Time and the Terraced Land*. Berkeley, CA: Howell-North Books, 1966.

Hanson, A.E. *Rolling Hills, The Early Years—February 1930 through December 7, 1941*. City of Rolling Hills, 1978.

Hedley, Marilyn. *How Daddy Became a Beachcomber*. Bloomington, IA: Authorhouse, 2006.

Morgan, Delane. *The Palos Verdes Story*. Palos Verdes, CA: Palos Verdes Peninsula Library Foundation, 1983.

Patryla, Jim. *A Photographic Journey Back to Marineland of the Pacific*. 2005.

Perkins, Jan David, N6AW. *Don C. Wallace: W6AM, Amateur Radio's Pioneer*. New York: Vestal Press, Ltd., 1991.

Reiter, Martin. *The Palos Verdes Peninsula, A Geologic Guide and More*. Dubuque, IA: Kendall/Hunt Publishing Company, 1984.

Smith, Sarah Bixby. *Adobe Days*. University of Nebraska Press, 1987.

Vanderlip, Elin. *Eccentric Obstinate and Fabulous!* Los Angeles: Donegal Publishing Company, 2009.

Young, Donald J. "Wartime Palos Verdes." *Palos Verdes News*, 1985.

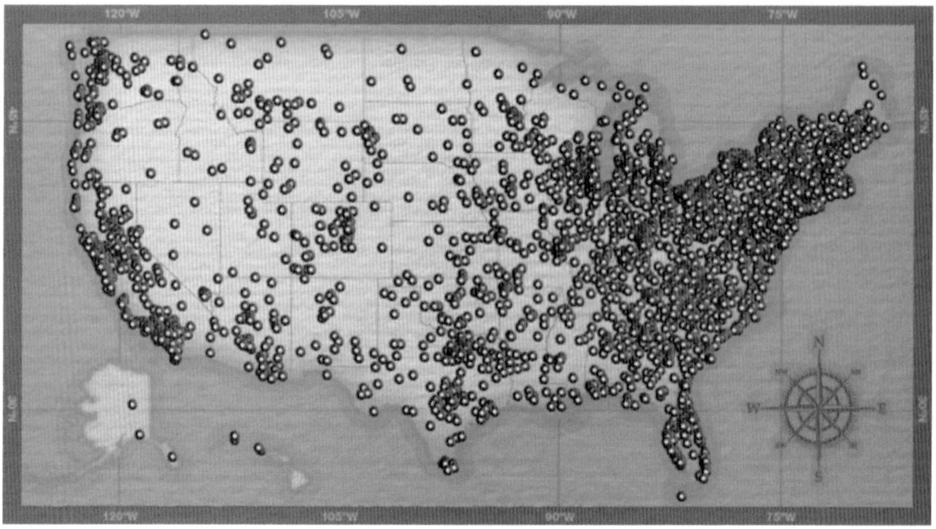